THE

RISE

OF

MARCO
RUBIO

Manuel Roig-Franzia

SIMON & SCHUSTER

New York   London   Toronto   Sydney   New Delhi

Simon & Schuster
1230 Avenue of the Americas
New York, NY 10020

First Simon & Schuster hardcover edition June 2012

SIMON & SCHUSTER and colophon are registered trademarks of Simon & Schuster, Inc.

For information about special discounts for bulk purchases,
please contact Simon & Schuster Special Sales at 1-866-506-1949
or business@simonandschuster.com.

The Simon & Schuster Speakers Bureau can bring authors to your live event. For more information or to book an event contact the Simon & Schuster Speakers Bureau at 1-866-248-3049 or visit our website at www.simonspeakers.com.

Designed by Joy O'Meara

Manufactured in the United States of America

10 9 8 7 6 5 4 3 2 1

Library of Congress Cataloging-in-Publication Data

Roig-Franzia, Manuel.
    The rise of Marco Rubio / Manuel Roig-Franzia.
        p.   cm.
    Includes bibliographical references and index.
1. Rubio, Marco, 1971–   2. Senators—United States—Biography.
3. United States. Congress. Senate—Biography.   4. United States—Politics and government—2009–   5. Legislators—Florida—Biography.   6. Florida—Politics and government—1951–   7. Cuban Americans—Florida—Biography.
8. Florida—Biography.   I. Title.
    E901.1.R83R65   2012
    323.73'092—dc23
    [B]   2012015140
ISBN 978-1-4516-7545-0
ISBN 978-1-4516-7547-4 (ebook)

For Ceci

Contents

THE RISE OF

MARCO RUBIO

Introduction

THE HEIR

For an instant, she hurtled toward the floor. A slender, delicate right shoulder knifed downward, a cane flipped sideways. Nancy Reagan, tiny, fragile as a china figurine in an ivory-colored suit, was crashing.

Many in the capacity crowd at the Ronald Reagan Library in Simi Valley, California, couldn't see what was happening. They clapped lovingly, oblivious. But before their applause gave way to gasps the synapses of the young senator escorting the former first lady to her seat fired perfectly. Marco Rubio, his hair parted just so, a valedictorian's smile on his face, tugged the aging icon toward him. He leaned right and swung a hand beneath her left arm, catching the ninety-year-old just as she slanted forward, almost parallel to the floor and bound for a bone-chipping thud.

Rubio, a forty-year-old who looked a decade younger, moved with the sure agility that he once flashed on the high school football fields of Miami. He wasn't fast, but he was quick, his high school athletic director, James Colzie, always thought. On the football field there's a difference. Fast means you run at high speed; quick means you react at high speed. Quick means you get to the right spot on the field at precisely the right time.

Sometimes being quick is better than being fast.

It was August 23, 2011. The figurine didn't shatter.

Soon it was clear that this was *a moment*. A *Los Angeles Times* blog published a frame-by-frame sequence of photographs beneath the headline "Marco Rubio to the Rescue!" They showed Nancy and Marco smiling at each other, then Nancy happily looking into the audience, then starting a slow-motion tumble as the senator reaches over to pat her hand, then Rubio saving her. The former first lady's anxiety at that second is written on her face as she grimaces and closes her eyes. Later *ABC World News* dedicated a segment to what the guest anchor George Stephanopoulos introduced as "that video that made so many of us gasp today." He brought in the network's medical expert, Dr. Richard Besser, to soberly explain the dangers of falls for the elderly.

Conservative bloggers and their readers, who had been reliably laudatory about all things Rubio during his quick ascent in the Republican Party, praised him. "Hero! Marco Rubio Saves a Falling Nancy Reagan," said conservativebyte.com. The headlines might just as well have read "Marco Rubio Saves the Republican Party." "This feels like an omen," a commenter on The Blaze website wrote. "Saving Reagan I think is a sign from above," a Human Events reader observed. Another asked, "Now will Marco Rubio SAVE AMERICA from its DOWNFALL? Is this a sign or what? 'Ronnie' saved the world from the Communists. Rubio can save America from its leftover Communists."

Rubio, in a sense, was viewed as a political son of Reagan's, an heir to his legacy of conservative principles. One of Reagan's real sons, a cheeky liberal, reacted to the news more like a son worried about his mother than as a political enthusiast. Watching the video of Rubio escorting his mother before she tripped, Ron Reagan fumed: "He's playing to the cameras. He's not paying attention to her!"

Reagan, who calls Rubio "the guy who dropped my mom," planned to lay into the senator if someone from the media called. But, he told me, no one called.

Nothing was going to shatter this moment.

Rubio's reflexes had only sharpened the impression that a party looking for heroes had found a figure with great promise, an idol touched by serendipity. Rubio's team couldn't believe its luck. "We joked in the office that he tripped her," a top Rubio political advisor told me not long after the greatest interception of Rubio's career.

Extraordinary political careers can build momentum from an accretion of perfect moments, and this was just one more for Marco Rubio. American politics had never seen anything like him: a young, made-for-YouTube Hispanic Republican with realistic national prospects, establishment backing, and electoral appeal that extended well beyond his ethnicity. There had been Hispanic stars before. But they tended to be Democrats and they tended to fizzle like Henry Cisneros, the suave Mexican American housing secretary, or plateau like Bill Richardson, the Mexican American foreign policy maestro with the decidedly un-Hispanic-sounding name.

Rubio had arrived on the national scene at a time when both parties were—again—forced to confront the enduring and growing power of Hispanic voters. Could they be wooed with promises of immigration reform alone, or must they be courted with some mix of social issues and religion, and promises of jobs? Might Marco Rubio be the solution?

Good timing matters, but it isn't everything. Execution counts too. And each time Rubio's timing has been good, his execution has been even better.

It was a blessing for him to come into Florida's House of Representatives just when term limits were clearing away much of the competition for leadership spots. But then Rubio did something with his good fortune, strategizing behind the scenes and impressing his elders so that he could ascend. It was fortuitous for him to encounter a Republican primary opponent in a U.S. Senate race who had alienated the Republican Party. But Rubio also capitalized on that opportunity. He overcame polls that showed he had no chance and pulverized the once popular Florida governor Charlie Crist so effectively that Crist was forced to quit the Republican primary and run as an independent. Then Rubio found himself in a vote-splitting, three-way Senate race, and again he made the correct call, sweeping wide to the conservative right and finishing off Crist by trapping him on the left sideline.

In 2010 a national narrative evolved around the idea that Rubio was a product of the tea party, an amorphous movement of discontented Americans who wanted to wipe Washington clean. It was as if Rubio had sprung whole from a town hall meeting. Of course, nothing could have been further from the truth. His rise had actually been as conventional as they come. He'd climbed the staircase methodically, touching each step along the way rather than leaping from the landing to the top floor. In that same election season, there'd been a gusher of out-of-nowhere tea party successes. Christine O'Donnell, who had never won a major election, and Joe Miller secured Republican U.S. Senate primary victories in Delaware and Alaska before losing in the general election. Rand Paul, the son of Ron Paul, a Texas congressman and Republican presidential candidate, was elected to the U.S. Senate in his first attempt at political office.

But Rubio had been running for—and winning—elections for most of his adult life. West Miami city commissioner, Florida state representative, Florida house speaker, U.S. senator. Step, by step, by step.

A letter from Nancy Reagan inviting him to speak at her husband's presidential library only confirmed what everyone knew: Rubio had arrived. "You've been identified as someone to watch on the national political scene," the letter read. "I'm looking forward to watching you in your new role."

The Reagan Library speech was a prestige gig, a way for Republicans to walk their finest past the gallery for inspection. With Rubio's invitation to speak came an invitation to dinner, and as ever, he did not fail to impress. The meal was served in the library's personal quarters. Gerald Parsky, a trustee of both the Ronald Reagan Presidential Foundation and the George H. W. Bush Presidential Library Foundation who had served in five Republican administrations, watched approvingly during the dinner as the young senator charmed the former first lady. "Very relaxed. Easy dialogue. Not nervous at all," Parsky said of Rubio. "I was impressed."

Rubio, who has a knack for a kind of self-effacement that draws him closer to his audience while simultaneously showing off his importance, later shared an intimate moment from that meal. "Mrs. Reagan," he said—a bit formally, ever the polite young man—turned to Rubio's wife, Jeanette, and told her that "Ronnie" used to "send [her] mom flowers" every year on Nancy's birthday. The flowers were always accompanied by a note from Ronnie thanking Nancy's mother for giving birth to her. "And he'd written over 700 love letters or something like that," Rubio continued. "And I'm just thinking, man, I am in a deep, deep hole. I'll never catch up to the Gipper." Rubio was careful to note that *he* wasn't calling Ronald Reagan by the diminutive "Ronnie"—that would be disrespectful.

In his speech at the library, Rubio positioned himself as a Reagan for the twenty-first century. Reagan had wanted to properly define the role of government; Rubio wanted to properly define the role of government. Reagan understood that Americans wanted a nation that aspired to prosperity and compassion; Rubio understood that Americans wanted a nation that aspired to prosperity and compassion. Reagan had his Morning in America, an image of a country growing stronger and prouder; Rubio promoted American exceptionalism, the notion that the United States is greater than any nation on Earth and has a solemn responsibility to maintain that status. It was one of Rubio's mantras during his U.S. Senate campaign and it played well at a time when the housing market was a disaster, unemployment was soaring, and Wall Street chieftains were flying away in private jets with tens of millions of dollars in golden parachutes while their banks were collapsing.

Here was this young, Cuban American politician with dark brown eyes and a huge smile telling everyone that things were going to be okay in a manner that sounded off the cuff, like he really meant it.

On a phone call before his Reagan Library appearance Rubio explained to Parsky that he preferred to speak from notes rather than a full written text. "He made a point of that in the prediscussion," Parsky said. But Rubio's speech that day revealed a young star still finding his footing. He lacked the crispness that he'd displayed in previous addresses, as if he'd grown a little cocky, a little too confident in his ability to wing it. Several times he stumbled over key lines or groped for words, but he still managed to wow his audience.

Rhetorically Rubio had given himself a complicated task. His message of optimism, his fixation on American exceptionalism, had to be reconciled with his assertion that the United States was headed for disaster. He would have to explain why the very generations that so many thought had contributed to the nation's greatness were also responsible for endangering its long-term solvency. Making that kind of claim required some rhetorical gymnastics. After all, the society that he was saying had screwed up so badly had done relatively well for itself in the twentieth century. It had defeated Hitler, built the largest economy ever seen, vanquished the Soviet Union, and landed on the moon.

"It is a startling place to be, because the 20th Century was not a time of decline for America, it was the American Century," Rubio told the audience. "And yet today we have built for ourselves a government that not even the richest and most prosperous nation [on] the face of the Earth can fund or afford to pay for."

He zeroed in on entitlement programs, telling his audience that when Social Security was enacted there were sixteen workers for every retiree, a ratio that had plummeted to three to one in 2011 and was headed toward two to one. Others had also been warning about impending doom. Special commissions had been formed and disbanded. The former U.S. comptroller general David M. Walker had been barnstorming across the country proclaiming that the exploding cost of Social Security, Medicare, and Medicaid would consume the entire federal budget as soon as 2025.

Rubio presented an idealized view of times gone by. In another era, he told the audience, "If someone was sick in your family, you took care of them. If a neighbor met misfortune, you took care of them. You saved for your retirement and your future because you had to. . . . We took these things upon ourselves and our communities and our families and our homes and our churches and our synagogues. But all that changed when the government began to assume those responsibilities. All of the sudden, for an increasing number of people in our nation, it was no longer necessary to worry about saving for security because that was the government's job. . . . And as government crowded out the institutions in our society that did these things traditionally, it weakened our people in a way that undermined our ability to maintain our prosperity."

That final observation—that entitlement programs had weakened Americans—was the point he clearly wanted to hammer home. He said it three times in the course of his twenty-three-minute speech. The senator from the state with the second highest number of Medicare beneficiaries was giving a speech in the state with the highest number of Medicare beneficiaries and calling American retirees—many of whom were members of the so-called Greatest Generation—weak. It seemed like sloppy speechifying.

"It's not as bad as calling Social Security a Ponzi scheme, but it's not the best way to express it," a prominent national Republican insider and admirer of Rubio's told me.

Or was it?

In the days after the speech, liberal groups and left-leaning commentators pounced. On MSNBC—which had become a counterpoint to the conservative Fox News Network—commentator Ed Schultz called Rubio "a political hack." "For Marco Rubio to say programs like Medicare and Social Security weaken Americans is flat out Psycho Talk," Schultz barked. On the same network host Rachel Maddow reminded her viewers about a previous speech in which Rubio had said that Medicare paid for his father's health care during the illness that led to his death in September 2010. The government program had "allowed him to die with dignity by paying for his hospice care," Rubio had said. Maddow argued that there was a glaring inconsistency. "What would he run as, the guy who says Medicare saved his father and his family but it's also turned you weak and helpless?" she told her viewers. Yet the address she cited was an impassioned plea to save Medicare by reforming it. Rubio specifically stated that he would not advocate changing the system for anyone over the age of fifty-five. But by using an inflammatory word like "weakened" during his Reagan Library speech he had given his opponents an opening. It didn't really matter that most of the criticisms ignored the substance of the point he was trying to make. He wasn't advocating abolishing entitlement programs for current recipients, and he told the Reagan Library audience as much: "My mother just—well she gets mad when I say this—she is in her eighth decade of life and she is on both of these programs. I can't ask my mom to go out and get another job. She paid into the system." But he was calling for change to the system so that it had a chance to endure.

"The truth is that Social Security and Medicare, as important as they are, cannot look for me how they look for her. My generation must fully accept, the sooner the better, that if we want there to be a Social Security and a Medicare when we retire, and if we want America as we know it to continue when we retire, then we must accept and begin to make changes to those programs now, for us."

As the clamor grew louder on the left, Rubio pushed back hard. He portrayed the criticisms as just another bout of whining from lefties. Here was a glimpse of another side of Marco Rubio—not the Florida politician who spoke about finding common ground with his political opposites—but the political brawler born of South Florida's caustic campaigns. During his rise, Rubio had surrounded himself with scrappers, men who envisioned politics as a slugfest. Rubio did not like being challenged, and when he was, his reflex action was to punch back. He used the opportunity to argue for reforming entitlement programs and sought to hold himself up as a sage of fiscal responsibility. So confident that he'd gained an upper hand, he even used the hubbub as a fundraising pitch. "The speech drove extreme liberals crazy, and they are on the attack," read an email sent by Reclaim America, Rubio's political action committee. "We need your help to fight back and support limited government candidates who share Marco's conservative vision for America."

Rubio was working from a time-tested political strategy: attack the media, especially outlets perceived as liberal. His base loved it, and Republican Party wise men such as Parsky applauded. "I think that he demonstrated courage in terms of a willingness to address the importance of addressing entitlements, especially Social Security," Parsky said.

The controversy invested in Rubio more stature as a conservative with substance and pluck. He'd already become one of the best-known Cuban Americans in the United States. His family history, their journey from Cuba to the United States, had become a core element of his political identity. And though that history, as he related it, would not entirely stand up to close scrutiny, its essence—that he was the product of the Cuban American experience—would prove resilient. But his popularity transcended and, in some ways, defied ethnicity. His national support seemed to derive as much from his conservative credentials as from the vowels at the end of his names.

Two weeks after Rubio's Reagan Library speech, Rush Limbaugh predicted, without equivocation, that Rubio would be elected president someday, the first Hispanic to hold America's highest office in the land. The commentariat bubbled with speculation that Rubio would be a future Republican vice presidential or presidential nominee.

An heir apparent had been crowned. It had happened, as Rubio's old football coaches might say, "real quick."

Chapter One

THE ISLAND

In a village hard among the sugarcane fields of north-central Cuba, a woman named Ramona García y de León gave birth to a baby boy on the night of January 31, 1899. The infant gulped his first breath of air in a humble dwelling built from the thatched leaves and stringy wood fibers of palm trees, *guano y yagua*, as the locals called them.

Residents of the island had been building houses from palm leaves since before the time of Christopher Columbus. In 1492 the explorer marveled in his journal about the "beautifully constructed" thatched palm structures on the island. After four centuries of colonial rule, palm-leaf huts were still commonplace in poor, rural areas such as the one where Ramona's child was born.

The Spanish language, lyrical thing of beauty that it is, employs the most sublime of phrases to declare that a woman is giving birth. *Dar a luz*, Spanish speakers say—literally, "give unto the light." If there was illumination in Ramona's home in Cuba's

Santa Clara Province that night at 9 P.M. when she brought her child into the light it was probably the flicker of a candle or the sputter of an oil lamp.

One hundred twelve years later, the baby's grandson, Marco Antonio Rubio, would be sworn in as a U.S. senator. The Senate clerk would call out four words, "Mr. Rubio of Florida," and Rubio would stride across the blue carpet in a dark suit and red power tie, navigating an aisle bracketed by mahogany desks. The vice president swears in groups of four senators at a time, their names called out alphabetically. Rubio—who would have the ascendant politician's knack for perfect placement—would walk at the head of the group by virtue of where he fell in the alphabet. In the well of the Senate chamber, Vice President Joe Biden would wait with an outstretched right hand.

The ceremony represented an inspiring culmination of immigrant dreams fulfilled, from thatched-roof house to the U.S. capitol in just three generations. But on that long ago day in Cuba, the prospects for the infant born to Ramona and the generations that would follow him could not have seemed particularly promising.

Ramona García, Marco Rubio's great-grandmother, lived in a small village called Jicotea, which shared its name with a species of tortoise that thrived in Cuba's lakes and marshes. Just over twelve hundred people called Jicotea and the nearby village of San Bartolomé home, according to a census conducted in 1899 that combined the two locations. The villages were satellites of Santo Domingo, a town about seventy miles inland, where the island's spine begins to arch toward the setting sun. The landscape flattens out there, watered and made fertile by the Sagua la Grande River as it meanders north before tumbling into the Atlantic Ocean among hundreds of cays and a constellation of coral reefs.

Ramona waited five months to make her child's birth official. On May 25 she took him to Nuestra Señora de la Esperanza — Our Lady of Hope — the Catholic parish church six miles to the southeast in the town of Esperanza. There she declared that his first name was Pedro and his middle name Víctor. What's missing on the baptismal certificate produced that day is a last name. The document, signed by an interim priest, underscores the uncertain provenance of the boy with its description of Ramona: she is a *soltera*, an unmarried woman.

Ten years later Ramona appeared at 7:45 A.M. before a municipal judge and his secretary in Santo Domingo, seven and a half miles north of her home. No father is listed on the civil registry documents that she went there to have inscribed. In the registry Ramona declared that Pedro Víctor would be given her last name, García. When it came time to sign the registry, she told the judge that she couldn't; she was unable to write her own name. A man named Ramón Ramírez signed for her. His relationship to her is not stated.

In the years before Ramona gave birth, she lived in a region shredded by conflict. Cuban rebels, led by the poet-soldier José Martí, soon to be a martyr, had sparked a rebellion against Spanish colonialists in 1895. During the uprising, Santa Clara Province evolved into a strategically important and fiercely contested region because it could serve as a base of operations to prepare attacks against the capital, Havana, 160 miles to the west. Rebels massed there in hopes of avoiding being trapped at the eastern fringes of the island as they had been in two other wars of independence, fought during the preceding three decades.

When the pregnant Ramona looked up at the sky, she would frequently have seen smoke. Santa Clara (which would later become known as Las Villas, then be carved up and parceled into the provinces of Villa Clara, Cienfuegos, and Sancti Spíritus) cultivated 40 percent of the island's lucrative sugarcane crop. The rebels took to burning fields owned by the Spaniards. The cane fields and sugar mills relied on the underclasses for labor in those days, primarily blacks, as well as white peasants whose ancestry traced back to Spain. The rebels called themselves Mambis, a name derived from a black Spanish soldier, Juan Ethninius Mamby, who had defected and fought against the Spanish in the Dominican War of Independence. *Mamby* was a Spanish slur. The Cubans defiantly adopted it as a badge of honor.

Revolutionary leaders such as General Máximo Gómez hoped that burning the sugarcane fields would distract workers from the harvest and turn their attention to the Revolution. The rebels were bent on "destroying a social and economic system built on racism and inequality," wrote the Latin America scholar Gillian McGillivray.

Spanish forces responded aggressively, descending on the province in great numbers, forcibly relocating villagers and laying waste to the countryside. Spain was not going to give up easily. It had beaten back two rebellions in the second half of the nineteenth century and was determined to protect this Caribbean stronghold, one of the last pieces of a once mighty empire.

Spain had ruled Cuba for most of the previous four centuries (interrupted by a brief period of British control in the 1760s), since the conquistador Diego Velázquez de Cuéllar established the first Spanish settlement in the early 1500s. But it was about to encounter a force much more powerful than the rebels fighting in the cane fields.

The U.S. government sent a warship to Cuba in the winter of 1898, after riots in Havana caused alarm that U.S. citizens on the island, and their business interests, could be in danger. The ship, which anchored in Havana's port, weighed 6,600 tons and was painted a brilliant white. It was the USS *Maine*.

At 9:40 on the night of February 15, 1898, two explosions ripped through the vessel. Witnesses on nearby boats saw bodies catapulted into the night sky. A survivor, Lieutenant John Blandin, later described what he saw as "a perfect rain of missiles of all descriptions, from huge pieces of cement to blocks of wood, steel railing and fragments of grating." The death toll reached 266. For perspective, consider that the number of dead on the *Maine* was more than fifteen times the number who would die in the October 2000 bombing of the USS *Cole* in Yemen, an attack that prompted worldwide outrage.

The cause of the explosions on the *Maine* is debated to this day, with theories ranging from Spanish mines to accidental sparks from cooking fires on board, and even conspiracies that the United States purposely destroyed the ship to justify going to war. But at the time public sentiment was shaped by William R. Hearst's influential American newspapers. "Remember the Maine, to Hell with Spain!" became a rallying cry. By April that year U.S. ships were blockading Spanish-controlled Cuban ports, and the United States had declared war against Spain. It was a conflict that added to the legend of a future president of the United States, Theodore Roosevelt, whose Rough Riders famously captured San Juan Hill. The war also added to the domain of the United States.

It took U.S. forces just four months to so thoroughly humble the Spaniards that the battered European power sought a peace treaty. The pact, which ceded control of Cuba, Guam, Puerto Rico, and the Philippines to the United States, was signed in December after negotiations in Paris. On January 1, 1899, John P. Wade, a second lieutenant with the U.S. Army's 5th Cavalry, raised the first American flag over Morro Castle, the imposing sixteenth-century stone fortress that guards the entrance to Havana's harbor.

Cubans had been shut out of the peace treaty negotiations, and the rebel general, Máximo Gómez, seethed. He refused to attend the flag-raising. "Ours," he wrote, "is the Cuban flag, the one for which so many tears and blood have been shed. . . . We must keep united in order to end this unjustified military occupation."

Ramona was in her last month of pregnancy when the U.S. flag first rose above Morro Castle, signaling the beginning of three years of U.S. control of the island through a military governor. In the province where she lived, more than half the population, including Ramona, would not have been able to read the news reports, according to a census ordered by U.S. president William McKinley and overseen by the U.S. War Department in 1899. The younger generation would have been of little help to the illiterate adults. In Santo Domingo and its satellite villages, only 243 out of 2,071 children under the age of ten attended school.

When U.S. forces inspected Santa Clara Province after the war they found a scene of ruin and disarray. A drought and the corrosive effects of war had led to a scarcity of food, wrote Major General John R. Brooke, the island's military governor, in an October 1899 report to the adjutant general of the U.S. Army in Washington. "The country roads, mail service, public instruction and local governments were in a state of almost complete abandonment," he wrote. "Agriculture and trade had practically disappeared."

One fourth of the men in Santo Domingo and its villages were unemployed, and the bulk of those who did work were engaged in backbreaking labor in sugarcane and tobacco fields. Fieldwork, though, would be impossible for Pedro Víctor. As a youth he was stricken by polio, an affliction that left him with one leg shorter than the other. "He couldn't work the fields, so they sent him to school," his grandson, by then a U.S. senator, told a California audience in 2011.

Unlike so many of the children in the region where he was born, Pedro Víctor gravitated toward the written word. "He became the only member of his family [who could] read," his grandson said. "And he would read anything and everything he could." Pedro Víctor went to work in a cigar factory, where his affection for words was put to use each morning. "They didn't have radio or television, so they would hire someone to sit at the front of the cigar factory and read to the workers while they worked. So, the first thing he would read every day, of course, was the daily newspaper. Then he would read some novel to entertain them. And then, when he was done reading things he actually went out and rolled the cigars because he needed the extra money."

Pedro Víctor badly needed to supplement his income during his lifetime in Cuba. In 1920, at the age of twenty-one, he married a young woman named Dominga de la Caridad Rodríguez y Chirolde, who was five weeks shy of her seventeenth birthday. The couple would have seven children, all girls.

By 1921, they'd settled in the south-central province of Camagüey. One of the places where they lived was Jatibonico, a town that represented relative prosperity in the Cuba of that era. It boomed during the First World War when demand for Cuban sugar grew. A large eponymous sugar mill and several major tobacco plantations dominated the town. Its population doubled to more than ten thousand between the censuses of 1907 and 1919. "This municipality will have a great future, as its territory is a very fertile one," a provincial inspector wrote in the 1919 census. The family lived in Camagüey for at least a decade, suggesting that Pedro Víctor was able to find a solid means of supporting them there. At least five of his daughters were born there, according to U.S. immigration documents: Olga, Elda, Irma, Dolores, and finally, on November 2, 1930, in Jatibonico, Oriales. It was Oriales who, four decades later, would give birth to a future senator of the United States.

In his later years Pedro Víctor would talk of his love of history, sharing with his grandson what he'd learned in all those books. His life had spanned a period of painful political upheaval, a legacy imparted to every Cuban and every Cuban American. He was born while the repercussions of the Cuban War of Independence were still being sorted out and he lived the first three years of his life in a nation controlled by a U.S. military governor. The United States eventually turned over the country to the Cubans in 1902. By the time he was six there had been another revolt, and a U.S. military governor was back in charge for another three years. He had seen the Cuban president Gerardo Machado deposed and pushed into exile in Miami in the 1930s. Then Pedro Víctor

watched Carlos Prío, one of the men who had helped depose Machado, himself deposed and sent into exile in the 1950s. Prío later quipped, "They say that I was a terrible president of Cuba. That may be true. But I was the best president Cuba ever had." When Pedro Víctor was in his early fifties a coup gave power to Fulgencio Batista, a corrupt dictator whose authority derived in part from friendly relations with the United States. It's no wonder that in 1956 Pedro Víctor, by then living in Havana and making shoes for a living, thought he could find a better place for his family. A better place ninety miles north, in the United States.

Pedro Víctor's coming-to-America story involved risks not unlike those still experienced by millions of immigrants who equate the United States with a better life. His narrative has the potential to resonate broadly in the twenty-first century, long after his death.

But his grandson had another story that he was also eager to tell.

Chapter Two

A PATH TO CITIZENSHIP

National Airlines Flight 352 touched down at Miami International Airport on May 27, 1956, completing the short trip from Havana. For a time in the mid-1950s, the airline operated as many as ten flights a day between the two cities, flitting back and forth across the Florida Straits as routinely as the Delta and U.S. Airways shuttles now hop between Washington and New York.

In the current era of travel restrictions to Cuba, it's strange to think of the island as if it were any other Caribbean destination, rather than the nexus of a highly emotional political standoff spanning eleven U.S. presidencies and a single Cuban dictatorship. On one vintage poster promoting flights to and from the island, National Airlines invites travelers to, "Go by National to Gay Havana. Route of the Buccaneers." A jet glides blithely above the lighthouse at Morro Castle at the mouth of Havana's harbor as a nattily dressed couple looks up from below.

The young family on Flight 352 was traveling in the opposite direction, away from gay Havana. Nine days earlier Mario Rubio y Reina, who was twenty-nine at the time, had walked into the U.S. Consulate in Havana and applied for an immigrant visa and alien registration. The key question on the form was number 25: Purpose of going to the United States?

"To reside," he answered.

On his passport photo Mario gazes straight ahead. He doesn't smile, but he looks proud, his left eye arched ever so slightly. He had gelled and combed back his thick brown, wavy hair into a perfect peak. On his upper lip is a neatly groomed, pencil-thin mustache, the fashion of the day. He is dressed in a jacket and tie. His twenty-five-year-old wife, Oriales, traveled with him that day, and they brought along their only child, Mario Victor Rubio; he was six years old. More than half a century later, a controversy would erupt over the circumstances of their arrival and the version of it that their youngest son told during his spectacular political ascent. But on that day in 1956, the small family arrived as did many other Cuban immigrants: unremarkably.

———

The Rubios were avid baseball fans, and all Cubans knew that the players who came to the United States represented one example of how the huge nation north of their island could transform lives. The lineups in the next day's papers detailed the exploits of their countryman, the four-time all-star Chicago White Sox leftfielder Minnie Miñoso, known as the Cuban Comet. At Fenway Park in Boston two young Cuban American pitchers, Pedro Ramos and the scintillating curveball maestro Camilo Pascual, had struggled. But the duo still managed to deliver a victory for the Washington Senators.

Cuban ballplayers were common in the United States, arriving without the anguish and political defector dramas that now accompany each appearance of star players from the island. By the time the Rubios arrived no fewer than sixty-six Cuban-born players had made their debuts in the Major Leagues. The Senators alone debuted seven Cuban-born ballplayers in the 1955 and 1956 seasons.

Like all those shortstops and centerfielders and fireballing starting pitchers, the Rubios crossed into the United States looking for opportunity. But their arrival would not be greeted by cheering crowds or professional contracts. In the reductive language of immigration forms Mario Rubio y Reina described his occupation as "laborer."

In 1956 the attention of U.S. immigrant agents was tuned more acutely to the East than the South. Precise quotas limited emigration from European nations, as well as China, India, and the entire African continent. No more than 225 Turkish immigrants were allowed, for instance, and 438 Portuguese and 17,756 Irish. The most startling restrictions to read from the distance of half a century, though, are the limits placed on emigration from two nations that are now the most populated on Earth. Only 100 immigrants from China were allowed (plus another 100 Chinese who lived in other nations) and 100 from India.

No such quotas existed for nations in the Western Hemisphere. But that's not to say there were not barriers. Cubans were typically asked to provide proof of financial support, either in the form of a job or the support of a relative. Their character would be scrutinized too. In the month before he emigrated Mario Rubio collected testimonials. The Cuban National Police Department attested that there was nothing in its files that would call into question his morality or conduct. A prison archivist confirmed that Mario had not been incarcerated. The head of the local recruitment office affirmed that he had registered for military service.

It also helped to have someone waiting for you in the United States. On Mario's visa application, he said his family would live at the home of one of his wife's sisters, Dolores Denis. Dolores, who was two years older than Oriales, lived in Miami on Southwest Sixth Street in an area that was still years away from becoming widely known as Little Havana. Like the Rubios, Dolores and her husband would also produce a political son, though his leanings would not coincide with those of Mario's boy.

In Cuba the Rubios left behind an existence defined by adversity. Mario's mother, Eloísa Reina y Sánchez, died when he was young. Mario was either six years old or just a few days shy of his ninth birthday at the time of his mother's death, according to conflicting accounts given by Senator Rubio. On the same day that his mother was laid to rest, Mario went to work selling coffee in the streets of Havana. He would face another family tragedy at the age of twelve, with the death of his father, Antonio Rubio. Mario was now an orphan.

As a teenager Mario made his living humbly, working as a security guard at a store similar to a five-and-dime called Casa del los Tres Kilos, which translates roughly to Three-Cent Store. He slept in a storage room. Senator Rubio has said his parents "were not political people." But it seems the young Mario Rubio was capable of some political engagement. In 2012, Marco Rubio claimed his eighteen-year-old father had participated in a failed military plot to overthrow Rafael Trujillo, the dictator who ruled the Dominican Republic.

In Havana, Mario Rubio met and fell in love with a seventeen-year-old cashier named Oriales. They married the next year and had a son the year after that. Mario gave his child his first name and his father's middle name, Victor.

Cuba at that time was a paradox. By some measures it was one of Latin America's most stable and prosperous nations. It had the region's lowest infant mortality rate and the second highest percentage of individual car owners. Its national finances were in order, boasting the third highest level of cash reserves in Latin America. But good jobs were scarce; 30 percent of Cubans were unemployed or underemployed. Upward mobility was difficult, and the political situation was becoming more tenuous. The dictator Fulgencio Batista was unpopular, but powerful. Large demonstrations were staged in 1955. Then in April 1956, the month before the Rubios left the island, a popular military officer, Ramón Barquín, led a coup that came to be known as the "conspiracy of the peers." Batista quickly squelched the uprising. Barquin was court-martialed and Batista began purging the officer corps.

With unrest on the island and poor prospects for economic betterment, the Rubios and other Cuban families looked to the United States and its aura of prosperity and hope. In the mid-1950s Cuban migration was merely a trickle compared to what it would become in the years after Fidel Castro took power. Earlier migration patterns were generally tied to political upheaval on the island and economic conditions in the United States. Migration spiked around 1886 with the emergence of cigar factories in Tampa and reached new highs in the years before and after the Cuban War of Independence, a period that coincided with the heyday of Tampa's cigar industry. During the Great Depression,

Cuban migration almost came to a halt. An annual average of only 396 Cubans emigrated to the United States from 1931 to 1935. Compare that to the annual average of more than 4,200 between 1906 and 1910, a period that included an uprising against the Cuban president Tomás Estrada Palma that prompted the United States to send troops back to the island and install the second military governor in a decade.

Those patterns repeated themselves in the 1950s, when the Rubios were deciding whether to leave the island. By then Cuba was ruled by Batista, a charming and venal strongman. Lagging in the polls in the 1952 presidential campaign, Batista led a successful coup three months before the election. He ousted the outgoing president, Carlos Prío, and put himself in charge. (Prío, as was the norm, fled into exile in South Florida.)

In 1953 the average Cuban was making just $6 a week, and in 1956—the year the Rubios left—and the following year nearly a third of the population was unemployed or underemployed. Batista, for his part, was enjoying a cascade of gifts from foreign companies, including an infamous gold phone given to him by the U.S.-owned Cuban phone company. That same year, while the Rubios were raising their three-year-old son Mario Victor, the revolutionary Fidel Castro led a failed attack on the Moncada Barracks near the city of Santiago de Cuba and was arrested. Two years later, in May 1955, he was released from prison and went into exile in Mexico, where he founded the July 26th Movement, named for the date of the barracks raid. He was giving few indications that he should be taken seriously. "Cubans had known Castro for years as a loud and ineffectual plotter, a loser," wrote Tad Szulc in *Fidel: A Critical Portrait.*

During those last months in Havana, the Rubios lived in Apartment C9 on a street called Maloja. A short walk away, through a quilt of angled streets, is one of Havana's most curious sights, a neoclassical structure that now feels jarringly out of place in a nation so at odds with the United States. A soaring cupola rises from its center, and columns stretch from its base to the right and left. It's called El Capitolio, and though it's a museum now, it was the home of Cuba's legislature when the Rubios lived on Maloja. There has been some dispute over the years about the inspiration for its design, but it bears a double-take-inducing resemblance to the U.S. Capitol in Washington, the unlikely future destination of the Rubios' son Marco.

The Rubios were somewhat itinerant in their early years in the United States. Like so many immigrant families, they followed family members. After leaving Miami, New York City was a logical destination. Oriales's sister and brother-in-law, Irma and Luís Enrique Lastres, had come to the United States in September 1955 and were living in New York City's West Village, a block and a half from the Hudson River. Irma was making $42 a week operating a Merrow sewing machine at Tama Sportswear on Sixth Avenue—nearly double the median income for women in the United States. Luís Enrique was making the same salary as his wife at Jollé International Jewelers on West Thirty-sixth Street. His salary was well below the median annual income for men in the United States, which had reached an all-time high of $3,600 in 1956, according to the U.S. Census Bureau. But that did not stop the extended family from clustering around the gainfully employed Lastreses. On the day before Mario and Oriales arrived in the United States, the Lastreses filled out an affidavit sponsoring Oriales's mother and two of her sisters, Magdalena and Adria García. The Lastreses weren't just vouching for their relatives. They were taking them in. The Lastreses had "living quarters prepared" for all three and pledged to "fully assist them in their maintenance and support until such [time] as they will have become self-supporting."

Six months later they were once again trying to help a relative come to the United States. This time it was Oriales's father, Pedro Víctor García. The father of seven daughters had been living in Havana just a short walk from the apartment that Mario and Oriales had last called home.

Pedro Víctor followed his family to the United States on December 18, 1956, aboard Cubana Airlines Flight T-605. When he arrived immigration authorities required that he undergo a medical examination. The report, reflecting the insensitivities of language in those days, noted that Pedro Víctor's right leg had a "deformity." He suffered from ankylosis of the knee, which is a stiffening of the joint, and his muscles had atrophied, leaving his right leg shorter than the left. Those conditions, which severely limited the function of his right leg, were probably the result of polio in childhood, the examiner noted. His spine was curved by a rare condition called cervicodorsal scoliosis and he had pulmonary emphysema.

Pedro Víctor's medical examination did not impede his entry to the United States. As they had done for his wife and two of his daughters, the Lastreses filled out an affidavit of support for the fifty-six-year-old father of seven. Even in the stiff language of legal documents, the moving American immigrant narrative of separation and aspiration comes through. "We are willing and able to receive, maintain and support our herein named father," the affidavit reads. "Our father's coming to the United States will afford him a much wider field for the further development of his capabilities and experience, and a more direct benefit for the direct assistance that all his children will then be able to give him, and will also provide his wife with his much needed conjugal relationship and his children with his much needed paternal companionship."

But being dependent on one's children can assault a man's pride. It took a toll on Pedro Víctor, so much so that he would later make a decision that once again cleaved his family. For the meantime, though, he went to work repairing shoes, which had been his profession in Havana.

His son-in-law Mario Rubio, the senator's father, had entrepreneurial dreams. Senator Rubio would later entertain audiences by saying that Mario had tried to make a living in New York, but found it "too cold," that he had found Miami "too hard," and that he found Los Angeles "too California." In the years after the extended family came to the United States, Senator Rubio said, his father opened several businesses, including a sandwich shop, a beauty supply store, and a dry cleaner. For a time, both the Rubios found work stitching nylon beach chairs. But Mario earned a living for most of his life as a bartender. It appears that by 1958 the family was living in Miami; a Mario Rubio is listed as an employee of the Roney Plaza Hotel in Miami Beach in Polk's 1958 Miami Beach city directory.

The Roney was a swank spot with formal gardens, 1,500 feet of ocean frontage, cabanas, and restaurants. In the late 1950s it was still years away from beginning its slide into decay and irrelevance. Walter Winchell spent winters at the hotel in the 1940s and broadcast his radio program from there, each night opening the show with his signature line, "Good Evening, Mr. and Mrs. America and all the ships at sea." Celebrities flocked to the Roney, drawn by the glamour of the guests and by their friendship with Mickey Hayes, a local character who ran a clothing store on the first floor. Larry Shupnick, who ran the hotel in the 1960s, convinced Jackie Gleason that the Roney would be a perfect headquarters for filming his popular television variety show. It was not uncommon for visitors to spot Bob Hope, Frank Sinatra, or Buddy Hackett walking through the lobby or meeting friends for drinks. Boozy late nights often ended in the hotel's Napoleon's Retreat, where Gleason's music conductor, Sammy Spear, would jam into the wee hours.

Bartenders at the better Miami Beach hotels typically wore black Eton jackets, a distinctive, waist-length style cut square at the bottom. Their jobs were prized not so much because of the 95 cents to $1.25 an hour in salary, but because of the $20 to $30 a night they could earn in cash tips. Frequent flights in and out of Miami International Airport made it possible for prosperous Cuban businessmen to pop up to the city for the day, stopping for a power lunch at the even swankier Fontainebleau Hotel, before returning for the evening flight. The most fashionable Cubans brought their wives along so they could shop.

While the Rubios were establishing themselves in their new country, their old country was coming undone. In November— six months after Mario and his family arrived in Miami and one month before Pedro Víctor arrived in the United States—Fidel Castro set sail with eighty-one rebels from Tuxpan, Mexico, in a creaky yacht, the *Granma*. Few could have imagined that barely two years later the dictator Batista would flee into exile on New Year's Day 1959, reputedly with millions of plundered dollars, leaving control of the island to Castro and his forces.

The signal event in the lives of millions of Cubans barely registered in the Anglo-dominated South Florida media. The struggle in Cuba didn't even make the front page of the *Miami Herald* on that historic New Year's Day. But as news of Batista's abdication spread, Cubans poured into the streets, many shouting "Viva Castro!"

Miami had yet to be transformed into the exile capital of the United States. In 1958 as few as 10,000 Cubans lived there. Many locals still pronounced the city's name with a southern accent, "myam-uh." There wasn't a single person of Cuban descent in the U.S. Congress or on the Dade County Commission. Reflecting the prevailing attitude of the time, Helen Muir, a well-known Miami newspaper columnist, wrote, "Miamians went to bed New Year's night with no more than passing interest in the fact that the dictator, Fulgencio Batista, had been deposed and that the thirty-two-year-old revolutionary, Fidel Castro, had come to power."

Half a century later it's remarkable to read Muir's account in her book, *Miami, U.S.A.* What's incredible is not so much the fact that Castro's victory was barely noticed by some, but that the word "Miamians" could be decoupled from Cuban Americans. Today the smells, tastes, rhythms, and passions of the city are distinctly Cuban American. But it wasn't that way on New Year's Day in 1959 when Muir noted that Miamians found it "far more interesting that Alaska was about to be declared the forty-ninth state in the union and that the European Economic Community, or Common Market, had gone into effect that day." Soon after Castro's ascension to power, U.S. authorities could not help but pay attention to what was happening in Cuba. Police supervisors were forced to send extra patrols to Miami International Airport because of the scuffles that were breaking out between the giddy *fidelistas* who were flying to Havana and the demoralized *batistianos* who were landing in Miami after fleeing Cuba. The *batistianos* were wise to flee. Castro and his junta were executing hundreds of their opponents.

In April 1959 Castro went on a victory tour to the United States. President Dwight D. Eisenhower snubbed him, sticking the vice president, Richard M. Nixon, with the task of receiving the revolutionary. Castro showed up in green fatigues. Nixon, in a buttoned suit, awkwardly shook the bearded revolutionary's hand as a photographer snapped pictures. A draft of Nixon's memo about the meeting, which was declassified in 2001, reveals his suspicions about the new Cuban leader: "His primary concern seemed to be to convince me that he was sincere, that he was not a communist." The vice president concluded, "[Castro is] either incredibly naïve about Communism or under Communist discipline — my guess is the former, and as I have already implied his ideas as to how to run a government or an economy are less developed than those of almost any world figure I have met in fifty countries." It didn't take long for Castro's assurances that he was not a Communist to be shown for what they were: complete baloney. But in the early days of his revolution, many Cubans in the United States thought he might be a kind of savior. After all, he'd toppled a corrupt dictator; he'd promised to transform a society.

One of those who saw possibilities in the new Cuba of Fidel Castro was Senator Rubio's grandfather, Pedro Víctor García. He was a proud man. In the two years since he'd emigrated to the United States, he had tried to make a living but never quite succeeded. After odd jobs in New York, he had found his way back to

Miami, the city where the Rubios were making a life, a city with a climate closer to his native Cuba's.

Pedro Víctor lived on Southwest Third Street, a five-minute walk from the address where his daughter Dolores had taken in Mario and Oriales Rubio. But Pedro Víctor never got a steady job in Miami either. He repaired shoes at his home and sometimes picked up a few extra dollars as a money collector in a parking lot. It was never enough, and eventually he grew tired of leaning on his daughters and their husbands. He was sixty years old. He had once supported the daughters who now cared for him. They had families of their own to worry about. In Cuba he could be his own man. So two years and two months after being admitted to the United States as a legal immigrant, Pedro Víctor reached a difficult conclusion. "I had to go back to Cuba to work there because I did not want to be supported by my daughters, my sons-in-law," he later explained. "They have families and I didn't want to be under their care."

On January 15, 1959, two weeks after Batista abdicated, Pedro Víctor flew back to the island of his birth. He had left behind a shoe store in Havana, which was rented to another man. Pedro Víctor planned to collect the rent owed to him. For the first three months he operated his shoe store, but in March he started selling off all his stock and materials. One of his daughters' husbands—it's unclear which one—offered a better option: he could get Pedro Víctor a real job, a job with a salary, vacation time, reliability. Pedro Víctor decided to take it.

His new employer was the Castro government.

The job was with Hacienda, Cuba's Treasury Ministry. It doesn't appear to have been a high-level post, nor does it seem that the position had anything to do with the governing of the nation. Pedro Víctor later described what sounds like a low-level bureaucratic or blue-collar position. He would say that he was tasked with recording payments owed to the Treasury by bus and truck drivers. His job was later transferred to the Transportation Ministry.

Years later, Pedro Víctor said through an interpreter that he was paid $175 a month, though this may have been a translation error. That sum would have been an astonishingly high level of compensation for the Cuba of that era and would have been more than his son-in-law Luís Enrique Lastres was making at the time in New York City. The only other possible explanation for such a lofty salary is that his job wasn't such a low-level position after all. But there is no evidence to support that scenario.

He rented an apartment four blocks from the Bay of Havana and just around the corner from the now elegantly decaying building where the critically acclaimed 1994 movie *Strawberry and Chocolate* was filmed. The building, with its graceful, winding staircase and lacy ironwork, now houses one of Havana's finest *paladares*, La Guarida, a restaurant where Queen Sofia of Spain has dined.

Pedro Víctor's description of the financing of his apartment illuminates the shell game that was real estate in Cuba after Castro took over. In 1960 Castro's government unveiled the Urban Reform Law, under which the government seized rental properties throughout the country. The law was part of a series of sweeping moves, including similar decrees allowing the government to seize rich agricultural land, that were designed to impose a socialist economic structure on the nation. The decree included an enticing inducement and a seemingly people-friendly come-on. Rents for the tenants of apartments were slashed in half, and the tenants were promised that they would become owners of the apartments in five to twenty years.

Pedro Víctor was skeptical. He didn't believe the government's promise. But it wasn't solely his skepticism toward the government's games that made him decide to return to the United States. Two incidents fundamentally altered his life in Havana. The first occurred on July 9, 1960, when he had a serious accident. His grandson has said that Pedro Víctor was hit by a bus. Six days later his wife, Dominga, traveled to Cuba to take care of him. In those days it was still relatively easy to travel back and forth between the United States and Cuba. She stayed for three months. Pedro Víctor tried to return with her. He requested vacation time from the Transportation Ministry, but his bosses denied him, saying it was a busy time of the year.

In April the next year, about a year after Pedro Víctor began working for the government, a group of CIA-trained Cuban exiles launched a failed invasion of the island at the Bay of Pigs, about 130 miles southeast of Havana. The quick defeat of the poorly backed exile fighters and the imprisonment of many of them would embolden Castro and humiliate the Kennedy administration. "How could I have been so stupid to let them go ahead?" Kennedy said not long afterward. The United States eventually had to capitulate to the dictator's demands and turn over $53 million worth of baby food and pharmaceuticals for the safe return of the captured exile combatants.

About two weeks after the Bay of Pigs fiasco, Pedro Víctor's growing unease with the Castro regime was further confirmed. At a ceremony commemorating May Day 1961, Castro stood beside Aleksandr Alekseev, the Soviet ambassador. The two were pals.

Alekseev liked to bring Castro gifts of Soviet vodka and caviar. As the band was getting ready to play, Castro turned to Alekseev and said, "You are going to hear some interesting music today." The band then swung into a rendition of "Internationale," the international socialist anthem. In his speech Castro declared that he was a Marxist-Leninist and that he would "remain one until the last day of [his] life." He went on to state, "Marxism or scientific socialism has become the revolutionary movement of the working class." Communism, Castro declared, would be the dominant force in Cuban politics: "There cannot be three or four movements."

Life in Cuba of that era was about looking over your shoulder. Castro loyalists eyed everyone suspiciously, searching for any sign of faltering loyalty to the regime. "They are watching you every day," Pedro Víctor later said. He was referring to the Comités en Defensa de la Revolución—Committees for the Defense of the Revolution. The block committees, which still exist today and are commonly referred to as CDRs, essentially serve as the eyes and ears of the government on every street in the country. They had been formed in 1960, before the Bay of Pigs invasion, a time when Castro anticipated attempts by U.S.-backed exiles to overthrow his government and wanted to root out sympathizers. He adopted the motto "In a fortress under siege all dissent is treason."

After the Bay of Pigs invasion the CDRs delivered an unnerving display of power. Within hours of the failed attack, thousands of suspected dissenters were arrested, many of them identified from CDR lists. "The CDRs paralyzed the counterrevolution, and they did it quickly," Norberto Fuentes, an exiled Cuban author and onetime friend of the Castros, told me in an interview at his Miami home.

All Cubans are expected to join their local CDR and participate in committee activities whether or not they are Communist
Party members. Each CDR has a popularly elected president
and separate secretaries of security, volunteerism, and education.
Some Cubans don't join or don't participate, but they do so at
great risk of being labeled an "enemy of the Revolution." CDR
presidents can organize "acts of repudiation," in which neighbors
stand outside the homes of those suspected of illegal activity or
disloyalty and scream insults—sometimes for days. The committees can insinuate themselves into almost every aspect of daily
life, even the birth of a child, which is often followed by a visit
from the CDR president. From that moment on, the CDRs enforce a life of indoctrination, making sure the children are attending classes, especially the courses on Cuban history that portray
the victory of Castro's forces as a moment of great triumph for the
nation.

The CDR system has atrophied over the years, a victim of the
waning enthusiasms of a population long deprived of basic goods.
But when Pedro Víctor was beginning to chafe at what was happening in his country, they were at the height of their power. And
he wanted out.

In the summer of 1962 he saw an opportunity. He asked his
bosses for a vacation, and this time they granted it. And so it was
that on August 31, 1962, he took an incredibly risky step. He
boarded Pan American Airlines Flight 2422 bound for Miami.

Pedro Víctor's troubles began not long after the plane landed.
He had a Cuban passport and a U.S. alien registration card, but he
didn't have a visa. A U.S. immigration officer named E. E. Spink
detained the sixty-three-year-old grandfather. Spink signed a form
that read, "You do not appear to me to be clearly and beyond

a doubt entitled to enter the United States." A photographer snapped a mug shot of Pedro Víctor with his alien registration number on a block in front of him. After more than three and a half years in Havana, he had aged dramatically. His cheeks were sunken, there were bags under his eyes, and his mouth was tight. He looked exhausted.

It had to have been a humiliating and unsettling experience, an undignified return to the United States for a man who had once been welcomed here. In a way Pedro Víctor's treatment was not unlike the present-day experiences of many Mexicans and Central Americans who come to the United States legally but later run afoul of visa laws and find their lives irreversibly upended. The immigration authorities who detained Pedro Víctor at the airport would have been well within their rights to send him back to Cuba immediately, explained Bill Yates, a former top immigration official who served under Republicans and Democrats during his thirty-plus-year career. Instead, they were willing to give him a chance to argue that he should be allowed to stay. The paper trail is inconclusive about whether he was forced to spend time in a detention facility. If he did, he must have eventually been released because six weeks later he received a summons to appear at an immigration hearing. The mail went to the home of one of his daughters, an address two blocks from the place where he had lived in the mid-1950s, when Cubans were trickling, rather than gushing, into the area. People were starting to call the area Little Havana. The summons gave some indication of what was to come, and it wasn't something good.

That spring, the federal government had leased space in the old Miami News tower, a striking Spanish Renaissance Revival structure on Biscayne Boulevard with a jaw-dropping view of Biscayne Bay. The building's design had been inspired by La Giralda, the stunning bell tower at the cathedral in Sevilla, which had been a minaret during the period of Moorish rule in Andalucía. The cupola-topped tower was built in 1924–25 and was designed by the prestigious architectural firm Schultze and Weaver, which would count among its accomplishments the Pierre Hotel in New York and the Biltmore Hotel in Coral Gables. They also designed a hotel on Miami Beach: the Roney Plaza.

——

The old newspaper building was renamed the Freedom Tower because the federal government opened a Cuban refugee center there. In the years to come, hundreds of thousands of Cubans streamed through the building, receiving medical checkups, financial support, and a variety of other services aimed at easing their transition to the United States. It has been called the Ellis Island of the South, the southern Statue of Liberty, a symbol, a beacon.

Pedro Víctor García, however, wasn't being sent to the beacon. He was being sent up the street, to the Justice Department's Immigration and Naturalization Service offices, physically about three miles north of the South's new Ellis Island, but symbolically a million miles in the distance. The building to the south represented succor and welcome; the one to the north tilted more toward the punitive.

On October 4, 1962, Pedro Víctor appeared before a special inquiry officer, a kind of immigration judge, named Milton V. Milich. Pedro Víctor's hearing was recorded on an Edison

Voicewriter, a machine originally manufactured by the inventor Thomas Alva Edison's company. The Voicewriter promised "ear-tuned jewel action" clarity in its advertisements. Two vinyl discs, about the size of single phonograph records, contain audio of the proceedings. Now full of scratches and audible pops, the records are a remarkable artifact of another era. In thirty-three minutes of testimony they tell the story of a man caught in an immigration no-man's land, a lesson about the laws that decide who gets to stay in the United States and who must go.

Pedro Víctor's was the last case of the day. And before getting started, Milich, who spoke in a New York deadpan, wanted to know whether Pedro Víctor could speak English. When Milich learned that Pedro Víctor spoke only Spanish, a translator—a woman with a soft, gentle, almost childlike voice—began relaying the judge's instructions. Pedro Víctor didn't have an attorney and said he couldn't afford one. Milich offered to delay the proceedings, but Pedro Víctor opted to move forward without legal representation.

"Señor, levante su mano derecha," the translator instructed— "Sir, raise your right hand."

"I swear," Garcia said in Spanish, his voice a low rumble.

The prosecutor was Joseph W. Monsanto, an attorney who would go on to become a chief immigration judge. Monsanto claimed that Pedro Víctor had abandoned his legal resident status when he left the country in 1959 and stayed away for more than a year. At that time many Cubans were being admitted to the United States as refugees. All seven of Pedro Víctor's daughters were then living in the United States, and two of them—one in Miami and another in New York—had been designated refugees. (Pedro Víctor does not identify which of his daughters were so designated.) The designation was not automatic. It would be four years before Congress enacted the Cuban Adjustment Act, which made it far easier for Cubans to claim refugee status.

On the Voicewriter records, Pedro Víctor sounds calm and respectful. He speaks Spanish in a deep, smoke-cured voice, the product of the three-cigars-a-day habit he would maintain into his eighties. He answers plaintively when asked if he belonged to a political party in Cuba, saying, "We don't have any political parties." He claims to be apolitical.

"I wasn't really opposed to Batista," Pedro Víctor says. "I don't oppose anything."

But it seems his son-in-law, the one who had gotten him the job with the Treasury Ministry, had a more antagonistic relationship with the government in Cuba. Pedro Víctor says his son-in-law, who is never identified on the recordings, was forced to leave Cuba because of the Batista regime. He does not go into detail about the circumstances. The son-in-law returned when Castro took power, only to run afoul of the government again. "He's been declared a traitor in Cuba," Pedro Víctor says.

Milich and Monsanto seem intent on figuring out whether Pedro Víctor supports Castro, revisiting that theme throughout the hearing. One key sequence of events interests them: Pedro Víctor had moved back to Cuba in January 1959, the same month as Castro's takeover. But ten months later, Pedro Víctor had returned to the United States for a visit, entering the country claiming to be a returning resident. If he had been disillusioned with the Castro government at that time, it would have been a perfect opportunity to escape. Instead, Pedro Víctor returned to Cuba after three weeks, prompting Monsanto to question whether he had pro-Castro sympathies.

"It's not really that I was in favor of Castro's government," Pedro Víctor explains through the interpreter. "But I had a job and I had to keep working with the government who gave it to me. I knew it was not good what they were doing, and I knew it was going to be a dictatorship."

It wasn't until 1960, Pedro Víctor explains, that he thought about permanently returning to the United States. But by then, he says, the defense committees were everywhere and they were making it difficult for people to leave the country.

Pedro Víctor makes some attempt to explain that dire consequences await him in Cuba. "I am in more danger now," he tells Milich. But the prosecutor and the special inquiry officer do not sound persuaded.

Monsanto insists that Pedro Víctor abandoned his legal residency in the United States. But the prosecutor doesn't have the final say. Pedro Víctor has one more chance when he answers questions posed by Milich. And Pedro Víctor addresses his final plea to the man who is sitting in judgment of him.

"I always thought of being here in the United States as a resident, living permanently here," Pedro Víctor says. "But I had to go back to Cuba to work because I did not want to be supported by my daughters."

He was expressing a hard truth about immigration: Though the United States held the promise of jobs that paid a decent wage not every immigrant found them.

Yet Pedro Víctor still holds hope at that moment in 1962 that this time it would be better. He is sure of it. "I wish to say that I want to be a resident because by this status I will be able to work, get a job and get some money from here and there, and not be depending on my daughters."

Pedro Víctor must wait to hear what is going to happen to him. A court official halts the proceedings to place a new disk on the Voicewriter. Milich is ready to announce his decision. There's no hint of emotion as he begins a monotone recitation of the facts in the case.

Less than a minute after beginning, Milich gives Pedro Víctor cause for optimism. "I take official notice the U.S. consulates in Cuba were closed in January 1961, and from that time on no person in Cuba could procure a visa to come to this country."

But then Milich pivots. It turns out he agrees with the prosecutor that Pedro Víctor relinquished his legal resident status by remaining outside the country for more than a year before his detention at the airport.

But that isn't all. Milich says that when Pedro Víctor entered the country as a "returning resident" in late 1959, he really wasn't what he said he was. Pedro Víctor had moved to Havana months earlier and could no longer be considered a resident of the United States. "Actually at that time he was on a leave of absence/paid vacation from his employment," Milich says.

Milich also draws an important distinction about Pedro Víctor's identity. Even though many Cubans—including two of Pedro Víctor's daughters—had entered the country as refugees, the grandfather standing before him cannot be given that designation, Milich says. Because Pedro Víctor is trying to come into the country as a returning resident, "he must be considered an immigrant," Milich says. In the eyes of the United States government, he is not a political exile. He is a man who has broken immigration laws.

Without a refugee status, Pedro Víctor has no chance. He is in an immigration Catch-22—unable to get an immigrant visa because the U.S. consulate in Havana is closed and unable to enter the United States legally because he doesn't have a visa. "The applicant is subject to exclusion . . . as an immigrant not in possession of a valid, unexpired immigrant visa." At that point, Pedro Víctor is officially an undocumented immigrant, a man standing on American soil without permission to be there.

Then comes the crushing blow. Milich orders "that the applicant be excluded and deported from the United States."

How could a Cuban be deported under those conditions in that era? A little more than a year and a half after the Bay of Pigs invasion? After Castro's declaration that he was a Marxist-Leninist? It turns out that in those days a small number of Cubans were still being sent back to the island for violating visa requirements. According to an annual report of the Immigration and Naturalization Service, seventy-five Cubans were deported between June 1962 and June 1963, fifty-two of them for visa violations. Only twenty-three had been deported during the same period the previous year, and 126 the year before that.

But why Pedro Víctor García? A shoemaker by trade, the father of seven daughters, all living in the United States?

Yates, the retired immigration official, told me that Pedro Víctor's employment by the Castro government—even though it seems to have been a low-ranking position—would have been a big "red flag." The United States was still in the depths of the cold war, and suspicions about communist infiltration were pronounced. Even two decades later, Yates says he can remember CIA officials cautioning him to be extra careful questioning employees of the Castro government and other communist nations who sought to enter the United States. The presumption, Yates said, was that employees of those governments were required to join the Communist Party to gain employment and that they could remain loyal to the cause.

Milich was also adhering to a strict application of immigration law. No visa, no reentry. Many migrants get caught in similar conundrums today: When they leave the country and stay away for longer than one year, they have abandoned their residency. "Frankly, a lot of people don't understand the ramifications when they leave the United States," Yates said. "It's common. Still common." In Pedro Víctor's case, "the judge really would not have had a choice," Yates said.

Regardless of whether Pedro Víctor got a fair or unfair ruling, he did not leave the country as ordered. In those days deportees weren't necessarily thrown onto a plane the minute they were ordered out of the country. Instead they were told to leave the country and were expected to do so, Yates said.

Besides, any personal dramas that a sixty-three-year-old man from Cuba and his family were experiencing were about to be eclipsed by something that frightened an entire nation. On October 14 a U2 spy plane captured images of a missile site in western Cuba. The discovery became public eight days later, when President Kennedy went on television to address the nation. "Within the past week, unmistakable evidence has established the fact that a series of offensive missile sites is now in preparation on that imprisoned island," he said.

Once that news broke, how could anyone have faulted Pedro Víctor for staying? He had been fortunate at the airport on the day of his arrival that immigration agents didn't immediately send him back to Cuba. Now he was catching a break because the course of world events was making it almost inconceivable that he would be forced to leave. Commercial air travel to Cuba was suspended. The world was on the brink of nuclear war for another six days, until Soviet premier Nikita Khrushchev announced on Radio Moscow that the missiles would be removed.

Pedro Víctor's legal status would remain unresolved for years. He stayed in Miami, moving into a home on Northwest Second Street. Technically he was living in the United States without permission. In 1966, though, the legal climate officially changed in his favor. In November of that year the Cuban Adjustment Act was put in place, allowing Cubans who had been admitted or paroled into the United States since January 1, 1959, to be granted permanent residency after being in the United States for one year. (In the context of immigration, parole means admitting a migrant, who would otherwise have been inadmissible, for humanitarian reasons.)

The next summer Pedro Víctor returned to the immigration bureaucracy to ask, once again, to become a permanent resident. The photograph that accompanied his application is a tipoff that he was more upbeat about his prospects. His mouth, set so grimly when he was stopped at the airport five years earlier, spreads into an impish smile. He looks like he's about to laugh. His cheeks have even filled out a bit. There were more forms to complete, pages and pages of government fine print with questions translated into Spanish. Pedro Víctor appears to give a misleading answer to at least one question. He attests that he has not been charged with a violation of law, even though he'd been ordered deported five years ago for violating immigration law. After all he'd been through, he may simply have wanted to tell immigration authorities what he thought they wanted to hear.

The form he filled out states that he had been a Cuban refugee since February 1965. Refugee status may have been granted retroactively, Yates suggested. Medicare, a new federal program enacted the previous year, paid for a physical exam of Pedro Víctor.

On September 13, 1967, the signature of Robert L. Woytych, the district director of the Immigration and Naturalization Service, was stamped at a cockeyed angle on a sparse government form. The date stamp accompanying his signature strays over the previously blank line on the form, almost obscuring the numbers. But the meaning is clear—application approved.

Chapter Three

THE MIAMI SON

The arrival of May 27, 1971, marked a milestone for Mario and Oriales Rubio. Exactly fifteen years earlier they'd left Cuba and come to the United States. It was also the eve of a new phase in their lives. Their family was about to grow for the first time in twelve years. The next day Oriales gave birth to her third child, at Cedars of Lebanon Hospital in Miami. They named him Marco Antonio Rubio; the middle name was the same as his paternal grandfather, Antonio Rubio. Mario Rubio was forty-four when he became a father for the third time; his wife was forty.

In the first two years of Marco Antonio's life, the family lived two blocks from the Orange Bowl, the horseshoe-shaped home of the Miami Dolphins football team. The stadium loomed over the east end of Little Havana, by then well established as a destination for Cuban Americans and other Latinos, a place where Spanish was the language of choice. Football wove the immigrant community together with nonimmigrants. On game day the colors that mattered most were aqua and coral, the signature pastels of one of the most storied teams in National Football League history.

Game day meant hawkers. *Parqueo! Parking! Ten bucks. Come on!* The lawns in front of the homes on the east side of Little Havana, those compact bungalows on the crowded, mostly treeless streets, filled with Fords and Chevys wedged in like steel and chrome puzzle pieces. Fans spilled out of the cars, swelling the streets as they made their way to the stadium with the palm trees out front. Inside, the heroes had names like Csonka, Buoniconti, and Yepremian, men whose roots stretched to Europe rather than the Caribbean.

When Larry Csonka bulled into the end zone or the quarterback Bob Griese launched precision directed spirals, everyone outside the stadium knew it. A wave of sound washed over a neighborhood transformed. The cheers would have reverberated loudly in the house at 1271 Northwest Second Street, where the life of a Republican star began. Marco Rubio would come to love football, and especially the Dolphins. And in those first two years of life, before he was even conscious of what was taking place, historic games were being played. In 1972 the Dolphins completed the only perfect season in football history, winning all fourteen of the regular season and three postseason games, capped by a hardfought victory over the Washington Redskins in the Super Bowl.

The Rubio family moved the next year, relocating about four miles to the southwest. Their house sat a block and a half from Woodlawn Park Cemetery, the final resting place where, as Joan Didion wrote, "Havana vanities come to dust." In the cemetery, where frangipani trees bloomed, lay the graves of Machado and Prío, the deposed Cuban presidents who had fled into exile in Miami.

The Rubios would return often to the old neighborhood, to the stadium where the legendary coach Don Shula directed the men in aqua and coral. In later years Marco Rubio would fondly recall going to Dolphins games with his father after dropping off his mother and his sister, Veronica, who was one year younger than he, at the movies.

"As a young child, I wore braces on my legs to correct a knee problem," Rubio wrote in a moving open letter after the death of his father in 2010. "I hated to wear them. So my dad would call from work and pretend to be Don Shula telling me I needed to wear them if I wanted to play for the Dolphins. (I always wondered why Shula had a Cuban accent on the phone but not on TV!)" The stadium where they watched football played another, more conflicted role in the history of Cubans in Miami. It was inside the Orange Bowl, before an impassioned crowd of 40,000, that President Kennedy spoke directly to Cuban Americans about the disastrous Bay of Pigs invasion that had taken place twenty months earlier. In December 1962 they had packed into the stadium to celebrate the return of exile fighters who had been imprisoned in Cuba. Fidel Castro's ransom had been $53 million in pharmaceuticals and baby food, settled upon after negotiations with the Kennedy administration. It was a humiliation piled on top of a humiliation.

Kennedy took the podium to cheers and waving U.S. and Cuban flags. But the memory of that day would be wrapped in a sense of betrayal for years to come by Cubans who felt that a succession of U.S. leaders didn't keep promises to help them topple Castro. During the ceremony, surviving members of Brigade 2506, the unit that undertook the invasion, presented Kennedy with the brigade's flag. Kennedy accepted it and offered a promise in return. "I can assure you that this flag will be returned to this brigade in a free Havana," he said to loud cheers. "Your conduct and valor are proof that although Castro and his fellow dictators may rule nations they do not rule people, that they may imprison bodies but they do not imprison spirits, that they may destroy—that they may destroy—the exercise of liberty but they cannot eliminate the determination to be free." Nearly fifty years later the brigade is still waiting for the return of its flag.

In the two decades after Kennedy's speech, as the Rubio family grew, what came to be called the Cuban Miracle was taking place. By 1980 Cuban immigrants and exiles owned 18,000 businesses in Miami; they had owned 919 in 1967, the year Marco Rubio's grandfather, Pedro Víctor García, finally cleared up his immigration status and was granted permanent residence. On average, Cubans made more money than other immigrant communities—nearly double what Puerto Ricans made, for instance. The sociologist Juan M. Clark attributed the community's successes to the obstacles it had overcome: "It would have been difficult for them to leave the island . . . without such a motivation. [That motivation is what] enabled them to overcome the harsh deterrents imposed by the regime." Just two decades after the fall of Batista and the rise of Castro, there were an estimated two hundred millionaires within the Cuban community in Miami.

The Rubios were not among them. They belonged to a segment of hardworking, modestly compensated immigrants. Years later Marco Rubio would remember simple pleasures: his father talking the firemen into letting Marco sit on their truck, and Sunday breakfasts at the International House of Pancakes, which his father always called "Pancake House."

Nearly nineteen years after coming to the United States, Mario Rubio decided to become a citizen of the country where he'd lived since 1956. On March 4, 1975, he filled out a detailed questionnaire as part of a petition for naturalization. Mario had migrated to the United States after swearing that he intended to reside there permanently, and his naturalization proved he was a man of his word: During the 227 months since he'd emigrated, he had left the country exactly twice, spending five days outside the United States in 1957 and thirteen days in 1960.

The U.S. government kept him waiting seven months before sending him a notice to appear the next month before a naturalization judge at the auditorium of Barry College. A handwritten note on the summons reads: "MEN MUST WEAR COATS & TIES."

He was assigned a seat on the right side of the auditorium, Row N. When he left that day, he was no longer an "alien" in America. He was an American citizen.

For at least five and a half years prior to becoming a citizen, Mario had worked for the Sans Souci Hotel on Miami Beach, according to immigration documents. He started as a bar boy and worked his way up to bartender in less than five years, his son has said. The art deco hotel spread across an oceanfront city block on Collins Avenue between Thirty-first and Thirty-second streets. The hotel's pool stretched out steps away from the sand, and there were cabanas where tourists ordered tropical drinks while gazing at the ocean. The famed architect Morris Lapidus designed the hotel's striking lobby, which so impressed a New York developer named Fred Trump (who would later be better known as The Donald's father) that the businessman insisted on Lapidus designing lobbies for Trump Village in Brooklyn. In frothier times during the mid-1950s the stripper Gypsy Rose Lee had performed at the Sans Souci, and the hotel once painted four adjoining rooms robin's egg blue to match the shah of Iran's Rolls-Royce convertible when he stayed there with Queen Soraya.

Mario Rubio had the misfortune of working at the Sans Souci as the hotel, and the rest of Miami Beach, slid into decline. By 1977 the situation was so dire that the local tourism development authority was demanding that the Sans Souci put up a bond just to ensure it would pay its taxes. Two more years passed before Mario reached the conclusion that Miami no longer could provide for his family. It had been twenty-three years since he came to the United States searching for a better life. He now had two grown children, twenty-nine-year-old Mario Victor and twenty-year-old Barbara, and two young children, Marco, who was about to turn eight, and his seven-year-old sister Veronica.

When the Rubios first came to the United States they had followed Oriales's older sister, Dolores Denis, to Miami. Dolores had come to the United States in either 1955 or 1956, according to the first five digits of her Social Security number, which are coded to indicate where and when the number was issued. She had worked as a nanny in New England after emigrating, and met her husband in New York City. Now the Rubios were going to follow Dolores again, this time to Las Vegas.

Before saying goodbye to Miami, Mario wanted to give his family one last Florida-style treat. He took them to the Kennedy Space Center, the vast complex where grand American ambitions launched a man to the moon. The visit was a birthday gift for Marco, who was turning eight in May. Later that same month they moved west.

The six years the family spent in Las Vegas "were among the best of our lives," Marco Rubio would later say. In the 1970s the Strip glammed up with the construction of a succession of fancy new hotels, including the Marina, the Maxim, Harrah's, and the Imperial. In 1980, the year after they arrived, Steve Wynn built a thirty-four-story place called Fitzgeralds, the tallest building in the state. And even though there were setbacks—a fire at the MGM Grand that killed eighty-seven people in 1980 and increasing competition from Atlantic City—there were opportunities in abundance for a man who was willing to work.

Mario secured a job at Sam's Town, a western-style resort that catered to locals on Boulder Highway. It had been built by Sam Boyd, a Las Vegas legend who had arrived in Nevada with $80 in his pocket and created a gambling empire that eventually spanned six states. Mario had to take a step down to support his family. Despite twenty years of bartending experience he found himself working as a bar boy again, assisting younger men who had just graduated from bartending school. "He took it all in stride," his son would later say, and eventually Mario worked his way back up to bartending duties during the most coveted shift. Oriales took a job as a hotel maid.

They set up an above-ground pool in the backyard and installed a basketball hoop in the front yard. Mario served as the equipment manager for Marco's Pop Warner youth football team. At home, Marco always studied the game. He kept a notebook on his lap when the Dolphins played. "He would write down all the plays," his sister Veronica recalled. "He would be coaching from home."

Throughout his childhood, Marco was the relentlessly talkative one, the kid who not only had opinions but made them known. "I remember when he was in the third grade and a teacher sent him home with a note saying he should become a lawyer," his sister recalled. In neighborhood games of tag, Marco made the rules and selected the teams.

Like the Rubios, Dolores's family found work in the hotel industry. Her husband, Armando Denis, worked at the Sands Hotel and joined the Culinary Union. The Denises were deeply committed Mormons. Dolores and Armando completed Mormon missionary work at the Las Palmas Mission in the Canary Islands. Dolores served as a temple worker and held several other positions in the Church of Jesus Christ of Latter-Day Saints. She liked working in the church's nursery.

The Denises had one son; they named him Moisés, which he would later point out means Moses in English. But everyone calls him Mo. He is ten years older than his cousin Marco, and he differs from his younger cousin in both temperament and political philosophy. Marco can be combative; Mo is more mild-mannered. Marco is a conservative Republican; Mo is a Democrat and served in the Nevada Assembly from 2004 to 2010, when he was elected to the state senate. Marco has national ambitions; Mo's ambitions seem more modest, though in 2011 he sewed up an important leadership slot, consolidating support to become the first Hispanic Democratic leader of the Nevada Senate.

"[Marco] has much bigger political aspirations than I do—like being governor," Mo said in a 2005 interview. "The only offices I have ever considered running for were the Assembly and the [Las Vegas] city council." Later it would be clear that he had undershot the heights of both his own and his cousin's trajectories.

Like his parents, Mo served as a Mormon missionary, spending two years in Uruguay. In the years since, he has been a leader in the LDS Church, holding the positions of bishop for his local ward and second councilor to the presidency of his stake, which is an umbrella grouping of local Mormon congregations.

The Denises brought the Rubios into the Mormon Church during the years both families lived in Las Vegas. Well, at least some of them. Mario, who had worked as a bartender for years, couldn't embrace a faith that wouldn't let him drink and smoke. In November 2011 Mo Denis addressed the religious history of his cousin's family in a taped interview with Univision. "When they lived, when Marco lived here, they were members of the Mormon Church," he says in the interview, which sat for months without being broadcast in the files of the network's Miami offices.

Not long after arriving in Las Vegas, Marco—along with his mother and sister Veronica—began reading the *Book of Mormon*. Eventually, Marco, his sister Veronica, and their mother were baptized as Mormons. Marco converted to the Church of Jesus Christ of Latter-Day Saints with enthusiasm.

"He was totally into it," his cousin, Michelle Denis, told BuzzFeed.com's McKay Coppins. Marco attended LDS youth groups and often walked to chapel with his family because his mother could not drive.

The cousins idolized the Osmonds, the family singing group whose chart-topping success made them the most famous Mormons of their era. The *Donny & Marie* show, featuring two of the siblings, had been a television hit in the three years before the Rubios moved to Las Vegas.

Marco, Veronica, and their cousin Michelle liked to perform Osmond songs at family get-togethers. "Tony"—as the cousins called Marco, referencing his middle name, Antonio—was so entranced by the Osmonds that he joined the Denises for their annual trip to Utah to tour the pop group's recording studio. "It was just the thing to do," Michelle Denis said. "Then we'd go hang out at BYU."

Those years in Las Vegas made an impression on the young Marco Rubio that later helped shape his political philosophy. The Vegas economy relied heavily on gambling, drawing riches from the men and women who flocked there to play the slots or roll dice at the craps table. As a rising politician Marco staked out an antigambling public persona that derived, at least in part, from what he witnessed as a boy. "When he was a kid in Vegas, what he sees is all these jaded women playing slots," a former close associate of Rubio's told me. Once he rose to a leadership position in the Florida legislature, "he would be very emphatic" about his distaste for gambling and would reference his days in Las Vegas. "I've seen another side of gambling," he would say.

The mid-1980s delivered two life-altering events to Marco Rubio. The first came in August 1984, when his grandfather Pedro Víctor García died. The first person in his family to learn to read, Pedro Víctor had spent hours talking to his grandson, especially about history. Pedro Víctor lived with the Rubios for much of Marco's childhood. He liked to sit in an aluminum folding chair on his porch, smoking Padrón cigars in a suit and tie. "He would just talk on and on," his grandson would later say. The grandfather's loquaciousness was matched by the grandson's inquisitiveness. "He asked a lot of questions you wouldn't expect from a kid that age," his brother Mario says. "He spent a lot of time with my grandfather, just sitting there and talking."

The second key moment came the year after Pedro Víctor's death, when the Rubios decided to return to Miami. The parents had found steady employment in Las Vegas, but they worried about the future. "My parents feared that if we stayed in Las Vegas we would be drawn into the same employment they had," Marco later wrote. "They wanted us to have dreams and to be in a place where we would have more success pursuing our dreams."

At around the same time, the family made a shift in its spiritual life. Marco, his sister, and his mother returned to the Catholic Church that they had left behind for Mormonism. The exact date of their return is in dispute. Michelle Denis and her brother, Mo, say the Rubios didn't return to Catholicism until later. "When they returned to Miami they returned to the Catholic Church," Mo Denis has said. Marco says the family converted back to Catholicism while still living in Las Vegas and distributed a communion certificate dated Christmas Day 1984 from a Nevada church.

Regardless of the chronology, Michelle Denis says the Rubios went back to Catholicism at the urging of Marco, which would have meant he was guiding the family's faith around the age of thirteen. "He really convinced the whole family to switch religions," she said.

After leaving Las Vegas, the Rubios returned to a city in evolution. During their six years away, drug wars bloodied Miami's streets and savaged its reputation. Cocaine millionaires danced in discos and their hit men sprayed bullets in broad daylight. Traffickers took to dropping large packets of cocaine from small planes into the waters off South Florida. There were so many packets that they earned the nickname "square groupers" because they bobbed in the same waters as the common Florida fish.

Just two months after the Rubios' departure for Nevada, assassins shot up a liquor store at the Dadeland Mall, firing off eighty-six rounds and killing two men while horrified shoppers ran for cover. The real magnitude of the crisis began to sink in when investigators found a Ford Econoline van abandoned in a nearby parking lot with the motor running. The stenciling on the side of the van said it was from Happy Time Complete Party Supply, but it was armored with reinforced steel and had windows that popped out for use as gun ports. If there were any doubts that a drug war raged in Miami, the so-called War Wagon resolved them.

Miami had entered the era of the cocaine cowboys. Its homicide rate soared, until it was declared the murder capital of America. There were so many bodies that the coroner needed to borrow a refrigerated truck from Burger King to store them. "What I see going on here would make Chicago in the days of Prohibition look like a Baptist Sunday School picnic," the county medical examiner Joseph Davis said at the time.

At the same time, the city was taking in the largest and most sudden exodus of Cuban migrants in its history. Between April and September 1980 more than 120,000 Cubans poured into the region. They were herded into compounds set up by the U.S. military, a tent city rose up beneath Interstate 95, and others were packed into the Orange Bowl. They were refugees from a repressive state, but the reaction among some locals was indignation. "For Fidel Castro, it was tantamount to an act of genocide," the prominent television news anchor Ralph Renick said in one of his nightly commentaries. "With one fell swoop, he rid Cuba of thousands of undesirables. He emptied his prisons, he cleared the bums off the streets of Havana. Murderers, thieves, perverts, prostitutes, the retarded, the crippled, winos—they all were rounded up, sent to Mariel Harbor and put aboard boats bound for Miami. Fidel Castro publicly stated, 'I have flushed the toilets of Cuba in the United States.' He bragged about it."

The Marielitos, as the refugees were called, were tarred as crazies and criminals. It was an unfair label. "Mariel was very bad in the beginning, but it was very good in the end," the former Miami mayor Maurice Ferre told the *Miami Herald* for the paper's excellent retrospective on the thirtieth anniversary of the boatlifts. "The vast majority of these people were honest, decent, hard working, industrious people . . . who are now doctors, bankers, entrepreneurs and who really uplifted the community."

When the Rubios decided to return to Miami, they settled farther west than they'd lived before. They bought a home in the quiet city of West Miami, just past Coral Gables. Mario found a job tending bar at the Mayfair House, a new hotel in Coconut Grove with suites going for up to $800 a night, Japanese hot tubs, and twenty-four-hour butlers. The *Herald* called it "unbearably ritzy."

After the drug savagery of the previous few years, commentators were beginning to take a new measure of Miami, and they were detecting an upswing. One review that year declared that Miami was "emerging a stronger, more vibrant international city despite its worries." The Mayfair was a small part of that turn toward optimism.

Of course, Miami retained its tolerance of those with colorful pasts, whether the deposed dictators of the previous era or this one's nouveau-riche drug kingpins and their entourages. Even a hotel such as the Mayfair flaunted its ancestral sinners, though it had to reach far back to find them. The hotel manager, Jaime Torquemada, liked to brag that he was a direct descendent of Juan de Torquemada, brother of the infamous Tomás de Torquemada, who had tortured and killed hundreds during the Spanish Inquisition. It was all part of the allure.

West Miami, where the Rubios settled, was too small to have its own high school, so Marco enrolled at South Miami High, a short drive away. Built in the previous decade to relieve crowded conditions on nearby campuses as the region's population exploded, the school sits in a quiet residential neighborhood. An enormous statue of a cobra, the school's mascot, now rises from the bulky concrete building.

After living in Las Vegas, far removed from the center of the Cuban immigrant experience in the United States, Marco found himself in a school saturated by it. The Mariel exodus had swelled Miami's Cuban population, and South Miami took some of the overflow. Seventy-five percent of South Miami's 2,410 students were Hispanic, 10 percent were black, and 13 percent were identified as "Anglo," according to an article from Rubio's senior year in the *Serpent's Tale*, the school newspaper. "It was an Hispanic culture," said Fran Cosgrove, who taught at the school when Marco attended. "Many were first-generation immigrants." At any news of Castro, chatter filled the hallways. "They absolutely cared," Cosgrove said.

The future senator did not follow the pattern of some budding political stars, joining every club and topping every list. In the school yearbook he appears less as an exclamation point than as a parenthetical phrase: wearing a string of pooka shells around his neck and laughing at another student's joke, donating blood, standing in the back row of the class photo of Mrs. Nott's fifth-period class. Rubio has said that he "struggled to fit in," and that "some classmates mocked him as 'too American.' " He was a good student, but he wasn't the big man on campus. He wasn't going to get elected King Cobra. That was a role that would be played by his future brother-in-law, the actor and Latin singer Carlos Ponce, who was one class behind him.

Marco's wedge into the school's spotlight came on the football field. He loved the game. South Miami boasted a powerhouse team, a perennial contender for conference titles and playoff slots. Only a few years before Marco arrived, Derrick Thomas, a future NFL Hall of Fame linebacker, had been lowering his shoulder pads into the midsections of opposing running backs for South Miami. James Colzie, who was the athletic director while Marco was playing football, liked to call South Miami "Linebacker High," inspired by Penn State's "Linebacker U" nickname.

The team's colors were orange, black, and brown. "One of the best-looking uniforms in the country," recalled Sam Miller, who was head coach of the team and is now retired in Greenwood, Louisiana. Miller, who is African American, said there had been some racial tension at the school prior to his arrival, and he was brought in to calm it.

In the team photos from the era, Rubio is one of the little guys. He wasn't going to play linebacker. "He wasn't the most physical kid on the field," recalled Otis Collier, his defensive backfield coach. "He wasn't going to hit somebody and put them in the hospital." But he was tough enough and smart enough to earn himself a starting spot on one of the region's strongest defenses, a high-energy unit led by Joey Veargis, a ferocious tackler whom his coaches call one of the greatest Florida high school football players ever.

Marco played in the defensive backfield, roaming as a safety and cornerback, according to Collier. (Colzie only remembers him playing cornerback.) "He was not fast, but he was quick,"

Colzie recalled. "As a cornerback you do a lot of coverage. You don't do a lot of hitting."

The team's practices could be brutal, hours spent in the wilting Miami heat and humidity. If a player didn't want it badly, it would show. Some couldn't hack it. Marco kept coming back. "He pushes himself to the limit," his older brother, who was a star high school quarterback, later said. "He just does not stop."

Defensive backs seldom garner headlines, not like quarterbacks throwing winning touchdown passes or running backs sprinting down the sideline into the end zone. Marco doesn't appear in the scant coverage of the team from that period. But his coaches and teammates remember him as a hard-nosed player they didn't need to worry about. "You could always tell he understood the game from an intellectual standpoint even if he wasn't the fastest guy or the biggest guy out there," said Octavio Matamoros, a defensive lineman on the team.

Football coaches are forever fretting about the positioning of their defensive backs. A nose tackle stares straight across the line of scrimmage at his foe, the opposing team's center, his objective distilled to a collision of one helmet against another. A defensive back has to scan the field, sorting through crisscrossing receivers whose routes are intended to confuse them, get them out of position, leave them standing alone, stiffed. The objective can be to outsmart the defensive back as much as to outrun him. That's why the coaches liked the little guy wearing number 46. Marco didn't outsmart easily. "We played it deep," Collier said. "He was always in the right place. It goes back to the intellect. He played smart. He never was out of position."

The South Miami boys took pride in being blue-collar scrappers. Their biggest rivals were from Coral Gables High School.

The Gables kids were the sons of an earlier generation of migrants, more deeply established, wealthier. The South Miami players tended to be more recent arrivals or the kids of working-class parents who weren't among those two hundred Cuban millionaires. Kenneth Dodd, who also coached at South Miami when Marco played on the team, recalled watching "Marielitos" on the squad with a sense of pride. The youthful refugees who had come over in the boatlifts talked about deprivations back in Cuba, a society growing poorer and more deeply controlled by an omnipresent and repressive government. The boys would tell Dodd how the Castro government used to drop off toys sometimes; if boys ran all day, from one neighborhood to the next, they could stay just far enough ahead of the truck to collect toys in two or three spots. The kids would return home exhausted, but at least they'd have something to play with. Once they got to the South Miami football fields, Dodd said, "They definitely were hungry. The influence of young Cuban kids trying to establish themselves, I'm sure had an effect on Marco. They were coming here for an opportunity."

A player Marco looked up to was a tough kid named Humberto Miret, Dodd recalled. One day at school, an upper classman cut in line. Dodd watched as Miret, then just a freshman, walked up to the kid and punched him. It earned Miret, now a high school principal himself, a trip to the office. Dodd sought him out afterward and encouraged him to join the football team. He liked that fierce spirit. "That type of atmosphere of a guy like Miret certainly rubbed off on Marco. [The two of them] were very close."

In Marco's junior year the team made the playoffs, only to be eliminated in a heartbreaker after the kicker missed three extra points. Players shed tears in an otherwise silent locker room after the game. "Gentlemen," Miller told them, "let's pick up our heads and walk out of here proud."

Two weeks after that disappointment, the Rubio family suffered a far, far more painful blow. On December 16 police and federal agents swept across Miami making arrests. The front page of the next day's *Miami Herald* and the wire services told the story of the bust of a major drug ring. The ring was accused of killing a federal informant, dismembering his body with a circular saw, dumping the pieces into a horse trough, and burning it with charcoal and lighter fluid. The gang was also accused of smuggling half a million pounds of marijuana and two hundred pounds of cocaine worth $75 million.

The alleged leaders were a father-son team, Mario and Guillermo Tabraue. Deep in the stories about the big bust, almost as if it were an afterthought, was a list of four other men who had been arrested. One of those men was Orlando Cicilia. He was married to Marco's older sister, Barbara. The stories made no mention of the fact that Cicilia was not a member of the gang when the murder of the informant took place, so readers certainly might have thought that he had had something to do with the vicious slaying. The indictment paints Cicilia as a kind of middleman, making a huge number of trips in 1985 and 1986 to deliver cocaine—six trips to Cleveland, eight to Boston, five to Honolulu, and as many as ten to Indianapolis. He held meetings at his home to discuss drug deliveries and received at least one cocaine shipment there, according to the indictment. But the gang orbited around the Tabraues. When police got to Mario Tabraue's walled estate in Coconut Grove on the day of the arrests, someone tossed a $50,000 bundle of cash out a window. "It almost hit one of the agents in the head," said FBI spokesman Paul Miller. "Could have hurt him."

Inside the walls of the compound, Mario Tabraue lived in a 6,949-square-foot mansion. He owned an Uzi and a MAC-10 sub-machine gun. Neighbors were accustomed to loud noises coming from behind the walls, for Tabraue was in the exotic animal business and liked to keep some of his most prized possessions close to home. The agents sent to arrest him found two spotted leopards on the grounds. The authorities called the task force assigned to bust Tabraue and his gang Operation Cobra, coincidentally assigning the same name as the mascot of Marco's high school.

The other Tabraue, Guillermo, then in his sixties, had serious bona fides in Little Havana, where he ran a jewelry shop. He had been a member of the fabled Brigade 2506 from the Bay of Pigs invasion, and he was pals with high-ranking policemen. Prosecutors suspected him of funneling drug money through the store, and of cutting good deals on rings and necklaces to police officers in return for their looking the other way when he was involved in more nefarious forms of commerce.

The drug bust would remain an unexamined episode in the Rubio family's story until a television news report by the Spanish-language Univision network aired in 2011. The senator, who speaks so frequently about his family, had not mentioned it publicly, nor had his political rivals publicly used it against him. Marco was only sixteen at the time of the arrest, and there has never been an accusation that he was involved in his brother-in-law's criminal activity.

The case inched toward trial for the next eleven months, as Marco completed his junior year and became a senior at South Miami High. The school was known as a mostly placid locale, barely touched by the drug problems experienced in some schools of the day, current and former teachers say. But there were occasional flashes of disquiet. In September of that year the football team was forced to leave school earlier than usual for a game against its rival, Coral Gables. Instead of the standard Friday night game time, kickoff was scheduled for 3 P.M. at a neutral field, Tamiami Park. Several days earlier gangs with links to the two schools had fought at a concert. Bullets hit two kids and twenty others were injured. Administrators worried about more violence on game night, so they scheduled the contest at an inconvenient location and an inconvenient time. Police officers lined the field. The mood was tense, and the players were antsy.

The administration's move worked. There were only forty-six fans present for the National Anthem at the beginning of a game that had been expected to draw five thousand before the switch. The fans who couldn't make it missed a virtuoso performance by South Miami's defense. Marco stepped up, seizing a leadership mantle. "Marco Rubio was like Tom Brady, character-wise," his teammate Matamoros said. The Cobras held Coral Gables to minus-34 rushing yards in a 35–7 rout.

Again the South Miami team made the playoffs, and again its kickers let the team down. On October 27, a 39-yard field goal attempt that would have handed them a win in the final seconds sailed wide, and they were eliminated. Years later Rubio would say he still had nightmares about it. "We should have won but the referees called back a play, we missed a field goal and our team lost," he later said.

One week after that defeat, Orlando Cicilia went on trial. He was a minor defendant in a major case. The allegations in the trial were explosive enough that they led to the demotion of a high-ranking Miami police official after testimony alleging he cooperated with bribe-paying smugglers.

The case began under U.S. Attorney Leon Kellner, who had gained national attention for winning an indictment of the Panamanian strongman Manuel Noriega and for prosecuting a string of high-profile drug cases. But Kellner stepped down in June 1988 and was replaced on an interim basis by a familiar name in Florida politics: Dexter Lehtinen. The new top prosecutor was a state senator and former member of the Florida House of Representatives who was married to the Havana-born Republican politician Ileana Ros-Lehtinen. Dexter was a Democrat when they met, but switched to the Republican Party shortly before they married. Ros-Lehtinen would win an election the next year, becoming the first Hispanic woman elected to Congress. Later, she became the most senior Republican woman in the U.S. House of Representatives.

In the first month of what came to be referred to as the Tabraue drug trial, some of the biggest local drug dealers testified against the gang as cooperating witnesses. Their testimony retraced the history of the South Florida drug industry, from marijuana in the 1970s to the cocaine cowboys of the early 1980s. If it had been a miniseries, it would have been called "Drugs and Remembrance," the *Miami Herald*'s Frank Cerabino wrote. Mario Tabraue's attorney, Richard Sharpstein, saw it more as a "case woven through the fabric of scoundrels, weasels and snitches—a veritable rat-fink parade."

The case went to the jurors in January, and after seven days of deliberations they delivered eight guilty verdicts. The ringleader, Mario Tabraue, was later sentenced to one hundred years in prison. Cicilia received the second longest sentence—thirty-five years, according to press reports at the time. It appears his sentence was later reduced to twenty or twenty-five years. The government seized his house after saying it could not find $15 million that he'd earned in the drug trade. The other alleged gang leader, Guillermo Tabraue, won a mistrial after a former CIA agent testified that Guillermo was helping the feds look into allegations that former members of Brigade 2506 were dealing drugs. They later got him on tax evasion charges.

With his brother-in-law headed to prison, Marco completed his senior year and looked ahead to college. This was the end of the 1980s, a vapid decade of junk bonds and cocaine rings. Everyone wanted to make an easy bundle. The cover of the high school yearbook depicts a coiled cobra clutching $100 bills in its tail. "South Miami Lotto," a headline reads. "How to play: Simply attend South Miami Senior High. Student body goal: To win the jackpot."

The yearbook staff compiled a recap of the past year. One item notes that Vice President George H. W. Bush had selected Senator Dan Quayle from Indiana as his running mate in 1988. "The public opinion polls showed that the inexperienced 41-year-old senator was not a popular choice," the staffers wrote. Of course, they couldn't have known that almost a quarter century later another forty-one-year-old senator would be considered for a national ticket, and that this time he would be one of their former classmates.

One of the rituals of the senior year at many high schools around the country is the writing of senior wills. Outgoing students write a few lines, granting something they own to the younger students. In Marco's senior will he wrote, "I, Marco

Rubio, hereby bequeath my hairstyling secrets to Freddy." Even as a high-schooler, Marco combed his hair neatly and conservatively. Tim Elfrink of the *Miami New Times* aptly described the style as reminiscent of Alex P. Keaton, the insufferable but somehow endearing young conservative character played by Michael J. Fox in the popular 1980s television show *Family Ties*. Marco also added a cryptic joke about bequeathing "my ability to avoid getting killed to Angel."

For many players on the Cobra football team, senior year was consumed with the hunt for scholarships. Talking colleges into taking his players was a particular obsession of head coach Miller. "We sent out postcards all over the country." The coach lugged projectors for 8mm film to national coaches conferences, always hauling an extra bulb in his carry-on luggage in case the one in his checked bag cracked.

In those days a South Florida high school football player's options were limited. Several colleges that now have football programs, such as Florida International University and Florida Atlantic University, didn't have teams back then. This wasn't a problem if you were a stud like Derrick Thomas, blessed with a body made for football. But skinny defensive backs from West Miami, well, they weren't going to be suiting up for elite national powerhouses such as Florida State University or the University of Florida. Still, the chance to play a few more games can mean everything to a high school kid who loves to strap on shoulder pads and a helmet. It's not easy to give up the buzz you feel when you run onto a field under the lights, a crowd cheering you on. It certainly wasn't easy for Sam Miller's boys to let go.

Miller helped line up dozens of interviews for his players.

One afternoon a young man named Mike Muxo showed up at South Miami High School to chat with a few players. Muxo had grown up in Miami, and he was an ace at recruiting local players. Since leaving South Florida he had moved to Missouri, where he was coaching at a tiny Presbyterian-affiliated university called Tarkio College.

Tarkio rose out of the cornfields of northwest Missouri, one and a half hours southeast of Omaha, Nebraska, and more than two hours northwest of Kansas City. Muxo sat down with Marco at South Miami to persuade him to come to Tarkio, but not without making clear what he would be getting himself into. "I explained to him that it was very different from South Florida," recalled Muxo, now the director of the police academy in St. Louis. Tarkio was in a tiny town, far from the culture of South Miami. Muxo's pitch to his recruits was twofold: come to Tarkio and you can keep playing football, plus you'll get an education, mostly for free. Tarkio did not award full football scholarships, but players often were able to bundle a partial football scholarship with federal grant money and attend the college for free or at least at very low out-of-pocket cost. Muxo told Marco and the other recruits about Tarkio football players who had gone on to become surgeons and attorneys. Marco was sold. He was beating the odds. According to a 1989 article in his high school newspaper, only 14 percent of the previous year's class were attending four-year colleges.

———

Marco showed up at Tarkio, which had 550 full-time students, in time for the start of classes in August 1989. Everything about the place was a culture shock, even on the football field. When placekickers booted the ball through the uprights it literally landed in a cornfield. The population of the small town where the school was seated was 2,243. "If you blink you're not going to know you went through it," said Doyle Slayton, the head coach, now retired in Texas. The nearest McDonald's was twenty-seven miles away. To catch a first-run movie the students had to find a ride to Omaha, eighty-five miles away. Winters were brutal, with temperatures dropping well below zero. The football players ended up hanging out most of the time in the weight room.

Tarkio played in the Heart of America Conference, a conglomeration of small religion-affiliated colleges that included Evangel College in Springfield, Missouri; William Jewell College in Liberty, Missouri; Baker University of Baldwin City, Kansas; Missouri Valley College in Marshall; MidAmerica Nazarene College in Olathe, Kansas; Culver-Stockton College in Canton, Missouri; and Graceland College in Lamoni, Iowa.

At Tarkio, which took its cues from Presbyterian teachings, students were taught "the Old Testament one semester, New Testament the next," Slayton, the head coach, said. Besides football players, the school was particularly adept at recruiting aspiring actors. It was known for its Mule Barn Theater, an octagonal building that had once been used to house mules and burned to the ground the year that Marco enrolled. The theater majors tended to be flamboyant. Muxo, the football coach, remembers sitting in the cafeteria with Marco laughing at their antics. The cafeteria food was mediocre, of course, and Marco missed the meals from back home in Miami. One afternoon he turned to Muxo and cracked, "I know I must be part of the control group in an experiment where they put you in the middle of nowhere and they feed you this food to see how you react to it. I know this has got to be some kind of government experiment." The government experiment became their running joke.

The state of the school's finances, however, was no joke. The month before Marco started classes, *U.S. News & World Report* published a list of the colleges with the highest default rates for federally granted student loans. The headline of the chart was "A Class of Deadbeats." Tarkio College topped the list, with a staggering 78.7 percent default rate. In November, three months after Marco started classes, administrators made an announcement to the student body: The school had been placed on probation because of its troubled finances and problems with its extension campuses. The year before, the school's once well-regarded teacher education program had been decertified.

Tarkio had essentially been on a recruiting binge for years. Coach Slayton was one of their best recruiters, attracting students not only for the athletic program but also for the theater program. His wife, Catherine, helped create a squad of scholarship cheerleaders. The couple adored the college, its small-town atmosphere and tranquil ways, and their enthusiasm was infectious. The Slaytons and other recruiters were so effective that the campus outgrew available housing, and Doyle Slayton started buying houses for the college. He remembers one property owner telling him the school would have to come up with $16,000. "Is that the down payment?" he asked. No, it was the full price of the house. Slayton, a Texan, couldn't believe it.

But another kind of recruiting was about to sink the college. The school's primary problem seemed to be its aggressive recruiting of students for its extension programs. Most were poor urban youth who were coaxed into signing up for vocational courses and taking out federal loans that they had no hope of repaying.

Recruiters helped them fill out the forms, though many of the prospective students had no intention of ever attending classes. "Basically what you had was a small college acting as a front," Kent Kraus, the dean of institutional advancement at Tarkio, would later say.

The college's financial troubles took a toll on the student body. Football players feared they would lose their scholarships. Some began to make noise about quitting the team. In 1990, at the end of his first year at Tarkio, Marco himself decided to go home. Muxo believes the school's troubles played into the decision, but there were other factors too, including just plain culture shock. The next year Tarkio was gone. The college, which had survived for more than 109 years, closed amid the ballooning scandal over its questionable loan practices. When the damage was tallied auditors determined the college had handed out $22 million in loans to ineligible students.

By then Marco had left Missouri and enrolled in Santa Fe College, a community college in Gainesville, Florida, known as a place to burnish academic credentials for students who wanted to enroll at the University of Florida. The college's website touts the campus as "the Gateway to the Gators," the University of Florida's mascot. He also met a girl. In 1990 a pretty Colombiana named Jeanette Dousdebes caught his eye at a party in their neighborhood in Miami. He was nineteen, and she was seventeen. They had both attended South Miami High School but hadn't known each other there. He teased her at the party and she thought he was funny. They would marry eight years later.

After a year at Santa Fe, Marco transferred to the University of Florida. He lived on student loans and grants and took a part-time job. He also scored a prime internship, working for Ileana

Ros-Lehtinen, the first Republican woman elected to the U.S. House of Representatives. She would become a fixture on the South Florida political scene, but at that time she was relatively new to Washington. It's unclear whether she knew that the young man she was bringing on as an intern was the brother-in-law of a man that her husband had sent to prison.

After graduating from the University of Florida Marco returned to Miami, where he enrolled in law school at the University of Miami. He has said he graduated cum laude. "He would always say how he admired and respected his parents and the sacrifices and struggles they had gone through to give him opportunities," a classmate, Marlene Quintana, said. "Cuban parents have high expectations. It was inbred in us since we were little."

Even before he graduated Marco was being inculcated in Republican politics. He got a spot as a floor manager at the GOP convention in San Diego, and when it came time to hand out local jobs for Bob Dole's 1996 presidential campaign, Marco snagged the role of campaign chairman in Miami-Dade and Monroe counties. Even at that formative stage in his career, he was displaying a knack for delivering a smart sound bite. "If this election was an audition for host of a talk show, Dole wouldn't stand a chance," Marco, then twenty-five, told *Maclean's* magazine. "This is a campaign that will truly test whether we're a nation of style or substance."

His oratorical skills were already evident, too. At an event for Dole volunteers in Little Havana he upstaged the other speakers, including several well-known elected officials, with a stirring speech. "It kind of took the thunder away from the elected officials," said David Rivera, the future state lawmaker and congressman who is one of Rubio's closest confidants. "But that was

Marco. It was an indication of his potential charisma in public life."

Dole got trounced by the incumbent, collecting just 159 electoral votes to 379 for President Bill Clinton. Dole lost Florida by six percentage points, 48 percent to 42, figures that mirrored those in Monroe County. In the other county Marco was tasked with overseeing Dole was thrashed even more thoroughly, losing 57–37 to Clinton, who was popular in that area. Clinton won Florida, in part, because he fared unusually well with Cuban American voters who had traditionally supported Republican candidates but this time favored Dole by a slimmer than usual margin.

Marco Rubio had gotten a taste of defeat. But his turn on the ballot was coming, and he was done with losing.

Chapter Four

THE APPRENTICE

Rolling down Calle Ocho, past the stainless steel counters where they sell *lechón*, that luscious slow-roasted Cuban pork, and the wheel-shaped sections of fried snapper called *ruedas de cherna*, the city of West Miami sort of sneaks up on you. It's somewhere past Coral Gables, they might tell you downtown. Somewhere south of the airport, somewhere out west. Somewhere. It's not just easy to miss; it's almost impossible to spot, barely demarcated before one block of urban sprawl blends into the next, and then just as quickly you've passed it. The entire community encompasses three-quarters of a square mile laid out roughly in the shape of a triangle with one swollen corner. It would fit easily inside the footprint of Miami International Airport. In fact five cities of its size would fit, with room to spare.

The electoral career of Marco Rubio begins here, on that swollen triangle of land, thirteen miles inland from the sands of Miami Beach. From the beginning, powerful, more experienced people saw his potential, his innate gifts, his energy and over-whelming drive, and they guided him forward. Often they were pushing him toward places well beyond their own reach. As he rose, Rubio perfected the art of political apprenticeship.

This pattern would repeat itself on larger fields of play, but in 1998, when the apprentice was twenty-six, the goal was a mod-est one: win a seat on the West Miami City Commission. The job gave Rubio a platform, a place for him and his mentors to consider the next move — for they all envisioned big things ahead.

Just over 5,800 people live in West Miami. Excluding the is-land of Cuba itself, it is one of the most Cuban places on Earth. In 2000, two years after Rubio's first run for elected office, more than 61 percent of the residents were Cuban and 84 percent were Hispanic, according to the Census. Only three other U.S. cities, all in Florida — Westchester, Hialeah, and Coral Terrace — claim a greater percentage of Cubans.

There was a time when Spanish wasn't the native language of so many West Miamians. The city was born of a taste for vice. Back in the 1940s a small group of businessmen took offense when the county reduced the number of hours a person could legally drink and gamble, so they carved out a town that tolerated a bit more sipping and wagering. But the town, which was later incorporated into a full-fledged city, evolved as a place that em-braced small-town virtues more than late-night debauchery. Sol-diers returning from World War II flocked there for free building lots and stayed to start families; the flyboys from the air force base to the south came too. The lots were smaller and the houses were far less grand than next door in Coral Gables, George Merrick's banyan-shaded homage to Andalucía. But the place was cozy, filling eventually with cottages topped by beryl tile roofs and streets lined with black olive trees, oaks, and mahoganies. Its real estate was considered more desirable than the rougher streets in nearby unincorporated Miami-Dade County.

The military vibe gave over in years to come, replaced by a Latino and heavily Cuban culture. It became a haven for "professionals who wanted to live like they were in Coral Gables, but couldn't afford it," said Tania Rozio, a community activist and former city commissioner who bought a home there in 1966. Longtime residents talk about West Miami as if it were an island of old-fashioned values floating on a sea that is greater Miami. "A small town within a giant city" is the way Rozio puts it. Now when West Miami families go on vacation they're invited to call the police station and provide the dates they'll be gone; officers stop by a few times a day just to make sure everything is okay until they return.

A few months before the 1998 election, Rubio sought out a woman who could help make everything okay in his campaign. Rebeca Sosa was tending flowers in her front yard when Rubio walked over and introduced himself. Sosa, who was forty-two at the time, had been mayor for two terms and was so popular that no one was bothering to run against her in the April election.

Rubio was just twenty-six. Barely out of law school, he was living at home with his parents. "How many nights did I hear the keys of my seventy-year-old father at the door as he came home after another sixteen-hour day?" Rubio, by then a father himself, would later tell an audience in Washington. "How many mornings would I wake up and run into my mom, who was just coming home from the overnight shift as a stock clerk at K-Mart? When you're young and in a hurry, the meaning of those moments escape you, but as the years go by and as my own children get older, I understand it now."

Rubio was engaged to be married while running for his first political office. His future wife, Jeanette Dousdebes, was a striking blonde from a Colombian family who had been a cheerleader, along with her sister, Adriana, for the Miami Dolphins. Her demeanor counterbalanced Rubio's frenetic energy. "She has kind of a calm personality, very easygoing," said Dorie Grogan, the cheerleading squad's senior director of entertainment. "He seemed like a supportive, really nice boyfriend."

At first glance Sosa wasn't sure it was such a great idea for Rubio to attempt a run at public office. "I couldn't believe how young he looked," she recalled. "I said, 'You're too young. Why would you run?' "

But Rubio had that spark. And, as he would throughout his political career, he connected by telling stories about his family. "He started talking about everything he learned from his grandfather," Sosa said, "and I was just blown away." Within minutes Sosa concluded that she "had a star" in front of her. A star who was going places. "He was bigger than we were," she later said.

Sosa took to calling Rubio "Marcito" (pronounced mar-KEY-toe), an affectionate diminutive form of his name that friends say she continued to use as his stature grew. They shared similar heritages. Sosa was born in Camagüey, the province where Marcito's mother was born. Sosa had served on West Miami's city commission since 1990 and had been its mayor since 1994. She had credibility that stemmed from salvaging the city's finances from possible bankruptcy in the mid-1990s, when auditors recommended a government shutdown. And she could be an old-fashioned charmer.

Sosa likes to sing, and she's prone to croon in Spanish at senior citizens centers. Now a member of the Miami-Dade County Commission, she was the kind of low-to-the-ground local politician who didn't just know everyone's name, but also the names of their dogs. Getting Sosa behind him was a coup for Rubio. Not getting her support all but assured defeat for his opponent, César Carasa. By the time Sosa and Rubio met, the young man with all the promise had already accumulated a cadre of influential admirers, including Al Cardenas, a Republican kingmaker in Florida and successful attorney. Cardenas had taken Rubio into his law firm.

On January 13, 1998, Rubio wrote a check for $25, the first contribution to his campaign treasury and a modest start for a politician who would go on to raise millions for electoral contests. In the next four months he raised more than $11,200, according to his campaign finance report, a remarkable figure for a political seat in such a small town. Cardenas tossed in $250, and David M. Rivera, a future congressman who would become one of Rubio's closest friends and a target of state and federal investigators, added $100. Rubio also got $200 from Sergio Pino, chairman of U.S. Century Bank, a firm that the investigative reporting organization ProPublica would later accuse of handing out loans to insiders.

In March Rubio collected a real trophy. It was a small contribution, just fifty bucks, but a very big name: John Ellis Bush, better known as Jeb. Bush was the son of President George H. W. Bush and the brother of future president George W. Bush. Jeb

Bush would go on to make a significant impact on Rubio's development. It was the start of an important and lasting alliance.

"[Rubio] had a lot of people that were behind him—people in political positions in the city that saw a future for him," said Rozio, the longtime West Miamian who was also a candidate for city commission in the 1998 race. But for all his high-octane support, Rubio took nothing for granted. Friends who helped him couldn't keep up. He always wanted to knock on one more door, drop off one more flyer. "He was so charismatic and so endearing," recalled Danny Ruiz, a young political operative and aide to then-Florida house member Rudy Garcia who helped Rubio with his campaign.

Rubio's pitch was straightforward: he preached fiscal sanity and painted a picture of that idealized small town West Miami so wanted to be. "I'd like our officers to be closer to the people like they used to be years ago. I want our police to know everyone, from the guy in the corner whose dogs bark a lot to the woman whose car screeched," he said. "I want them all to personally know every single person who lives in West Miami."

When Rozio first met Rubio, she had the same impression as Sosa: "Too young!" But Rozio, who at fifty-two was twice Rubio's age on election day, quickly realized that she was wrong. "He was an instant sensation," she recalled in an interview more than a decade later. She and Carasa, who was thirty-nine, remember the election as a friendly competition. "He's always got a smile on his face," Carasa said of Rubio. "Women like him." The young man who was about to blow away Carasa and Rozio at the polls smiled and waved whenever they ran into each other. "Good luck," he'd say.

He was the Maserati; everyone else was a Pinto. Rozio, like

many to come, was particularly dazzled by the *idea* of Rubio—the well-spoken, handsome, hardworking Cuban American. On the night before the election, Danny Ruiz remembers, Rubio crackled with energy. Confident, but intense. They were out past midnight distributing door hangers together. "Nobody was out there," said Ruiz, who has since left politics and works in the flooring business.

On election night Rubio waited for results at West Miami's city hall. They were still coming in when the phone rang. "It was Jeb Bush himself, calling to congratulate Marco for winning our little race," said Enrique Gonzalez, a Rubio ally who won a commission seat in the same election. "He was the anointed golden child, even then."

The final results showed an electoral slaughter. Rubio collected 744 votes to win one of the two commission seats that were in play; neither Carasa nor Rozio cracked 300.

Rubio was on his way.

West Miami was going to be a short stop. The next phase of his career was beginning almost as the first was, well, beginning. Like many a good political tale from those days in Florida, this next one tracks back to an indictment, although not one involving Rubio. When all its consequences were tallied, Rubio was the politician left standing.

On June 12, 1998, a federal grand jury indicted State Senator Alberto Gutman, a thirty-nine-year-old political juggernaut from Little Havana who had once posed in a National Rifle Association ad with a .380 Beretta. Gutman proudly called himself a Jewban, the local nickname for a person who is both Cuban and Jewish, melding two powerful South Florida constituencies. Gutman could woo crowds in Yiddish and Spanish. He was a force.

The charges against him were serious. Gutman was charged with multiple counts of Medicare fraud, making him the fifth public official in Miami-Dade to be indicted or forced from office that year. U.S. Attorney Thomas Scott called the indictment part of "a weekly ritual." The day before his indictment, Gutman had been named Legislator of the Year by the Florida Police Benevolent Association. After the indictment the association's president shrugged and said, "What can you do?"

That week the *Miami Herald* reported that a top prosecutor in Miami-Dade County's major crimes division would resign because of allegations that he had fondled a secretary in his office. Three other secretaries were losing their jobs after being accused of engaging in phone sex with a hit man who had become a government witness.

And in March that year a federal court had removed Mayor Xavier Suárez from the office he had held for nearly four months. The incumbent mayor, Joe Carollo, was restored to office after thousands of absentee ballots were invalidated. The *Miami Herald* won a Pulitzer for its superb investigation of the balloting, including the discovery of a man named Manuel Yip, whose vote in the mayoral election was the fourth he'd cast since his death four years earlier. "This would never have happened in a Third World banana republic," Carollo said. A Florida newspaperman, Robert Andrew Powell, writing in *Newsday*, declared that it was "a golden era, a Pax Romana of Governmentus Corruptus."

Still, Gutman decided to take his chances in the November 1998 elections rather than pull out of the race. He wasn't going to let a little thing like an indictment, even if it was being touted as the nation's largest Medicare fraud investigation, stand in the way. Nor did the voters object. They reelected him for the eighth time, albeit by a much narrower margin than usual.

Alas, even a character as swaggering as Alberto Gutman couldn't hold on forever. Almost a year after being reelected, he pleaded guilty to conspiracy and resigned from office.

Jeb Bush, by then the governor of Florida, scheduled a special election to replace Gutman. This was a coveted seat, a spot that had been held firmly by one of the region's most politically adept figures. Savvy Republicans had seen it coming and were preparing to make their move.

At the same time a fundamental shift in the way politics was practiced in Florida was about to take place. Seven years earlier, Florida voters had overwhelmingly approved eight-year term limits for state legislators. Several state senators had fought the measure in court, but in September 1999, the month before Gutman resigned, Florida's Supreme Court upheld the term limits. The decision meant that in 2000 more than a third of the state's 160-member legislature would not be able to run for reelection.

One of those term-limited legislators was a Miamian named Carlos Valdes, another Cuban American with a great family history that led back to the island. Valdes had been born in Havana and claimed to be a descendent of Perucho Figueredo, a freedom fighter during the Cuban War of Independence in the late 1800s and the author of the Cuban national anthem, "El Himno de Bayamo." He was slated to leave office with all the other term-limited lawmakers in November 2000, but he decided to resign early and run for Gutman's open seat. That decision raised the risk-reward quotient for the politicians who had been eyeing Valdes's seat. One of those aspirants was Marco Rubio.

Valdes's early departure meant that his replacement would take office well ahead of the avalanche of new legislators who would arrive thanks to the term limits. It would be a nine-month head start on angling for leadership posts. The right ambitious pol could benefit greatly, especially in the Florida House of Representatives, which chooses its speakers years in advance of the date that they actually take office. Lawmakers who aspire to become speaker start campaigning for the job almost as soon as they are elected. "In the Florida legislature, they almost pick their speaker by ultrasound," said Dan Gelber, a Miami Beach Democrat who served eight years in the legislature.

But the change in the election date also put an incredible amount of pressure on the candidates hoping to replace Valdes. Rather than having more than a year to campaign, they had to be ready for a primary in six weeks.

Rubio started at a big disadvantage. A poll taken in November by the United Teachers of Dade union showed him trailing a former state representative, Jorge Rodriguez-Chomat, by a margin of 31 to 7 percent. Then again, more than 60 percent of voters were undecided. Rodriguez-Chomat had earlier made headlines by getting into a shoving match on the floor of the Florida house with Valdes, the man he was now trying to succeed. After the scuffle, which took place during a debate about school vouchers, Valdes said Rodriguez-Chomat called him a "jackass" multiple times. "By the third or fourth time, I just said, 'You must be looking at yourself in the mirror,' " Valdes recounted. The voters apparently didn't think much of the histrionics and bounced Rodriguez-Chomat in the next election. But he wanted another chance, and he tried for a comeback when the seat that Rubio coveted came open.

Since Rubio's first election nineteen months earlier, he had gotten married to Dousdebes. Among the groomsmen at the October 1998 ceremony at the Church of the Little Flower, a Catholic church in Coral Gables, was his brother-in-law, Carlos Ponce, a Latin heartthrob singer and actor who had married Rubio's sister Veronica. (In the forgettable 2009 film *Couples Retreat*, Ponce is the actor who steals one of the few funny scenes, portraying a buffed yoga instructor who makes the husbands jealous by performing sexually suggestive moves with their wives.) Ponce, who was recovering from a fall, wore midnight-blue casts on his left arm and right leg at the wedding, according to a small item that made the local gossip column.

The race for the house seat began, as so many Florida campaigns do, with the ritual of voter-registration hopscotch. Just a few days before the West Miami Commission race, Rubio changed his voter registration to an address two blocks away from his parents' house. This created a small kink when he filed to run for Valdes's seat, which represented Florida House District 111: Rubio's house wasn't in Florida House District 111. But it really wasn't a problem. Lots of people were doing it. Three out of the five candidates who wanted to represent District 111 didn't live there. And there was nothing illegal about it. By law the candidate only needed to be living in the district come swearing-in day to be eligible. One candidate, Jose Luis Rodriguez, brushed off the residency question, saying, "I'm about two blocks away from 111. I'm going to wait until after the election to move." Rubio, who said he lived three or four blocks away from the district, promised he would move into the district before the election. "Everybody's a carpetbagger until the election," Jose K. Fuentes, a Miami lobbyist, cracked years later in an interview.

With less than two years in office in West Miami, Rubio didn't have much of a record to run on. He had gotten some attention for establishing the city's first bicycle patrol officer. He called it the "cornerstone" of his campaign. He had also showed an inkling of a trait that he would display many times as he climbed: rather than go to war with the people who opposed him politically, he tried to reason with them or bring them into his circle. It wasn't an inviolable imperative, but there were many occasions when he sought to deal diplomatically with opponents rather than pound them in public settings. One night during a heated West Miami Commission meeting he sounded like the voice of reason, which was all the more noticeable given that the combatants were all old enough to be his parents. The tussle was over the city's covering the costs of an office for Pedro Reboredo, the county commissioner who had supported his opponents, Rozio and Carasa, against Mayor Sosa's preferred slate, which included Rubio. The city, which was trying to hold down spending, wanted to spend less on Reboredo's office. He felt slighted and smelled payback as a motive. "Now I know why I'm really here—because I didn't support you in your last election," Reboredo told Sosa. "Well, I'm sorry, but this is a democracy and I can do whatever I want."

But Rubio stepped in, looking to soothe the older politician's wounded pride. Barely two months in office, and having just turned twenty-seven, Rubio was sounding almost statesmanlike. "I don't believe the issue here has anything to do with how good a commissioner you are, Mr. Reboredo," Rubio assured him. "It's just about whether we want to continue access of our facilities free of charge."

Another trait that Rubio would foster over the years was the ability to bring the people he defeated and their allies into his camp. It helped that his elections seemed predestined by the Republican power structure. Because he seemed to be a chosen one, it was smart for people who had opposed him to get in line behind him. When Rubio decided to run for the legislature, Carasa, who lost to him in the West Miami Commission race, joined the Rubio team. Carasa remembers making phone calls for the young candidate at an office on Calle Ocho. The message Rubio wanted to transmit, Carasa said, was that "taxes were totally out of control."

In the Republican primary for the Florida house seat Rodriguez-Chomat may have had all the early name recognition, but Rubio had the money. His network came through big. In the days before the primary he managed to accumulate an imposing war chest of more than $70,000, compared to Rodriguez-Chomat's $29,000. Rubio also got a boost from the *Miami Herald*'s editorial board, which was impressed by his eloquence. "He can turn an anecdote about planting trees in one sun-parched neighborhood into a reverie about the power of public service," the paper wrote in its December 10, 1999, endorsement of Rubio.

He sounded like a moderate Republican. He was pushing for early education for at-risk children, and when asked about his views on the hot-button issue of abortion, the paper said, he pronounced himself "pro-life but says that he understands fully that a woman's right to an abortion is the law."

The education pitch was a central element of the campaign, and Rubio argued for change in clear terms that struck an emotional chord with voters. "Thirty percent of children enter Miami-Dade County Schools unprepared to learn," he said in one interview not long before the primary. "You do the most important learning the first five years of your life, but we don't even start school until age 6. We can't wait for the school years to intellectually challenge children. We have to do that in the beginning. I think the most efficient use of our money comes from investing in the front end."

Rodriguez-Chomat, the more experienced politician, turned out to be a nonfactor in the race. It was the novelty of someone even newer to politics than Rubio, though, that made things interesting. Rubio was pushed into a runoff by a political novice, a popular radio and television reporter named Angel Zayon.

Even though Zayon had never voted in an election before, he suddenly became a prohibitive favorite. Zayon's appeal was woven into the minds of Cuban exile voters because of his in-your-face television reporting in 1991, when Mariel detainees held hostages at a federal detention facility. The next year he organized a relief drive for victims of Hurricane Andrew, the Category 5 beast that leveled entire neighborhoods in South Florida and caused more than $20 billion in damage.

It looked like a race that Rubio couldn't win. "The thought process was that because of Angel's popularity, Angel was going to be able to walk right into office," Danny Ruiz said.

The race would give Rubio an up-close view of the political dark arts and the rough, no-holds-barred world he was diving into. During the race an attempt was made to discredit him by spreading rumors that he was gay. The rumor was not true, but it worried the young candidate. For a time he obsessed about it, frequently bringing it up in strategy sessions, sources familiar with the campaign said. Finally, a decision was made to douse the rumor by distributing a photo of Rubio with his attractive wife. The rumors went away.

The house district Rubio was seeking to represent stretched

through Hialeah, Miami Springs, Virginia Gardens, Little Havana, Allapattah, and parts of Miami and Coral Gables. Hialeah became a kind of incubator in the development of Marco Rubio, a test of his ability to overcome a formidable opponent. Hialeah is predominantly blue collar. Several longtime Miami political operatives described it as "the Bronx" of Miami. It was ruled for a quarter century by Raul L. Martinez, a Cuban-born populist who ran a political machine that catered to even the smallest worries of the residents who streamed into his office all day. In the full-contact sport that is Cuban exile politics, Martinez was an outlier because he dared to be a Democrat. That put him on the opposite team from Rubio. But even though he was a Democrat, he would take sides in Republican races. And in Rubio's contest, he backed Zayon.

Martinez had a historical grudge against Ros-Lehtinen, who had brought in Rubio as an intern earlier in the decade. The congresswoman's husband, Dexter Lehtinen, had won a conviction of Martinez in 1991 in an election fraud case. Lehtinen was the interim U.S. attorney at the time. The investigation was launched at a time when Martinez was expected to challenge Lehtinen's wife, who was then a state senator, for a spot in the U.S. Congress. Lehtinen would have to battle perceptions that he was using his prosecutorial powers to damage his wife's political rival—it was a suggestion that he denied.

Rubio's mentor from West Miami, Mayor Rebeca Sosa, knew right where to send him in Hialeah: the Tropical Restaurant. There, he was ushered into a circle of well-to-do Cuban American businessmen who loved the political game. The Tropical perches in a strip mall next to a coin laundry. Diners sit in bright orange booths or on round bar stools fixed firmly to the floor along the length of a U-shaped stainless steel counter. Mechanics eat next to cops, who eat next to used car salesmen, who eat next to guys wearing JC Penney's slacks but who also happen to be multimillionaires. The menu, complete with pictures, hangs on the wall behind the counter.

I was sitting there with a veteran of the back stages of Miami politics for approximately five minutes when an older Cuban American gentleman came by with cards promoting a candidate for a local office. Politics is a 365-days-a-year proposition at the Tropical. The conversation took place in Spanish, as did the ordering. Regino Rodriguez, a tall, silver-haired seventy-four-year-old, presides over the place. Rodriguez served in the Cuban military prior to Castro's takeover. He fled to Spain and came to the United States in 1981. He's a likable man with a confiding manner, a sly smile, and an air of mystery. With a raised eyebrow here and a grin there, he gives the impression that he possesses many secrets. He understands his role in the sociodynamic world of Cuban American politics. The people at the counter seek his advice come election time. "I say, vote for *fulano*"—Spanish slang for "so-and-so"—because "fulano es mi amigo," Rodriguez says.

In Rubio's uphill race to win a seat in the state house, he needed friends, and Rodriguez became one almost immediately. "I saw in him a great politician. Behind his looks is a great human being, very humble, a man with abundant professional ethics," Rodriguez said. Then he cracked that sly, knowing smile of his and shrugged his shoulders, raising his hands, palms up. "He's a product that's easy to sell because whoever sees it is going to buy it."

At the Tropical, Sosa introduced Rubio to Modesto Pérez, a small businessman with a scrappy, engaging demeanor. Pérez calls Sosa *la madrina principal*, the main godmother, of Rubio. When I went to see Pérez at his building supply store a few minutes' drive from the Tropical, he was holding court with three older gentlemen arrayed on wobbly chairs and stools in front of a counter. Behind him there were large open shelves, cardboard boxes filled with metal parts, and a row of water coolers labeled for export to the Caribbean.

Our conversation would have to wait a few moments. Pérez nodded and one of the men slipped out, only to return a few minutes later with a Styrofoam cup filled with ink-thick *cafecito* and a stack of small plastic cups reminiscent of oversized thimbles. Once we finished the *cafecitos*, we wandered to his office in back, leaving the counter unattended.

Visitors to Modesto Pérez's back office pass through a hallway lined with photographs of politicians and political events. In one of them, Pérez hands a long-handled replica samurai sword to Marco Rubio. Pérez delights in giving out the swords; he says he has presented dozens over the years. Like Rodriguez, Pérez saw a wealth of potential in Rubio, and he fancied himself as a kind of instructor who could shape a politician still in his formative stages. At first it wasn't easy. "It was a project," Pérez said. "He was like a wagon with square wheels. I had to push him."

Pérez nudged the young aspirant to target older people and working folks. In the beginning, Pérez said, Rubio was cautious and "didn't have anything to say. He was mute." Pérez would say, "Go to the little grandma and kiss her, the old guy, shake his hand." Rubio followed instructions.

Ruiz, the political operative, watched admiringly as Rubio mastered the art of charming voters, especially the senior citizens who were so important in that district. Rubio "came across as the loving grandson who listens to his parents, always respectful of his elders, will always do his best for his parents, his grandparents, his elders," Ruiz said. "I've seen other candidates who have tried hard to convey that message but couldn't."

Rubio's Hialeah backers thought his opponent wasn't so much Zayon, the broadcast journalist, but Martinez, the mayor. "I did not know Marco; nobody *really* knew Marco," Martinez recalled a decade later in an interview. "Zayon and I were friends." On paper, the odds seemed insurmountable: Zayon was popular, Martinez was powerful, and Rubio was unknown. "We had a monster against him," Pérez said, referring to Martinez. "It was the hardest election of my life. The only one that was with us was God. Even the Devil was against us."

Looking back, Rodriguez expressed a grudging admiration for Martinez's politicking skills. "He knows how to throw a rock and hide his hand," Rodriguez said. But Pérez had moves of his own. Once, he said, he took Rubio to meet a well-liked Catholic priest. Pérez told the priest that he understood he "can't do politics" at the church. But, Pérez recalled, the priest responded by saying, "Jesus Christ was a communicator. He said to the masses, 'How can we do better for the community?' " On Sunday Pérez made sure Rubio was in the pews. The priest told his congregation something like "Here at mass sits a young man who aspires," Pérez recalled. "It was an informal presentation. He couldn't do it a hundred percent." But it couldn't hurt.

On the day of the runoff only 13 percent of registered voters cast ballots, less than the turnout for the first round. Rubio ended up with sixty-four more votes than his opponent, 51.2 percent to 48.8 percent. One of the areas he won, by a sliver, was Hialeah. He had beaten Pérez's monster. Now he wanted Martinez to throw rocks for him. "[Rubio] came over right after the election, and we made peace," Martinez recalled.

Alex Penelas, the Miami mayor and a Democrat, stopped by for a few minutes to congratulate Rubio at the office of the police union, where he was celebrating. Penelas had hosted a fundraiser for Rubio. Penelas was another era's Marco Rubio, another telegenic young Cuban American political star for whom great things were being predicted. His appearance at a victory party for an aspiring legislator who had only held elected office in the small city of West Miami was another signal that Rubio was a star in the making.

At that point Rubio was all but elected. Democrats just didn't win in his district, and he went on to destroy his opponent, the Democratic Party activist Anastasia García, in the fundraising contest. Rubio amassed more than $99,000, four times the money Garcia raised. Among those making contributions to Rubio were the megalobbyists Ron Book and Chris Korge, a fact noticed by the *Miami Herald*, whose coverage was frequently crucial to the outcome of legislative races. Rubio had a lucid and persuasive answer when reporters asked about the lobbyists' donations: "Whenever I receive any contribution, I make it very clear: They buy into my agenda; I don't buy into theirs."

It was unseasonably cool on election day, 64 degrees, a full 13 degrees below average. But not a drop of rain. The contest, already a foregone conclusion, was the blowout everyone expected. At the age of twenty-eight, Rubio was headed to Tallahassee.

Chapter Five

THE ALCHEMIST

The door swung open. Joe Pickens found a seat. He scanned the room. He couldn't believe what he saw. Arrayed around the conference table at the Hyatt Hotel in Orlando were eleven other state legislators. He made twelve.

The twelve disciples of Marco Rubio.

Pickens was amazed to be there because he hadn't been a Marco Man. He had backed Andy Gardiner, another candidate in the Byzantine contest to become the speaker of the Florida House of Representatives, a race that Rubio had sewed up in 2003. Now, two years later, Pickens was being ushered into Rubio's elite circle of advisors, shoulder-to-shoulder with Rubio uber-confidants such as Ralph Arza and David Rivera, two tough political infighters from Miami.

Pickens knew a little about politics; he had served as a school board attorney in rural Putnam County and he had been in the legislature for more than half a decade by the time the twelve gathered in Orlando. He understood the risk of reward or banishment that comes from committing to one candidate over another. And he wasn't the only former dissenter in the room. He recalled, "Half [of] us were people who had openly supported the other candidates" and at least three—Jeff Kottkamp, Marty Bowen, and Dennis Baxley—had been rivals for the job. Years later his voice still carried a tinge of wonderment that he was in the room for the meeting. "In politics, you know, it's the supporters of the successful candidate that reap the benefit," he said. But sitting there, he realized that he had been "welcomed back into the fold."

Rubio had summoned the lawmakers to the Orlando hotel to help him plan his two-year tenure as Florida speaker, a post he would ascend to in November 2006. Pickens doesn't recall the exact date of the meeting but remembers it was about a year or so before Rubio was to take office as speaker. Since coming to Tallahassee as a virtual unknown in 1999, Rubio had learned how to accumulate and manage power in Florida. He had learned that Miami couldn't serve as a singular base, but that he had to extend his influence throughout the state. He had learned that he had to think three moves ahead of his opponents.

The political game could be played like his beloved football, with helmet-to-helmet collisions and spine-snapping force, but it also paid to bring a chess master's sensibilities to the field. When Rubio arrived in Tallahassee he was eager to make his mark, and he found an interior passageway to power that others could easily have missed.

In his second year at the capital, a committee was formed to redraw voting district lines. Redistricting is a meticulous politi-

cal art. Shaping and reshaping district lines is tedious: it sometimes involves snaking a district in and out of neighborhoods or
stringing corridors along freeway medians and other unpopulated
places. It's mind-numbing work but essential. Political fortunes
are shaped in those backrooms, where politicians and their aides
can draw their rivals out of the legislature and draw their friends
in. The work distills politics to the level of electrical engineering,
a wiring and rewiring of circuits on the motherboard.

As usual, Rubio's timing was good and his instincts were
spot-on. Redistricting was a once-in-a-decade ritual, and it presented him with a once-in-a-decade opportunity. Not yet thirty,
he volunteered to help. In doing so he took the same route he
had traveled before, positioning himself as an apprentice, well
situated to impress the older generation. Volunteering for the task
meant substantial face time with the leaders of the state house.
And the leaders noticed him.

Rubio logged hours in the map room, fueled by can after can
of Mountain Dew. He tapped his foot beneath the table, beating
out some rhythm that was in his head alone. He remained clear-
eyed while others flagged. His energy caught the eye of Johnnie
Byrd, a rising power on his way to becoming house speaker. Byrd,
who was from Plant City in central Florida, was two decades
older than Rubio. He was a conservative Christian and was in the
habit of walking around the state capitol with a Bible in his hand,
sometimes reciting Scripture verbatim to make a point. His voice
dripped with the honey of his Alabama roots, and he spoke slowly,
a counterpoint to the younger lawmaker's rapid-fire banter. Years
later Byrd remembers that he had to tell Rubio "to stop drinking
Mountain Dews some days." At the time, Byrd marveled that "if

he drank two or three more Mountain Dews a day, we'd never be able to control him."

In Tallahassee, as in every government town, information is the currency of power. And Rubio was starting to know things. Knowing things allowed you to add friends, and Rubio was in the business of adding friends, even if sometimes they were from the opposite party. He took one nugget of information he had gathered in that stale conference room and gave a heads-up to Dan Gelber, a Miami Beach politician with big ambitions. "They may take you out of your seat," Gelber, a Democrat, recalls Rubio telling him. "They may draw the lines around you." Gelber was a bit surprised. Because they were members of opposite parties, the laws of nature dictated that they should always be in conflict. But regional fealty often matters just as much as party loyalty in state house politics, and the men shared a certain kinship as fellow representatives from the Miami area. Rubio's tip seemed motivated less by politics than by something else. "He [tipped me off] as a friend to a friend," Gelber recalls.

Gelber eventually survived the threat to his political future; the map wasn't crimped to send him into oblivion. For years he would remember the kindness shown to him by the young Republican who had alerted him to potential trouble. "I knew immediately," Gelber recalled telling his wife not long after meeting Rubio, that "he was the pick of the litter. He seemed to be very disciplined in how he spoke and what he said. Pleasant guy. Funny. Knew when he had to smile."

Johnnie Byrd was so impressed with Rubio that he asked him to join his team, eventually selecting him as majority leader. He liked the younger man's tactical abilities—"He understood politics"—and he loved Rubio's drive. "He just made himself available," Byrd recalled.

———

Byrd came from a completely different Florida. It is said that in Florida, to get to the South you've got to go north. In other words, South Florida doesn't feel much like the Deep South, but as you travel north the vibe becomes more distinctly southern, as if you have left the state altogether and entered Georgia. Byrd was looking for ways to connect better with voters in the South Florida neighborhoods, where Spanish was the language of choice. A politician with higher ambitions of his own, he was positioning himself to run for the U.S. Senate, and the young Cuban American from Miami was helping him dredge a channel to supporters in South Florida as well as helping expand his legislative power base. In 2002, Rubio ingratiated himself with the influential Republican by loaning one of his staffers to help tutor Byrd in Spanish. He tapped a staffer whose connections traced back to Hialeah, the city where he had pushed so hard to win votes in his first legislative election. Rafael Pérez, who became Byrd's tutor, was the son of Modesto Pérez, the Hialeah businessman who had been one of Rubio's early political tutors and patrons. Rafael, whom everyone calls Ralph, was an exacting language instructor, once demanding that Byrd order his dinner in Spanish at a Miami restaurant. "I know Ralph is pretty hard on him," Rubio once remarked. "He doesn't talk to him like he's the speaker when it comes to learning Spanish."

Rubio was more likely to read the sports page than weighty philosophical tomes. But by the time he finished his first legislative term, he had devoured Ayn Rand's *Atlas Shrugged* twice. Rand's 1957 opus—an homage to individualism and entrepreneurship that warns of the dangers of an overly aggressive, meddlesome government—had attained cult status and was practically required reading for an aspiring conservative. Byrd nudged Rubio toward more contemporary fare. "I spent a lot of time inculcating him and the newer legislators in laissez-faire economic ideas," he said. Byrd cofounded the Club for Growth, an organization that had just been founded in 1999 by Stephen Moore, an economic analyst and writer who went on to join the editorial board of the *Wall Street Journal.* The organization promoted a pro-growth agenda focused on reducing taxes and pushed for a balanced budget amendment and for private retirement accounts as an alternative to Social Security. One of the group's early board members was Arthur Laffer, a champion of supply-side economics. He was best known for the Laffer Curve—a graphic representation of the theory that lower tax rates stimulate economic growth—which had been named for him.

The club is enormously influential, in part because of its active role in promoting and providing financial support through campaign donations to fiscally conservative candidates. Yet it is not rigidly partisan. It occasionally backs Democrats and has a long history of expressing its displeasure with Republicans it deems incorrect on fiscal issues. Such nonconforming politicians are called RINOS—Republicans in Name Only.

Rubio embraced the tenets of the Club for Growth. And the club embraced him, eventually becoming one of his largest sources of campaign donations. Still, it took a while for the doctrine of low spending and small government to take hold in the young Miami lawmaker. During his early years in the legislature, he made heavy use of earmarks, which are often considered pure budget pork. In 2001 he asked for a total of $101.2 million for seventy-two projects. The next year he requested $43 million for thirty-seven earmarks. There was money for autism treatment, flood mitigation, brain and spinal cord injury research; but there were also small, less vital sounding projects such as money to design the restoration of an historic home and to build a park picnic shelter. Only four lawmakers in Florida's 120-member house sought more money.

But then he stopped. Cold.

In 2003 he made nary a penny of earmark requests, known officially in Florida as Community Budget Issue requests. And he wouldn't seek a single one for the rest of his tenure in the state house.

Stuffing the budget with goodies could be damaging to a politician whose record would be scrutinized from top to bottom. Stripping the goodies from your record could make you look like a fiscal purist. The education was sinking in. Later, Rubio would campaign against earmarks during his run for the Senate and after being elected, Jim DeMint, the South Carolina senator, would put Rubio on his "wall of fame" for early support of anti-earmark proposals.

Byrd's decision to give Rubio a top post on his leadership team placed the star student at the center of almost every important and controversial issue facing the Florida legislature. In years to come, as Rubio's fitness to serve on a national ticket was weighed, there would be a temptation to compare him to Barack Obama. Both were heralded as possible headliners on a national ticket during their first term as U.S. senators; both had served in state legislatures and were strong orators. But the comparison is imperfect: although Obama wasn't exactly a backbencher, he never ran the Illinois Senate. Rubio—as a lieutenant of Byrd and of his successor, then as speaker himself—was at the center of the daily head-butting and deal-making that defines state politics. The experience steeled him for future combat, gave him a deep understanding of how budgeting works, and established his image as the ultimate government insider. It was an invaluable experience, but it also made him enemies. Deciding who gets money and who doesn't is a process that can make a politician a lot of friends but also creates a group of alienated people who are ready to pounce if things don't turn out the right way. "All those deals," an advisor to a Republican presidential candidate responded when I asked about Rubio's prospects of joining the national ticket in 2012. "That's what we're worried about." In Tallahassee, as he had from the moment he entered politics, Rubio displayed a knack for elevating political discourse, the same eloquence on matters large and small that the *Miami Herald* editorial writers had noticed during his first legislative campaign. He impressed less with his ideas about policy than with his oratorical skills.

Byrd could be opaque and inaccessible; he once blasted the Don Henley song "Dirty Laundry," a condemnation of shallow, scandal-obsessed reporting, while a pack of journalists waited outside his closed office door. Rubio for his part, would woo reporters by inviting them into his office for evening *cafecitos*.

Byrd could be effective in corralling his colleagues at one moment, then alienate them the next. Once he said, "The members are sheep," a remark that didn't sit well with headstrong lawmakers. When Byrd's style began to irk impatient colleagues and lobbyists, Rubio was there to both defend and interpret him. "I don't think he's hard to read, but he takes time to make up his mind,"

Rubio said. "Everybody up here wants a quick answer, and I think that throws people off a little bit."

Rubio gravitated to the spotlight. Frequently it was Rubio rather than Byrd who made the public announcements about the positions of GOP leaders. Keeping their fellow Republicans in line was something Rubio began to excel at, and he could deliver that message in a variety of ways, both publicly and privately. He showcased that ability in 2003, when he and Byrd were attempting to execute a deft bit of political maneuvering.

Florida Democrats had come up with a plan to expand prescription benefits to low-income seniors. This was a weak spot for Republicans. Polls had long shown that seniors smiled upon Democrats for their stance supporting health care benefits for retirees. Rubio and Byrd wanted to reverse that perception, and they came up with their own drug plan, albeit a more modest version. Still, some Republicans were reluctant, so Rubio sent a message: if Republicans weren't willing to get behind the plan, "then they haven't been paying attention," he declared in a newspaper interview. Message delivered. They had managed to take an issue that had been a Democratic strong suit and make it their own. A version of the proposal passed in the house and, in a bit of a surprise, also won approval from the senate.

Paying attention wasn't a problem for Rubio. He seemed to be everywhere and involved in everything. With his gift for the clever turn of phrase, he became the public face of the house Republicans. He could be affable and charming, accessible and relaxed. But when the budgets tightened or the Democrats pushed back, it was Rubio who played the role of Byrd's partisan bulldog. At the height of one budget battle he declared, "The brazen deception and misinformation in the statements by the

Democratic Caucus today is stunning." Another time he chided Democrats for being reductionist: "Their constituents would be better served if they spent more time concentrating on policy and less on sound bites."

But behind the scenes many Democrats considered Rubio someone with whom they could work. The most skilled politicians understand that their opponents need to perform for their constituents, but they still can be reasonable negotiators behind closed doors. They deliver piercing lines when the audience is present or the video cameras are rolling, but are less strident when the paying patrons have gone home and the klieg lights are dimmed. Rubio earned a reputation as someone who understood this, and it only helped him raise his stature and spread goodwill.

Rubio could be careful on controversial issues. Conservative lawmakers tried to engage him on voluntary school prayer and abortion, but "he was nowhere to be found," an influential conservative Florida lawmaker said. "I always thought it was a shame because Marco was obviously the most gifted orator." At times, the young rising star could be strangely disengaged. During a heated budget floor fight, a small group of conservative lawmakers were hoping to get him involved on their side. But Rubio's eyes hadn't strayed from a large three-ring binder that seemed to have captured his undivided attention. Several lawmakers walked past to peek at what was so consuming—it was a list of draft-eligible college football players. He was trying to figure out who the Dolphins were going to draft.

Even as Rubio's public profile increased, his youthful appearance sometimes caught capitol veterans off guard. Once, Florida's lieutenant governor, Toni Jennings, handed him a sheaf of papers and asked him to make copies. She had mistaken him for a clerk. "I was more than happy to make them," Rubio later said.

From the moment he entered politics, Rubio grasped the significance of money. Even during his first year in the legislature, he was building alliances by raising cash for colleagues. In late 2000, when Jeff Kottkamp, a future lieutenant governor of Florida, made a runoff in a house race, Rubio showed up with a couple of checks for him. "It was the first time I'd met him," Kottkamp recalled. Even then, Rubio "had in mind that he was going to run for speaker ultimately, so he was getting a head start." He'd outhustled and outraised his opponents while winning races for the West Miami Commission and the Florida legislature. Now the rising legislator needed a bankroll to match his grandest ambition yet.

With his sights set on the speakership, Rubio made use of a loophole—a generous quirk of Florida law that all the candidates for leadership posts were using. He created an organization that resembled a political action committee but was known in Florida as a "committee of continuous existence." Florida lawmakers came up with all sorts of lofty-sounding names for their political fundraising arms: Principled Leadership Committee, Floridians for Effective Government, Committee for Responsible Government. Rubio called his Floridians for Conservative Leadership.

For a time the committees operated in a kind of ethical gray zone, a blind spot in a state that prided itself on transparency. Special interests and other donors could give the committees unlimited amounts of money; some of the donations were called "dues" and some of the donors were said to be "members" of the committee. But the lawmakers were allowed to keep the names of the donors secret.

That practice continued without controversy until September 2003, when Gary Fineout, then an investigative reporter for the *New York Times* regional newspapers, exposed the loophole. The secrecy of the donor lists was contrary to the state's spirit of open government, and after much public outcry the law was reformed in 2004 to require more disclosure.

In 2003, while Rubio was running for speaker, some lawmakers were voluntarily disclosing the names of their donors. Rubio initially defended keeping contributors anonymous, saying, "It makes people feel comfortable." But with public outrage about the committees increasing, he backed down, announcing that he would reveal the names of his donors at the next filing deadline. When the names were unveiled, the public discovered that Rubio had received a $50,000 lump sum from a political group run by Alan Mendelsohn, a politically active eye doctor from Broward County. The donation matched the size of the largest single donation received by any of the committees. It wasn't the last time that Mendelsohn would pitch in to help Rubio.

The stated purpose of Rubio's committee was to "support state and local candidates who espouse conservative government policies." But Adam C. Smith of the *St. Petersburg Times* and Beth Reinhard, then of the *Miami Herald*, figured out that the committee spent $150,000 on administrative costs in 2003 and only $4,000 on campaign contributions.

Later Rubio founded another committee, Floridians for Conservative Leadership in Government. Its stated purpose was to advance conservative ideas, but about two-thirds of the $386,000 it raised went to political consultants, including more than $100,000 to Rubio's ally, Richard Corcoran, who helped with a project Rubio later launched to collect ideas for improving

state government. "I am proud of the work we have done to advance conservative ideas and principles," Rubio would later say. "The purpose of the committees was to provide a platform to pay for the costs associated with this work."

Rubio's committees were plagued by accounting glitches and perception problems. There was an unusually high amount of credit card spending that was not itemized, a departure from the more detailed reports filed by many other lawmakers. Payments were also made to Rubio's nephew, his mother-in-law's transportation company, and his wife's half-brother and cousin. Rubio and his staff defended the payments as perfectly legal and legitimate campaign costs. Rubio named his wife treasurer of one of the committees, and paid her $5,700, mostly to cover meals and expenses. He and his wife failed to disclose $34,000 in expenses, the newspapers found.

Rubio and his staff tended to explain away such discrepancies as clerical errors. "The bookkeeping . . . was not always perfect," Rubio's political advisor, Todd Harris, later said of one of the committees. There would be other questions raised over the years about Rubio's handling of campaign money, and there would be similar rebuttals. His defenders promoted what would become a stock narrative that was wholly accepted by Rubio-friendly reporters and publications: Rubio was simply sloppy, but not corrupt. "He's not the kind of guy who sets up file systems," a former close advisor told me. "He signed campaign treasurer reports, financial disclosure reports without looking at them intensely. He never had anybody who worked for him who said, 'Are you sure you want to do that?' "

With the money he raised, Rubio was well positioned to mount a serious campaign for house speaker. The speaker races weren't decided by the public; they were internal house contests. Because the campaigns took place years before the speaker actually took office, in 2003 Rubio was gathering support in hopes of becoming speaker from 2006 to 2008.

The campaign worked almost like a pledge drive. The candidates traipsed across the state gathering pledges from fellow lawmakers and keeping a running tally of who was with them. Rivera, Rubio's friend since the Dole campaign days, handled the hard sell with lawmakers. At one gathering, Rivera surprised a group of legislators by placing pledge cards in front of each of them and insisting they sign. Most felt they had no choice—to not do so would mean incurring Rivera's wrath, and he was a consummate behind-the-scenes strategist feared for his ability to influence the outcome of elections. Rubio faced formidable competition, most notably from Dennis Ross, a Florida house colleague who would later go on to win a seat in the U.S. Congress; Kottkamp; and Gardiner, a future majority leader of the Florida senate.

Byrd encouraged Rubio to expand his network beyond South Florida, to make an effort to connect with lawmakers in central and northern Florida. With their differing styles and conflicting allegiances, the three regions of Florida sometimes functioned almost as if they were separate city-states at war with each other over money and power. Rubio portrayed himself as a candidate willing to put regional differences aside, and, as he had done in those conference rooms where he helped redraw district lines, he impressed with his energy and relentlessness. "Marco actually ran an incredibly effective campaign," said Joe Pickens, who lived in the small town of Palatka, fifty miles below the north Florida hub of Jacksonville. "Marco's uniqueness was that he had the ability to appeal to geographic areas of the state that previous South

Florida candidates had less success appealing to. Between North and South, urban and rural—Marco was able to bridge those gaps."

As candidates started to fall, Rivera stepped up the pressure on behalf of his friend. Ross, Kottkamp, and Gardiner still stood in his way. So Rubio and Rivera spread out across the state, pulling votes one by one from Rubio's opponents in face-to-face meetings, offering promises of prime committee chairmanships or support in future speakers races to ambitious lawmakers who had gotten behind other candidates. "It was like the night of the long knives," one of the speaker candidates recalled. A key convert was Ray Sansom, a north Florida legislator who could deliver a bloc of votes. Sansom was later indicted in a corruption case that was eventually dropped by prosecutors. Rubio and Rivera promised to back Sansom in the next speakers race, several legislators involved in the race said.

With the race still very much in play, a state lawmaker named Kevin Ambler hosted a dinner party at his home in Tampa for several of the candidates and their top lieutenants. Food and drink were placed out on the patio so the men could smoke cigars during the meal. "We kind of had a kumbayah," one participant said. When they left that night Rubio was well on his way to becoming speaker.

In that tight race, Rubio benefited from a smart move he'd made years earlier. His decision to make peace with Raúl Martinez, the Democrat and influential Hialeah mayor who had opposed him in his first legislative race, worked in his favor when he was looking for help gathering pledges. Martinez, who had come to admire the ambitious young lawmaker, opened a door for Rubio to meet with John Thrasher, a former house speaker.

Thrasher "had the Jacksonville delegation, which Marco needed," Martinez said in an interview.

North Florida lawmakers were eager to change a formula that paid state workers more in south Florida counties that had higher costs of living than counties in the north. Support for the formula might make the difference between Jacksonville lawmakers siding with Rubio or lining up behind another candidate. "Marco agreed to that," Martinez said.

"I was kind of upset . . . you don't negatively affect people's livelihoods," Martinez said, "but he agreed to it."

One of the key issues preoccupying central and northern Florida lawmakers in those days was school funding. Florida allotted its state funds based on a complicated formula that gave extra money to schools in highly populated areas, including the big South Florida counties of Miami-Dade, Broward, and Palm Beach. Lawmakers from other parts of the state wanted to tweak the formula to divert more money to less populated counties, and they would go on to succeed in making changes that cost the South Florida school systems tens of millions of dollars. While Rubio was speaker—a time when the economy was weakening and he was remaining steadfast against increasing taxes—he presided over a record cut to public education of $2.3 billion, including more than $120 million taken from his home county's school budget.

A notion has evolved—and been quietly and enthusiastically promoted by Rubio opponents—that the young lawmaker cut a deal with central and north Florida lawmakers to change the school funding formula in return for their support in his speakership race. It's a serious charge; it would mean that Rubio sold out his own constituents to win a personal political prize. The theory goes thus: prior to becoming speaker Rubio didn't do enough to stop the formula from being changed even though he was a key Republican leader, and after rising to the top spot in the house he didn't do enough to restore the funding for South Florida schools. The theory has gained such traction among anti-Rubio Republicans that it's worth examining more closely. I asked three state lawmakers, two ardent Rubio backers and one former ally who later split with him politically, to comment. "There were a lot of north Florida legislators who did pledge to Marco, and you've got to wonder if that was part of it," said J. C. Planas, who served with Rubio in the legislature and was an ally before intraparty disputes chilled their relationship. "But that's Monday-morning quarterbacking. . . . Whether or not he did everything he could to try to bring it back, I think that's where the question lies. . . . Only Marco can answer that. Do I think as speaker he could have done it? Yes. But it's a difficult pull."

When I asked Dennis Baxley, Rubio's friend and ally in the state house, about the theory, he didn't address it directly, but responded that Rubio "refused to be parochial. He allowed this discussion to evolve about disparate views. I was proud of him." Rubio, Baxley said, was concerned about "what's the fair thing for the whole state. There was a lot of sentiment in the Miami-Dade delegation that they should protect their own."

Pickens, who served as the house education appropriations chairman and is now president of St. John's River State College, echoed Baxley: "I would say Marco Rubio was willing to be open-minded about those processes. Marco Rubio declined to be purely territorial when he governed the state of Florida as speaker of the house." Pickens in fact thought Rubio's handling of the school funding and other regional conflicts demonstrated skills that he could apply at a national level. "For those who are thinking Marco Rubio could be president some day, he's already demonstrated in the microcosm of Florida that people in Iowa don't need to worry that Marco Rubio would be a president for all Americans and not a president for some parts of America."

As the months went by, Rubio was amassing so many pledges in his race for the speakership that his rivals began to drop out. By November 2003 he was being declared the unofficial winner. But looking back, key lawmakers calculate he had probably sewed up the contest even earlier. He had mastered the subtleties of the inside game. "It's fair to say we were beat—we, the Gardiner team—long before we knew we were beat," Pickens said.

Later Rubio gave some of the credit to the head start he'd gotten by coming to Tallahassee early via the special election in early 2000. "[It] allowed me to come in right before term limits, so that gave me an extra year over my class," he said. "Clearly, that was beneficial. Coming in with term limits, at a moment in time when all these people who had served in government for so long had to leave at one time, created a vacuum. And having that extra year here obviously helped me distill it quickly."

For all his political skills, he sometimes got the optics wrong. In the midst of his speaker race he was caught up in an embarrassing episode during the Major League Baseball World Series. He and a few other Republican lawmakers skipped an important vote—touted by some as one of the most important in Florida history—to watch the hometown Marlins play a World Series game.

Rubio bristled at the criticism and said he had taken an afternoon flight because he had to attend to a family matter the next morning. But what's interesting is not so much his reaction as the attention that he was getting. He attracted criticism because his star was glowing so brightly. "There are people making much to do about nothing because it's Marco," his close friend David Rivera said at the time. Rivera blamed the attacks on rivals in the speaker's race and noted that the bill passed easily, though some press accounts suggested its fate had been in doubt for much of the day.

Baseball plays a curious role during Rubio's tenure in Tallahassee. His rhetoric was staunchly small government and low spending, but he was an ardent backer of state money to help the Marlins build a new park: in 2004 he was deeply involved in trying to push a $60 million tax subsidy. That meant he had to get past Fred Brummer, a stubbornly antisubsidy legislator and certified public accountant from Apopka, a midsize town near Orlando. Brummer detested tax giveaways for sports teams. In the circus that the Florida legislature sometimes appears to be, he had once dressed as a ballpark vendor and sold peanuts on the house floor while trying to kill a stadium funding measure by offering an amendment to move the team to the tiny Panhandle town of Carrabelle and rename it the Florida Mullets.

Still, Rubio was intent on trying. He ushered a group of business leaders into Brummer's office, then excused himself. Looking back, Brummer remembers being impressed by Rubio's persistence, and the fact that the younger lawmaker didn't make a scene meant there wouldn't be hard feelings between them. He got the drill. "There wasn't any cajoling or whining," said Brummer.

But there wasn't going to be a ballpark deal either.

A chartered Falcon Air jet waited on the ground in Miami on the morning of September 13, 2005. Nearly two hundred people would come aboard for the 9 A.M. flight. They were going to Tallahassee.

Today was the day that Marco Rubio, the embodiment of so many hopes in Miami, would lay claim to the powerful office of Florida house speaker. Settling into the seats on the jet were an array of Rubio supporters, from Rebeca Sosa, the guiding hand in his first political race, to the chairman of the school board and the head of the Miami-Dade Republican Party.

Rubio's speech before the Florida house was a historic moment: he was to be the first Cuban American house speaker in Florida's history. Radio Martí, the U.S. government–sponsored broadcaster, beamed audio of the address to Cuba. The guests wore laminated floor passes around their necks inscribed with a quote from Ronald Reagan: "There's no limit to what a man can do or where he can go if he doesn't mind who gets the credit." Years later Modesto Pérez, the Hialeah businessman who pressed so hard to help Rubio win his first state house race, still keeps his hanging in his office and shows it off proudly.

Rubio walked to his place at the head of the chamber in a dark suit, a red flower tucked into his lapel. He placed one hand on each side of the dais, his palms open and his fingertips resting on the polished wood. And for once the rapid-fire talker slowed down. He was calm, intimate, nearly perfect in tone. His voice betrayed his emotions. In the audience grown men wiped tears from their cheeks.

———

On that day Rubio gave gifts and received them. He offered each lawmaker a blank book and asked them to fill it with ideas for improving their state. And he was given a sword by Governor

Jeb Bush, who took to the lectern and said, "I can't think back on a time when I've ever been prouder to be a Republican, Marco." The sword belonged to "a great conservative warrior," Bush told the audience to peals of laughter. The "mystical warrior" was named "Chang." "Chang is somebody who believes in conservative principles, believes in entrepreneurial capitalism, believes in moral values that underpin a free society. . . . I rely on Chang with great regularity in my public life. He has been by my side, and sometimes I let him down. But Chang, this mystical warrior, has never let me down."

The goofy, tongue-in-cheek (we can only hope) description baffled some listeners. Rubio would later say the mystical warrior was an invention of Bush's. A possible origin dates back to the late 1980s, when Bush's father, then president of the United States, was known to sometimes ask "Should I unleash Chang?" as a means of incapacitating tennis opponents "through sheer verbal audacity," as a *Washington Post* writer put it.

The sword itself was nothing special, an inexpensive object bought off the Internet by aides in Bush's office. But it would hang in a place of honor in Rubio's office, a symbol of his deep bond with a son and brother of presidents.

The system of selecting speakers so far in advance of taking office gave Rubio ample time to plan. The meeting he scheduled in Orlando with the group that came to be known as his disciples was part of an extensive plan that included traveling around the state staging "idearaisers" to gather input from Floridians and focus groups organized with the help of the nationally known consultant Frank Luntz. The meeting was both a culmination of Rubio's political education and an affirmation of his innate savvy. Better to take enemies and transform them into allies. They would be grateful for his largesse, and they would exhibit the zeal of the converted.

They would become Marco Men.

For months the disciples met around the state, helping Rubio plan how he would run the Florida House of Representatives. (Baxley and another group member mentioned "the disciples" nickname in 2011 interviews. Baxley said the group has also been called "the cardinals" and "the apostles." The nickname was the brainchild of Rubio's ally Ralph Arza, said Richard Corcoran, a close Rubio confidant. During his 2010 Senate campaign, Rubio denied using those terms.) The group was trying to get into the heads of Florida voters, to understand the people they served. Focus groups were assembled, and the disciples listened for clues, hints about what they could do when they all took power together. Sometimes the lawmakers sat behind one-way glass, observing without being seen, as focus group coordinators asked Floridians what they thought of state government. The sessions were designed to set priorities, and education kept coming up as a major concern for Floridians across the political spectrum. They were worried that the state wasn't doing enough to ensure that their kids succeeded. Broadly speaking, by 2005 Florida's education system was starting to make improvements but still lagged in key indicators such as graduation rates, test scores, and funding.

Occasionally the sessions were tough on Rubio's ego. Some of the focus group members "viewed him as manufactured, not down to earth. That was a shock to him," a participant said.

The lawmakers also learned that they were not held in high esteem. "One of the big things was just this sense that we were up here entertaining ourselves," Baxley said. "That everybody was making six figures and living the high life." The public might have been excused for thinking the politicians up in Tallahassee were just having fun, given the carousing that some of them were known for. The Miami-Dade County delegation had a particularly wild image. Lawmakers from Miami hosted an annual party, serving paella and rum. They crowned some of their hotshots Mambo Kings, an honorific bestowed on Rubio early in his tenure.

But the legislators certainly weren't making six figures. An analysis by *Florida Trend* magazine in 2009 showed that Florida lawmakers, earning $29,600 a year during the period the publication analyzed, were the most poorly compensated of ten states with similar legislative workloads.

Rubio's income, however, had improved considerably since he'd arrived in Tallahassee; he reported $124,700 in salary from a job at a law firm and his legislature salary in 2002, but by 2008, his last year as speaker, he was making $414,000. Still, during his time in the legislature, Rubio's personal balance sheet frequently looked unhealthy, twice teetering into negative territory as it was weighted down by debt from a house, a car, and student loans. In 2002 he listed a net worth of negative $103,100 and in 2004 of negative $46,100. His net worth once reached as high as $415,000, but he left office in November 2008 with a net worth of just $8,351. His personal finances seemed out of whack with the fiscal conservatism he advocated for the government.

Starting in 2004 and continuing through his two-year term as speaker, from 2006 to 2008, Rubio was sustained financially primarily by a job at the law firm Broad & Cassel, which paid him a yearly salary of $300,000. The firm did $4.5 million of legal work for the state between 2002 and 2005—the year before he became speaker—according to an analysis by the *Sarasota Herald-Tribune*.

The work Rubio and his allies were doing to prepare for his speakership and take the temperature of Floridians was getting attention and starting to earn raves. The idearaisers were the building blocks for a book that Rubio titled *100 Innovative Ideas for Florida's Future.* "Rubio's approach came straight from the concept" of Newt Gingrich's mid-1990s Contract with America, Luntz said, referring to a list of legislative goals Gingrich sought to enact while he was speaker of the U.S. House of Representatives. Gingrich and Rubio met and had a meal in Tallahassee in 2006 and talked about health care. "They really hit it off," said Gayle Harrell, who served with Rubio in the Florida legislature. Gingrich praised Rubio's book. "This is as smart an idea as any I've heard in the country . . . a work of genius," Gingrich said in an address to the Florida house. He took a copy of Rubio's book with him back to Washington. "I think they could learn a heck of a lot from what Marco Rubio is doing here," he said. He predicted that some of the ideas Rubio collected would be "totally whacked out. Some are going to be fascinating, and a few are going to be brilliant."

By November Rubio was promoting his *Ideas* concept with vigor. He would eventually say his "personal favorite" was an idea to replace the standard state curriculum with a "world class curriculum" to be developed with input from communities and business leaders.

The book lays out an ambitious agenda, focused heavily on privatization and public-private partnerships, tax cuts, greater school accountability, school choice, and limiting the size of government. The ideas range from the familiar, such as encouraging doctors to use electronic records to reduce errors (Idea 84) and moving up the date of the Florida presidential primary (Idea 37), to the unexpected, such as granting whistleblower status to hookers as a way of uncovering prostitution rings and helping the women escape to a different life (Idea 43). Perhaps hinting at his grander ambitions, the final suggestion, Idea 100, was to create a national "Idea Bank" to collect ideas from across the country.

In general the book steered away from hot-button social issues, but when Rubio was asked about some of them, he didn't shy from responding. In April 2006 the state was being criticized for its inability to place foster children with families, a problem that had become so acute that some foster kids were forced to sleep in a state conference room. Rubio dismissed expanding the program to include gay couples who wanted to take in children. "Some of these kids are the most disadvantaged in the state," Rubio said. "They shouldn't be forced to be part of a social experiment."

Once he became speaker, Rubio's ambitions were made all the more difficult by a darkening economy. For once, his timing was off. In the previous few years Florida's budget had been flush with money from a real estate boom. "Documentary stamp tax revenues were raining from the sky," said Brummer, referring to a fee the state received on real estate transactions. "2005, 2006, you just couldn't figure out what to do with the money." But by the spring of 2007 state economists were scrambling to revise their tax revenue projections downward. The real estate market, which had been so kind to the state treasury, was starting to taper off. It was not an easy situation for a lawmaker enthused about cutting taxes.

Rubio would need more friends.

As he'd done before, he reached out to his natural enemies. Dan Gelber, who was taking over as minority leader, went to see Rubio with a laundry list of requests, and the new speaker granted most of them. They were small things, such as control of offices and parking spaces. But they meant a lot to Gelber.

It was clever magnanimity. Rubio's party had a huge majority. Why antagonize the minority? "You deal the cards," Gelber told Rubio. "If you want us to simply go after you, we'll go after you. We'll throw grenades for two years."

The men decided to hold their fire. They fell into an amicable understanding about how and when to be confrontational. Before a big issue came up, Gelber would walk into Rubio's office and say, "I need thirty minutes to scream about this stupid thing you're going to do." Rubio would smile and come back with something like "Can you do it in twenty?"

Rubio assembled an inner circle of politically adept allies that included Ralph Arza, the teacher turned legislator, and David Rivera, the skilled political operative and state lawmaker who came to be seen as controlling the flow of legislation to the new speaker's desk. Gelber described Rubio's confidants as "charming ne'er-do-wells" and said he liked to refer to them jokingly as Badenovs, after the devious spy in the black hat in the cartoon *Rocky and Bullwinkle*. "Marco was always above it," Gelber said. "But his crew were pretty good guys you'd want in a foxhole. Pretty good brawlers."

The men whom Rubio chose to surround him differed from him in style. Arza, a thickly built former football coach, could be an intimidating presence. "A bully," Brummer called him. "He was even physically threatening. His way or no way at all. Not the kind of guy you would want to do business with at all." Rivera was craftier, a consummate political operator who knew how to get things done in campaigns and in the statehouse. "One of the most charming people I've ever met," a person who knows Rivera well told me. "He and Marco are like brothers." Fellow legislators joshed that Rivera resembled "Mr. Bean," the comic British character.

Both Arza and Rivera would create political perception problems for Rubio. But he had a tendency to stand by them, sometimes to his own detriment. Loyalty was a trait that Jeb Bush, a political mentor of Rubio's, said he valued most. And when it came to Arza and Rivera, Rubio took the same approach.

In April that year Miami-Dade School Superintendent Rudy Crew, who was African American, accused Arza, a key player in state education policy, of calling him a "nigger." Half a year later—the month before Rubio was to take office as speaker—Arza was once again accused of using the racial slur, this time by a Miami lawmaker, Gus Barreiro, who filed an ethics complaint alleging that Arza said "nigger" in a drunken message left on his answering machine.

After the October allegation, Rubio tried to talk Arza into resigning, but his friend refused to step down. Rubio then announced he wouldn't appoint Arza to a leadership spot. But Arza didn't budge. Pressure intensified. Democratic lawmakers threatened to walk out of the chamber on the first day of the legislative session if Arza was not expelled. Such a display of discontent would have ruined an otherwise celebratory day for Rubio. He came under criticism for not taking action sooner. "He punted on first down. Rubio knew about this problem and did nothing. None of them did," said State Senator Tony Hill, a Jacksonville Democrat and member of the black caucus.

But Rubio defended himself, saying he had to allow the complaint process to run its course. "When you have two conflicting people making conflicting statements, that can't be the standard the Legislature uses," he said. "It opens up all members of the House to anything just because someone files a complaint." Finally, on November 1, a week and a half after the crisis began, Arza resigned. He was also charged with witness tampering for his expletive-laden call to Barreiro and turned himself in to police. Six months later he pleaded guilty and was sentenced to probation.

Much of the Arza drama had been outside Rubio's control; after all, he hadn't been the one using a racist term. But in a parable of the dangers of proximity in politics, he was taking a hit. What happened next, however, was all his own doing. And it threatened to upend any hopes of a smooth start. Rubio had preached a gospel of fiscal conservatism in the *100 Ideas* book, but some of his first acts as speaker were to spend a lot of money. He dedicated nearly $400,000 to office renovations and to build a members-only dining room. He hired a $10,000-a-month economic consultant who was a favorite of Jeb Bush's and a Club for Growth believer. He brought in staffers at higher salaries than normal, many of them holdovers from Bush's office that he argued would have left government service.

Rubio could be impulsive, and it was as if he hadn't thought through the way his actions would be perceived. His reasons for the spending were not entirely without merit, but he had misjudged the reaction. Newspaper editorials ripped into him for contradicting his rhetoric. The fiscal conservative risked being permanently tattooed as a big spender.

Counterintuitively some of the spending was the result of changes designed to clean up Florida government and prevent lobbyists from buying votes. In previous years lobbyists swarmed the capitol, lining up lunch dates with lawmakers. The lobbyists, of course, picked up the tab. "The joke was 'Will listen for food,' " Brummer said. Lobbying reforms changed all that. "Once you couldn't get your free lunch anymore, immediately the members' lunchroom became overcrowded. . . . The remodeling was more of a practical thing," Brummer said.

Rubio also wasn't the first speaker to spend on renovations. Three of the previous six speakers had been criticized for remodeling—some for spending much, much more than Rubio. But Rubio, in what would become a pattern, extended the shelf life of the controversy with his own reaction, writing letters to newspapers disputing the criticism. He argued, "There's no mahogany, there's nothing cosmetic, there's no whirlpool anywhere in the renovations we've done. This criticism is more fair if it's put into context. I want people to understand our motivations have nothing to do with self-aggrandizement or personal paybacks."

Rubio loved the give-and-take with the press. But he could be thin-skinned about what they wrote and fell into a habit of calling the home offices of some newspapers early in the morning, bypassing the local bureau chiefs, to register complaints. He did it so often that one capitol bureau chief quietly asked his staff to tell him to stop.

But this kind of hypersonic behavior was evident in everything he did: he was always on the move. He could swing from elation to fury in an instant. Yet he seldom seemed low. "For some people, he can make them nervous," Baxley says. "He's just pinging off the walls. He's bouncing, bouncing, bouncing. . . . It wasn't unusual to go into his office, he'd have a baby on his lap, watching something on TV, and have a serious conversation with you about a bill." What struck the people who worked with him was the resiliency of his outlook. "Once he was down, kind of mopey," a former close associate said. "He said, 'This will last a few more minutes and I'll be fine.' " He was right. A few minutes passed and he was back to his voluble, cheery self. Such an ability to process and move on is common among high-achievers.

Rubio's family was a frequent presence in the capital city. He was now a father and often brought his wife and kids to Tallahassee for long stretches during the legislative sessions. This differed from the habits of some lawmakers who preferred to keep their families far away and enjoy the pleasures of what several legislators described as a "hotbed of infidelity."

During his apprenticeship under Byrd, the two men's wives set about making the capitol "more diaper-friendly," as the former speaker put it. Gelber, who also had young children, delighted in sneaking tiny photos of his kids onto the shelves in Rubio's office. When Rubio realized what the Democrat had done, he laughed about it—and kept the photos.

Rubio always found a way to benefit when football stars came to the capitol. In 2006 the Miami Dolphins legend Dan Marino threw him a pass in the house chamber, and Rubio was so excited that he quipped to one lawmaker, "You know if I drop this pass, my political career is over." But that was nothing compared to the excitement that Tim Tebow produced when he visited. Tebow would later become one of the most popular and controversial athletes in America because he defied critics by praying on the field after his Denver Broncos scored big touchdowns. When he visited the Florida legislature in 2008 he was still a college star, having won college football's highest honor, the Heisman Trophy, the year before. Tebow was ushered into the chamber and took his place in the back. Up front, Rubio stripped off his jacket as lawmakers teased him. "He's nervous!" one called out. Rubio, who was an avid flag football player, milked the moment, hamming for the cameras. Laughter and good-natured catcalls filled the chamber as Rubio slapped his hands, jumped up and down in place, and stretched in an exaggerated manner. Tebow tossed him a soft pass that the speaker handled easily.

At the back of the chamber, Gelber says, he goaded Tebow, telling the quarterback, "Marco says you throw like a wussy, that your arm's not strong enough." Whether or not he heard the remark, Tebow zipped the next pass a bit harder, a spiral that came in low and fast, too tough to handle. He finished with another soft toss, and there were smiles all around. Rubio was still buzzing about it the next year during his Senate campaign, posting the video on his Twitter account and writing, "BTW I am the only US Senate candidate to ever catch a pass from Tim Tebow! See it yourself."

In some ways Rubio's time in Tallahassee can be viewed through the prisms of his relationships with two governors: a mentor in Bush and an adversary in Charlie Crist, who was elected governor in 2006 and took office in 2007. Bush, who served as governor from 1999 to 2007, was married to a Mexican-born woman, had lived in Miami, and understood the city's pulse and traditions. "He's practically Cuban, just taller," Rubio once said of Bush. "He speaks Spanish better than some of us."

Bush was not an imperious executive, shielded from legislators by a phalanx of gatekeepers. He was the kind of governor who roamed the halls. "He was all over the building, all over the details," Baxley said. "Jeb was highly interactive." Like Rubio, he could be an emotional speaker; he had a habit of crying during speeches. A policy wonk with seemingly boundless energy, Bush made great headway on his ambitious agenda to steer the middle-of-the-road state in a more conservative direction on both social and economic policy. He pushed through the first statewide school voucher program in the nation, as well as controversial school testing measures. During his eight years he vetoed $2 billion in spending and enacted state tax cuts totaling $19 billion, though many cities and towns have since been forced to raise taxes to fill the gaps.

An ardent proponent of privatization, Bush helped eliminate nearly 14,000 jobs, and by executive order he replaced affirmative action in university admissions and state contracting with his own "One Florida" initiative, a move that generated lasting ill will with many in the African American community.

Bush was alternately dubbed the "best governor in America" by admirers and "King Jeb" by detractors, but few would dispute the verdict of Professor Aubrey Jewett of the University of Central Florida, who concluded, "He'll go down as one of the most consequential governors in Florida history."

Rubio gravitated to Bush. "He really looked up to him," said Baxley, who watched a "big brother, little brother" bond form. And Bush was drawn to Rubio. "With Marco it was obvious from the beginning that he was smart, intelligent, going places," his fellow legislator Planas said. "They shared the same philosophical values." At times it was the little brother who led the way for the big brother. In 2005 Bush and Rubio raced across South Florida campaigning against a measure to allow casino-style slot machines. Bush said he got involved after hearing that Rubio was taking up the cause.

The relationship between the two men deepened over the years. By the time Bush was preparing to leave and Rubio was preparing to ascend to speaker, some were detecting another motive for their closeness. "The Bushes know how to get in behind a parade," said Byrd. "I attribute it more to Bush seeing the rising star of Marco." Byrd has heard the stories that "Bush helped Marco" but says, "I think the opposite is true. As Bush was waning, Jeb seized upon Marco as someone he should hitch to."

Bush's departure left Rubio lacking a key ally at the very top of state government. He could have used the support of the new governor, Crist, to help push for his agenda as speaker. But the two didn't get along. In the members' lunchroom Rubio would complain that Crist wasn't a true conservative, that he was leading the state in the wrong direction. Planas thought the complaints were sincere, but he also detected other possible motivations. "I wonder if some of Marco's challenges to Charlie were spurred by Jeb. It could have been a three-pronged thing," said Planas.

Crist, a preternaturally tanned former Florida attorney general, had been elected by a narrow margin in 2006. He too had football in his background. He'd been a high school quarterback and was good enough to make the junior varsity squad as a walk-on at Wake Forest University. For a time he was considered one of the nation's most popular governors, a short-lister for future national presidential tickets. His endorsement of Senator John McCain in the 2008 presidential campaign was followed breathlessly in news reports that portrayed him as a kingmaker. But Crist's standing in the popularity polls didn't translate into loyalty from ardent Bush supporters who remained in Tallahassee. Crist irked them by canceling hundreds of Bush appointments and failing—in the eyes of Bush enthusiasts—to give the former governor sufficient credit in his speeches. Writing in the *St. Petersburg Times*, Adam C. Smith dubbed Crist's approach the "de-Jebification of Florida politics."

"Charlie's a pleaser," said Baxley, who had supported one of Crist's opponents in the Republican gubernatorial primary. "You can't help but love Charlie. But Charlie doesn't really know what he believes. He does it with a good heart. But it's terrible leadership. He spent more time with the African American caucus and with the Democrat caucus than with the Republicans. With Jeb it wasn't like that at all. It left a huge leadership vacuum."

Crist's manner also bothered some in the capitol. He had a habit of sending thank-you notes that seemed more saccharine than sincere. "He was cloyingly friendly," a former top capitol aide told me.

As governor Crist was able to take charge of the state Republican Party, and he stumbled almost right away. He made the surprise selection for party chief of Jim Greer, a former lobbyist. Greer would later be indicted for allegedly skimming party money for personal use, charges he denied. Many establishment Republicans considered Greer a poor choice and were riled that Crist passed up other, more experienced candidates. "Jeb and a lot of people had every reason to be mad at Charlie for putting Jim Greer in as the head of the party," Planas said.

Within months Crist and Rubio were at war with each other over property taxes, and before the year was out the house speaker had engineered a lawsuit claiming Crist overstepped his authority by bypassing the legislature to allow the Seminole tribe to install blackjack tables and Las Vegas–style slots. The state supreme court eventually ruled in Rubio's favor, dealing an embarrassing setback to the governor.

The property tax dispute struck at the core of Rubio's legislative agenda. He wanted to eliminate property taxes on primary residences and replace that revenue with a sales tax. In his *100 Ideas* book he argued that eliminating the property tax would increase the value of Florida homes and would attract more retirees to the state, who would in turn fill the state's coffers by spending their income and increasing sales for items the state was taxing. Proponents hailed the idea as a way to give relief to Floridians, whose taxes had soared because of increasing home values; critics said it would benefit the wealthy at the expense of the poor.

Crist came up with a rival plan, and the two sparred in dueling media statements. In April, while he was caught in a traffic jam, Rubio called in to a Spanish-language radio program in Miami and accused the governor of being beholden to lobbyists for local governments who feared losing property tax revenue. "I am upset with the governor," Rubio said.

Later that year he tried another approach, suggesting setting a low cap of 1.35 percent on property tax rates. He even toyed with a petition drive. But his proposals kept meeting strong opposition from Crist and the senate, which also happened to be controlled by Republicans. As the debate continued, some state senators worried that Rubio was whipping up the emotions of the public for plans that had little chance of succeeding. Neither of Rubio's proposals became law, leaving him visibly frustrated. "That was a dumb one," Planas said of the property tax fight. "That was Marco and Charlie having the who-is-the-most-macho competition. I blame them both. Both he and Charlie were dead-set against agreement. That was a dumb thing to do. I think the war between them was unnecessary and harmful to the people."

Rubio's quick pace had been a virtue during his rise, but his tendency for impulsiveness could hurt him. In April 2008, he was caught slipping a provision into the state budget to help Max Alvarez, a campaign contributor who had said Rubio was "like a son" to him, bid on a $265 million turnpike contract. He'd done so without consulting key members of his staff, who were caught off guard and later lamented that they could have prepared him for the reaction if he'd only let them know what he was doing. Editorialists ripped Rubio. The uproar was a gift to Crist, whose staff stoked the controversy behind the scenes before the governor slapped his rival by vetoing the bill. Rubio had tried to defend himself, saying he was trying to open up the bidding to avoid "monopolistic" ties between the state and large corporations better positioned to bid on the contract. In this instance, Rubio had forgotten an important lesson from his past. In 2003, he'd been criticized for trying to set aside millions of dollars to buy the Freedom Tower in downtown Miami during a lean budget cycle when funding for universities and low-income housing was being slashed. He reacted angrily when the spending request was discovered, then made the problem worse by trying to justify it. "Just because a project maybe didn't go through the proper channels doesn't mean that it is unworthy of state funding," he said.

Although Rubio was unsuccessful in selling his property tax proposals, the legislature and Crist did eventually agree to modest tax relief. And dozens more checkmarks sprouted on Rubio's *100 Ideas* list. He notched significant victories on a corporate tax credit for private school vouchers, stricter penalties for child molesters, energy efficiency incentives, and a bill to overhaul Florida's elementary education system. In pressing his agenda, he could amaze his colleagues and staff with his ability to quickly learn some of the finer points of an issue, then distill it into understandable terms. It was a trait that gave credibility to his arguments and could shut off opposition before it arose because his antagonists weren't always as facile with language or as prepared to debate the minutiae. "He's a very quick study," Rubio's former press secretary, the venerable Tallahassee insider Jill Chamberlin, said. "He's very good at mastering stuff just enough to talk about it."

"All 100 ideas were passed by the Florida House," Rubio declared on his website. "Fifty-seven of these ideas ultimately became law." The award-winning PolitiFact Florida, a fact-checking project now jointly operated by the *Tampa Bay Times* and the *Miami Herald*, meticulously researched his claim and concluded that it was a bit of a stretch: twenty-four ideas became law and another ten were "partially enacted." Among the Rubio victories were property insurance reform, creation of a state investment pool for businesses, and an online health insurance database. Others, such as committing to having a "Top 10" public university and building a "model transportation system," are not a simple matter of passing a law but rather judgment calls on whether the lofty goal had been reached, PolitiFact concluded.

Rubio's inclination to compromise where others might have opted to stand on principle and lose is also a matter of interpretation. "He talked the talk, but he didn't walk the walk," the NRA lobbyist Marion Hammer complained after Rubio's house failed to pass legislation permitting employees to bring guns to work.

Even on his last day in office he faced frustration, settling for a narrow version of a disabled children's health insurance bill that covered only autism. He left office to mixed reviews, but with big goals for the future.

His colleagues gave him season tickets to Miami Dolphins games, an autographed football helmet, and a football jersey with his name on it. Arza, his disgraced pal, returned to the capitol to hear Rubio say good-bye. And once again Rubio moved an audience to tears with a powerful address, this time as a farewell. His voice cracking with emotion, he stood in front of the dais, speaking into a handheld microphone connected to a long cord. "The greatness of America," he said, derives from the "compassion of its people, a commitment to self-government and respect for the rights of all men. . . . Ninety miles from the shores of our very state are men and women of my ancestry and heritage who still do not have that. But they look to this country for the hope that they one day will."

He told the audience about savage taunts directed at his Cuban immigrant parents in Nevada during the Mariel boatlift: "You're a bunch of Cubans. Why don't you go back home? Why don't you go back to Cuba?" But, as he so often was able to do, he pivoted from talking about disgraceful behavior to celebrating native human goodness. "That's not reflective of America," he said of the jeers directed at his parents. He told the story of his parents' car breaking down in the Deep South in the early 1960s. They couldn't speak English and they had no money, but "they couldn't stop the number of people that came out and helped them."

He had never lost an election, but he had learned about losing battles in the legislature. In his round of farewells, he allowed an occasional wistfulness, a sense of what might have been. "In some ways," he said, "I wish I had been a little bit older." He was thirty-seven.

Chapter Six

A HIGHER CALLING

M arco Rubio needed advice. He picked up the phone and dialed Dennis Baxley.

Baxley was eighteen years older, ran a funeral home in Ocala, and was serving as the head of Florida's Christian Coalition. He'd bonded with Rubio a few years earlier while serving as the younger lawmaker's speaker pro tem, the second-highest post in the Florida house. They were friends, and friends will give it to you straight. Baxley, who describes himself as a fifth-generation Florida cracker with a "granddaddy who was a citrus grower," would tell Rubio what he really thought.

Rubio was contemplating a run for the U.S. Senate, but to get to Washington it was looking like he'd have to go through the sitting governor, Charlie Crist. The governor hadn't yet announced that he was going to run in the August 2010 primary to select the Republican nominee for the November general election. But even more than a year before voters went to the polls it was assumed that he would. And getting past Charlie Crist was going to be hard, a feat that the Miami lobbyist Jose K. Fuentes described as not so much David versus Goliath as "an ant versus Goliath." Crist was popular, a fundraising dynamo, and he had the power of incumbency. Rubio would be running as a former state house speaker who had gotten into the consulting business, a line of work that could easily be spun by critics as a way to cash in after leaving office, especially since he and his former legislative aide had signed $198,000 in consulting contracts with Miami hospitals.

"It's not very smart to take on a sitting governor with a 70 percent approval rating," Baxley told his friend. Rubio had heard this before from other advisors. At the time he seemed to have a clear path to a highly desirable government job: attorney general of Florida. "There was a lot of discussion about him really being able to get a walk-on as attorney general," Baxley said. "A lot of people were advising him to stake that out."

But Rubio didn't want to wait. He preferred to be quick, as he'd been on the football field. He saw bigger possibilities. "I said, 'Marco you need to follow your heart, talk to Jeanette,'" Baxley recalls.

Rubio's wife mostly stayed away from the glare of her husband's white-hot political career. The former Dolphins cheerleader and mother of four didn't give speeches and wasn't particularly enamored of crowds. She wasn't one of those spouses who tinkered endlessly with the work of the politician in her life. "She doesn't get involved in all the technical stuff," Baxley said. But in matters of "deep conviction" Rubio turned to her for guidance.

Rubio weighed his options at a raw moment for Republicans. They had suffered a dispiriting loss just months earlier in the

2008 presidential race, and Democrats had strengthened their control of both the U.S. Senate and the House of Representatives. The new president, Barack Obama, was enjoying high approval ratings and pursuing big goals. Democrats were basking in the afterglow of Obama's campaign message of hope and change. And the full fury of the tea party backlash against Obama's health care reform plans was still months off, even though there were beginning to be signs of grassroots discontent.

Florida always matters at the national level, in part because of its outsize role in presidential elections, but also because it is the ideal Petri dish for studying voting patterns. It offers insights about Hispanics, exurb Republicans, and the I-4 corridor swing voters between Tampa and Orlando. The Florida Senate race would shape up as a battle for the Republican soul: moderation versus conservatism, establishment versus insurgency.

Rubio kept talking about the Senate. He wasn't one to back off, even when the odds seemed to be against him. He'd won a city commission seat when everyone thought he was too young, a legislative seat when conventional wisdom assumed he couldn't, and a house speakership when history and geography dictated he had little chance. With time, Baxley detected something in his conversations with Rubio that is absolutely critical to success in the political arena: Rubio believed he could win. "He had that heart conviction that he could. He's not a guy to run at windmills."

Still, Rubio's first moves in the race were measured and cautious, not the impulsive actions of a neophyte, but the carefully choreographed steps of a cagey political veteran who had successfully orchestrated his rise from West Miami city commissioner to Florida house speaker. The speaker who had sometimes acted in haste had grown into the candidate for national office who thought things through a bit more. Quietly Rubio filed papers in the winter of 2009 to form a Senate exploratory committee that would allow him to start putting together a campaign team and raising money. No press conference. No announcement. No waving flags. No balloons. No questions.

While Rubio was tiptoeing into the race, Crist was busy creating problems for himself. In February Crist traveled to Fort Myers for an event with President Obama. Crist skipped a cabinet meeting in Tallahassee and lunch with former governor Jeb Bush to attend the event. Crist is a man-hug kind of guy, and on this day he committed one of the biggest errors of his political life: he embraced Obama with cameras rolling. What's more, he embraced Obama's stimulus package that delivered nearly $800 billion in tax incentives, unemployment benefits, and direct federal investments in education, energy, infrastructure, and health care. The Crist-Obama bear hug was described by the *St. Petersburg Times* as "the kind of bipartisan love that has eluded the president in Washington."

Crist was clearly in the Republican minority. The GOP members of the Florida congressional delegation voted against the stimulus, and a half dozen Republican governors, such as Sarah Palin and Rick Perry, tried for several months to refuse the money. The hug was a giant gift to Rubio.

Rubio, who tangled so frequently with Crist in Tallahassee, knew that the governor also had other liabilities. Crist had vetoed merit-based pay for teachers, a favorite item of conservatives who railed against teachers unions and accused them of coddling underperforming educators. And he had bucked the conservative establishment when, as Florida attorney general, he stopped state efforts to maintain life support for Terri Schiavo, a brain-damaged woman who had been in a vegetative state for more than fifteen years. Her case drew international attention as her husband succeeded in ending her life support despite fervent efforts by her parents, Catholic leaders, Governor Jeb Bush, President George W. Bush, and the U.S. Congress.

Rubio's plans finally surfaced in March, a month after he filed exploratory papers, when Alan Mendelsohn, a politically connected Broward County eye doctor, held a fundraiser for him. Mendelsohn called it the "Marco Rubio Senate Kickoff," but the candidate-to-be was playing it more carefully. He said he was only "testing the waters."

The month before, Mendelsohn had been linked to a Ponzi scheme. He was later convicted and sentenced to four years in prison after admitting to paying off a state senator, siphoning hundreds of thousands of dollars from a political action committee, and failing to report more than $600,000 in taxable income. But both eventual top candidates in the Senate campaign—Crist and Rubio—had ties to Mendelsohn, muting the impact that his legal troubles might have had on the race. The doctor had steered $50,000 to Rubio's state house fundraising committee, but he had also been a staunch ally of Crist's and a member of the governor's transition team.

When Mendelsohn unofficially kicked off Rubio's campaign, few could have thought Rubio had a chance. A Quinnipiac poll the month before had measured Crist's support at 53 percent and Rubio's at 3, an extraordinary chasm to leap.

The long odds weren't all that was weighing on Rubio's mind. In his hometown of West Miami, his father's health was deteriorating from a recurrence of lung cancer. Rubio's sister Veronica

Ponce pegged the start of the decline to Easter Sunday that year. "He sat in my house and complained about shortness of breath," she wrote on her blog. "A few days later I got the call at work that he had asked to be taken to the hospital and instantly I felt that punch that blows straight through your gut and out your back and it cripples you and leaves you breathless because you know. You just know."

The doctors told Mario Rubio he had only eight to twelve months to live. The diagnosis meant that Marco would be running for Senate while his father was dying. As the senior Rubio declined, he spent hours monitoring Fox News to see if his son's face would appear on the screen. A few times he missed appearances because no one told him in advance, so he set the TiVo to capture every second of the cable network's broadcasts.

Rubio made his candidacy official on May 5, 2009. His strategy was already taking shape: link Crist to Obama. Rubio had announced first, and he was prepared to attack first too. His campaign team produced an advertisement that showed a spinning, fragmented image. "An election coming into focus," said a deep-voiced narrator in a classic voice of doom, movie-trailer style. "A choice for Florida's future. Some politicians support trillions in reckless spending, borrowed money from China and the Middle East, mountains of debt for our children, and a terrible threat to a fragile economy. Today, too many politicians embrace Washington's same old broken ways." As the voiceover proceeded, the rotating pixels were organizing into an image of Crist and Obama looking into each other's eyes. The narrator declared, "But this time, there is a leader who won't. Let the debate begin." The banner "Marco 2010" flashed on the screen.

The ad delighted Rubio. He dashed off a note of congratulations to his team:

Man, let me tell you guys something. I just ran this on my computer and three things happened. 1. I got chills. 2. My wife and children painted themselves up in blue face like Braveheart. 3. I went to the closet and got out my costume from Gladiator and I could hear the crowd chant: "Maximus! Maximus!"

Let's go kill the emperor! I love it.

Do we need a small buy to push this out? Do I need to sell my car and take out a second mortgage to pay for a bigger buy?

A week later Crist announced his candidacy, and it didn't take long for Rubio's supporters to have cause to despair. All of fourteen minutes after Crist's announcement, John Cornyn, head of the National Republican Senatorial Committee in Washington, released a statement endorsing the governor. It was an unusually early pledge of support in an intraparty contest and a clear signal that the establishment was sticking together behind Crist. Mitch McConnell, the Senate minority leader, endorsed the governor too.

The pair of endorsements had been solicited by Cornyn and McConnell's colleague in the Senate, Mel Martinez, the outgoing senator whom Crist and Rubio were vying to replace. Martinez, a former U.S. housing secretary, was also endorsing Crist. Martinez is a Cuban American who came to the United States in Operation Pedro Pan, a U.S. program in which 14,000 Cuban children were sent by their parents to the United States between 1960 and 1962 as Castro's dictatorship was taking hold on the island. In 2004 he'd become the first Cuban American ever elected to the U.S. Senate.

By coincidence Rubio had an appointment with Cornyn in Washington on the day of the Crist announcement. He had what he would later describe as a "respectful" meeting with the white-haired Texas senator. "I told them they were wrong," Rubio said. "I told them that I was going to win and they would be shocked in a year."

Rubio went from there to the office of Jim DeMint, the self-appointed leader of the ideological conservatives in the Senate who was in the process of becoming a hero to many of the grassroots activists who embraced the tea party label. DeMint supported a flat tax, private accounts for Social Security, and a constitutional amendment to outlaw abortion except when the mother's life is in danger. He had said that homosexuals and single mothers should not be permitted to teach school, and that summer he would memorably declare that if Republicans could block President Obama's sweeping health care legislation it "will be his Waterloo. It will break him."

As he'd done in Florida, Rubio moved his audience—in this case a senator whose backing he hoped for—with the story of his parents' migration from Cuba and their efforts to provide a better life for him. "I remember my eyes welling up," DeMint later said. "You get pretty hardened in Washington. But I thought this guy is for real. We don't meet many people like him in Washington."

While Rubio was looking for support in Washington, his staff was launching its attack on Crist. After the governor's announcement, they released the video that had put Rubio in a gladiatorial mood. He'd outhustled his opponents in every contest so far, and now he was going to try to get a head start in the race to define Crist.

Even though his poll numbers looked bad, spring 2009 offered a "perfect storm" for Rubio, in the words of Tom Tillison, the cofounder of a central Florida tea party group. The antiestablishment group and others around the country were looking for candidates who aligned with their movement, and Rubio—who still seemed to be searching for a base—embraced them. "He had the perfect opponent in Charlie Crist at a time when the tea party was adamantly opposed to the stimulus package, TARP, all the bailouts," Tillison said. "The tea party was looking for a more conservative option in that race, and Marco Rubio appears on the scene articulating a good strong conservative message. It had as much to do with Charlie Crist being who he was as who Marco Rubio is."

On April 15, 2009—tax day—Rubio rolled up the sleeves of his pale blue dress shirt and rallied an audience in West Palm Beach of about a thousand that waved posters saying "You can take my Constitution of the United States when you pry it from my cold dead hands" and "Free markets, not freeloaders."

"My parents lost their country to a government, I'm not going to lose mine," he told the cheering crowd. His voice rising to the level of a shout, Rubio declared, "The federal government has passed the mother of all toxic assets, a $9 trillion debt that our children and grandchildren will pay by being taxed into the Third World."

Rubio recognized early on that these disillusioned voters mattered. If a small group of them wanted him to give a talk, he'd drive hours to get there, recalled Tillison and Everett Wilkinson, chairman of the South Florida tea party. "People loved what he said," Wilkinson said. Despite his high profile in Tallahassee, Rubio was still a relative unknown in many parts of the state where voters were more concerned with their houses going into foreclosure and who in America was getting rescued with American tax dollars than who had been running the state house.

Looking back, Rubio would say, "I wish I could tell you it was part of some brilliant calculation, but it really wasn't. [Obama had moved] very rapidly on things like the stimulus plan and moved on from there, obviously, to the health care bills. So there was a counter reaction to that. It was an expansion of government's role that people weren't comfortable with. And I think what our campaign was able to do was give voice to an alternative to that."

In the early days of the race Rubio, who had been so skilled at raising campaign cash in the past, struggled to collect contributions. One night his children—whom he liked to describe as "half Cuban, half Colombian, and 100 percent American"—overheard him talking about his troubles. "The next morning, my children collected their allowance, which was largely quarters and single dollar bills," he would later recall. "It was in that moment that I was reminded what this race was really about."

Baxley found himself sufficiently inspired that in June he quit as head of the Florida Christian Coalition so that he could endorse Rubio. "Our nation is at a crossroads," he declared. "Marco Rubio is at the very tipping point of this defining hour." The two traveled to events together, and Baxley took to revving up the audience by calling out, "Do you want your country back? They'd yell back, 'Yeah!' "

Rubio was trailing Crist badly in the polls and in the endorsement race. But in June he picked up a key supporter: DeMint, the South Carolina senator he had brought to the brink of tears a month before. "My colleagues literally laughed at me," DeMint later wrote. Mike Huckabee, the former Arkansas governor who had been so appealing to Christian conservatives during his 2008 presidential campaign, came out in favor of Rubio too. In a video endorsement Huckabee touched on a theme that would be critical to Rubio's campaign: his opposition to Obama's stimulus and Crist's support of it. "There's no one I've seen on the Republican scene in a long time that is more committed to standing very, very firm on the things that matter to most of us, like holding down spending, keeping taxes low, and not believing that government handouts is the way to build an economy."

The two endorsements added to Rubio's appeal to national conservatives and gave his candidacy a much-needed jolt. But his prospects that summer still did not look bright, and more bad news was coming. A campaign finance reporting deadline was on the horizon, and Rubio's team would not be releasing an impressive number. Contribution tallies are important, especially early on, because they are portrayed as an early measure of a candidate's strength or weakness. Crist's report was going to show him as a Goliath: he had scooped up $4.3 million. Rubio's was going to make him look like an ant: he had gotten only $340,000.

Rubio's advisors gave him a blunt assessment. "The hard truth is that no one outside of a small number of activists cares about you right now as a stand-alone candidate," wrote his consultants Todd Harris, Malorie Miller, and Heath Thompson in a memo that was shared with the media after his victory. "And our 2nd Quarter fundraising numbers will make many care even less."

Harris is an affable Californian who collects wine as enthusiastically as he collects media friends in Washington, a city where the professional and social worlds are separated by the thinnest of membranes. He had worked for Jeb Bush and Arnold Schwarzenegger and is an artful spinner who can be hardnosed and confrontational if his client's reputation is attacked—but he always has a smile. "One of the best spinners I've ever seen," one veteran Florida reporter told me. Miller had worked in the Florida legislature. Thompson was the least visible of the group, a strategist prized for his work on President George W. Bush's 2004 campaign.

That month the trio of advisors also clarified the blueprint for the rest of the campaign. "You do not want to hear this," they wrote to Rubio. "The communications strategy for our campaign from now until we go on the air can be summed up in seven words: This race is not about Marco Rubio. Like it or not, this campaign is a referendum on Charlie Crist. Period. If August of 2010 comes around and voters think Charlie Crist is a nice guy and his positions are tolerable, he's going to win."

The sorry fundraising report was accompanied by a campaign shakeup. Rubio's young campaign manager, Brian Seitchik, left, as did Ann Herberger, a respected fundraiser who had worked for Jeb Bush. Rubio brought in Pat Shortridge, a former aide to Congressman Dick Armey, to manage the campaign, and media spokesman Alex Burgos, who had served on Mitt Romney's 2008 presidential campaign staff.

Amid all the bad news came even worse news. Reports began surfacing that the Rubio team was working on a deal to get him out of the race so he could run for attorney general—not the kind of signal that an underdog scrambling for financial support would want to send. Rubio denied the reports. But it seems the possibility was being discussed internally. Shortridge argued he should

Marco Rubio's grandmother, Dominga de la Caridad Rodríguez y Chirolde, in a photograph accompanying her July 12, 1956, immigrant visa and alien registration. She and her husband, Pedro Víctor García, had seven daughters. The entire family emigrated to the United States. (U.S. National Archives and Records Administration)

Rubio's grandfather, Pedro Víctor García, was born into rural poverty in Cuba and became the first person in his family to learn to read. He attempted to enter the United States on August 31, 1962, and was detained because of a visa violation. He was granted legal permanent residence five years later. (U.S. National Archives and Records Administration)

The journey from Cuba to the United States of Oria and Mario Rubio became one of the central elements of their son's political identity. As Marco Rubio rose to power, he connected with voters and with the politicians who helped him soar by emphasizing the sacrifices made by his parents. (AP Photo/Phil Coale)

Rubio gives a thumbs up as he and Mario Diaz-Balart, another star Cuban American politician, watch votes being tallied in the Florida House of Representatives, May 3, 2001. (Mark T. Foley/State Archives of Florida)

Jeb Bush was a mentor and an inspiration for Rubio. The governor, whose influence and political network had few peers in Florida, presented Rubio with a sword during the emotional ceremony designating his protégé as the next Speaker of the House, September 13, 2005, in Tallahassee, Florida. (AP Photo/Phil Coale)

Whether speaking to a small group of legislators or a huge auditorium crowd, Rubio captivates his audience, as he did during a debate on the house floor on May 2, 2006. Republican Dennis Baxley, standing, talked Rubio through his decision to retain his connection to his Catholic faith while attending Protestant evangelical services. (Mark T. Foley/State Archives of Florida)

Rubio confers with his friend, Representative Ralph Arza, in 2006. As Rubio was rising to the speakership of the Florida house, Arza created a major dilemma for Rubio when he was accused of using a racial epithet offensive to African Americans. (Mark T. Foley/State Archives of Florida)

Rubio confers on March 8, 2007 with Republican lawmaker Juan Zapata, with whom he sponsored a bill to give in-state tuition breaks to the children of some undocumented immigrants. The bill failed. Rubio later opposed broader in-state tuition proposals. (Mark T. Foley/State Archives of Florida)

Rubio, right, and David Rivera at the speaker's rostrum on April 25, 2007. The two "are like brothers." Their friendship survived even as Rivera was being investigated by state and federal prosecutors in corruption cases. (Mark T. Foley/State Archives of Florida)

During Rubio's campaign for the U.S. Senate, he used "The Hug"—an embrace between Governor Charlie Crist and President Obama—as a weapon to criticize Crist for accepting federal stimulus money, a decision attacked by conservative activists. In happier times, Crist and Rubio did the hugging when the legislature passed a property-tax cutting measure on June 14, 2007. (Mark T. Foley/State Archives of Florida)

In the Florida statehouse, Rubio could be a "partisan pitbull," but some Democrats, such as Dan Gelber, seen here with Rubio on March 5, 2008, considered him someone who could be reasonable behind the scenes. (Mark T. Foley/State Archives of Florida)

Rubio loves football. There was nothing like a football star visiting the capitol to put him in the best of moods. On April 2, 2008, NFL Hall of Famer Dan Marino visited with Rubio and Governor Crist to promote insurance coverage for autism. (Bill Cotterell/State Archives of Florida)

When he was growing up, Rubio watched Miami Dolphins games with a notepad on his lap to chart the plays. He still kept close tabs as he became one of Florida's most powerful politicians. On NFL draft day, lawmakers streamed into his office for updates. In his last days as speaker, colleagues showered him with football-themed gifts, including a signed Miami Dolphins helmet. (Mark T. Foley/State Archives of Florida)

A bit of immortality: Marco Rubio enjoys the unveiling of his official portrait on the floor of the Florida House of Representatives on May 2, 2008. (Mark T. Foley/State Archives of Florida)

It was a night to remember. A large crowd in Coral Gables, Florida, broke into cheers as Rubio—once a huge underdog—took the stage to celebrate his U.S. Senate victory on Nov. 2, 2010. At right, front, are his daughters Daniella and Amanda, and his son Anthony. At rear is his wife, Jeanette, holding his son Dominick. (AP Photo/Lynne Sladky)

TOP: Sometimes you just have to laugh. Al Franken yukked it up with Rubio before President Obama's State of the Union address on Capitol Hill on January 25, 2011. Lawmakers tried to foster a spirit of cooperation with bipartisan seating arrangements. (Chip Somodevilla/Getty Images)

CENTER: Washington was no easy place. After a year in office, Senator Rubio confided to a reporter that he couldn't think of a single highlight. Nonetheless, he paid special attention to foreign policy— a prerequisite for senators with an eye on the Oval Office. Here, Rubio and Senator Joseph Lieberman leave a May 11, 2011, news conference about the crisis in Syria. (Alex Wong/Getty Images)

BOTTOM: "Hero!" That's how the conservative blogosphere saw it when Rubio saved Nancy Reagan from a nasty fall while escorting her down the aisle at the Reagan Presidential Library. Rubio's quick reflexes on August 23, 2011, strengthened the impression that he was a star touched by serendipity. (AP Photo/Jae C. Hong)

stay in, writing in a memo, "If we can't get this thing figured out and on a clear path to victory by the end of October, then by all means pivot into another race. But then, you will have pivoted having fought the good fight to the best of your ability."

Throughout the campaign Rubio proved that he would go anywhere, drive any distance, speak to any group no matter how small in order to get votes. Florida stretches eight hundred miles from Key West to Pensacola, and that meant many sixteen-hour days in the car. Rubio liked to blast hip-hop on the stereo, Snoop Dogg and other edgy rappers. "He can spit!" one young staffer marveled to a friend, invoking the slang term for singing rap lyrics. A love of music that could be profane and sometimes celebrated drug use and violence wasn't exactly what they expected from the up-and-coming voice of righteous conservatism. "You know, I get in trouble when I talk about that a little bit, because maybe I shouldn't listen to that anymore, but the music is good," Rubio would later say. "[You've] just got to sometimes ignore what their politics may be and just enjoy the music."

In that summer of hip-hop and long car rides, the momentum was all Crist's. Even Al Cardenas, one of Rubio's early political mentors, couldn't see his way to getting behind his former protégé. Cardenas knew Florida politics as well as anyone, but he misread where the race was headed. In August he endorsed Crist. "I have strong personal feelings for Marco and his family and it bothered me greatly then that he was risking a brilliant future," Cardenas later said. "I spoke to him like I would to one of my sons."

Rubio is a disciplined politician, and he was sticking to a game plan that his advisors believed in. In effect they were running two campaigns. One reached out to Florida voters, while the other reached out to national media and campaign contributors outside the state. They wanted to make Marco Rubio more than a Florida senatorial candidate; they wanted to make him a national figure.

It was a risky approach, but the campaign didn't like its chances with the Florida media, so it was a gamble worth taking. Rubio's advisors were contemptuous of the Florida papers and broadcast outlets and thought they hadn't taken Rubio seriously enough. The locals had already formed an image of Rubio as a capital horse trader, and were less likely to embrace him as a national figure with a fresh approach. The national media might. What the campaign was hoping for was a ricochet effect: good press outside of Florida bouncing back into the state and influencing voters, the media, and contributors.

In September the Rubio camp got what it wanted. The *National Review,* an influential conservative magazine, put Rubio on its cover, his arms crossed and his jaw locked defiantly. "Yes, He Can," the headline reads, playing off Obama's signature campaign line, "Yes, We Can." The story framed the campaign as a showdown with implications for all Republicans. "Florida Conservative Marco Rubio's Play for the GOP Future," read another line on the cover.

The profile by the journalist and author John J. Miller hits all the notes the campaign was trying to hit. It calls Crist "one of the most liberal politicians in the Republican firmament," and casts Rubio as being "among the brightest young stars on the right." The article also includes a glowing review of Rubio by Jeb Bush, leaving little doubt where the former governor—who had yet to endorse a candidate in the race—stood. "He's got all the tools," Bush declares.

Rubio's supporters were thrilled. It was the turning point in the race, Baxley said. "People all over the country started falling in line with Marco before Florida even knew what it had." The *National Review* wasn't alone in identifying Rubio as the next big thing. Websites with strong conservative followings, such as Red State and Human Events, were blasting Crist in their postings and helping drive Rubio's fundraising efforts. Small donations were pouring in from throughout the country, and when Rubio announced his fundraising numbers in October his supporters could crow about topping $1 million in the previous three months. He was spending it almost as fast as it came in, but at least it showed he was in the game.

A December 2009 Rasmussen Reports survey confirmed that the race had shifted. Ten months after Rubio was down by 50 points, he managed to pull into a dead heat with Crist. The momentum was now Rubio's. And the shift in the polls in Florida coincided with an uptick in conservative Republican confidence farther north. In Massachusetts Scott Brown—another handsome tea party darling—stunned the Washington establishment by winning a Senate seat opened by the death of the liberal icon Ted Kennedy. The Brown victory in a special election broke the Democratic Party's filibuster-proof majority in the Senate and affirmed that something seismic was taking place in the Republican Party—the tea party mattered. Running against Obama worked. Rubio had made the right call, and Crist—with his man hug of the president—the wrong one. The embrace was becoming such a central image of Rubio's campaign that his staff took to referring to it simply as "Fort Myers" in strategy sessions. No further explanation was necessary.

Rubio's plan was working so nicely that he could even afford to jab a bit at the Florida reporters his campaign held in such low esteem. In January he tweeted, "I think FL Press corp was excited to see me today. LOL. Remember when toughest question I got was 'when are you going to drop out?' "

Around that time influential players in Florida politics and at the national level were cooling to Crist and warming to the idea of Marco Rubio as their senator, but they were doing so behind the scenes. In the same way that Rubio's opponents in the Florida house speaker's race were "beat before they knew it," Crist's support was discreetly draining away. "A lot of people connected with [Rubio] before they could go public," Baxley said. Jumping to Rubio wasn't simple because so many conservatives had already aligned with Crist, and dumping him would seem disloyal. Rubio supporters needed to make the case that Crist wasn't true to conservative principles.

Off on the side, José "Pepe" Fanjul, the Cuban American sugar and real estate baron, worked to convert Crist backers into Rubio backers. Marco Men. Fanjul invited one longtime national conservative power broker who had thrown his weight behind Crist to his home on Palm Beach to meet the aspiring senator from Miami for the first time. It was a small get-together, just three or four people, and it gave the political veteran who had come into town a chance to size up Rubio without distractions. "Two things came across to me," the venerable Republican told me. "In spite of his rhetorical gifts and his very agile mind, he's very modest. He has humility. That's a rare quality. The other 'H' quality—hubris—is in much larger supply."

Rubio's national strategy had its official coming-out party in February in Washington at the Conservative Political Action Conference, or CPAC, a kind of Lollapalooza for conservatives. Rubio had been invited to speak, another affirmation of his rising stature. He frequently spoke extemporaneously, but his address before thousands from the Republican base was critical, and there was no room for error. Rubio and his advisors wrote and revised, wrote and revised, going through ten drafts before they were satisfied. Minutes before he went on stage they were still tinkering.

That same month, Washington, a city that goes into a panic at the sight of a few snowflakes, was socked in by an honest-to-goodness snowstorm that came to be known, hyperbolically, as Snowmageddon. Rubio nimbly folded the storm that had been on everyone's minds into the opening of his address, using it to underscore his anti-Obama, anti–big government message. Rubio, who as Florida house speaker could sometimes come off as a bit overwrought and self-righteous, started with a laugh line.

"A week ago we didn't know we were going to make it here," he told an audience that might have been mistaken for a pep rally if not for all the suits and wingtips. "We were watching all the images of that winter weather, the extreme blizzard that even impacted government. I don't know if you know this but the Congress couldn't meet to vote on bills. The regulatory agencies couldn't meet to set new regulations either. And the president couldn't find anywhere to set up the teleprompter to announce new taxes. You know, now that I come to think of it, the blizzard might be the best thing to happen to the American economy in 12 months."

The Marco Rubio who was being formally introduced to a cheering national conservative audience that day delivered the speech of his life. Its appeal to conservatives and impact on Rubio's national profile is comparable to Barack Obama's speech at the 2004 Democratic National Convention, which catapulted the future president onto the national stage. As ever, he drew on the appeal of his personal history to transfix his audience: "I was not born to a wealthy or connected family but I have never felt limited by the circumstance of my birth." He outlined a political philosophy founded on the notion that the United States is "the single greatest society in all of human history." And he framed the months and years ahead as a struggle between people such as himself, who believe that to their core, and Washington politicians who don't. Us versus them. Nothing short of a battle to save America.

> *There have always been those who haven't seen it this way. . . . They think that we need a guardian class in American government to protect us from ourselves. They think that the free-enterprise system is unfair, that a few people make a lot of money, and the rest of us get left behind. They believe that the only way business can make its money is by exploiting its workers and its customers. And they think that America's enemies exist because of something America did to earn their enmity.*
>
> *Now, the problem is that in 2008 leaders with this worldview won elections. And now they know that the American people will never support their vision of America.*
>
> *So, instead, over the last 12 months they have used a severe economic downturn, a severe recession as an excuse to implement the statist policies that they have longed for all this time. In essence, they are using this downturn as cover not to fix America, but to try to change America to fundamentally redefine the role of government in our lives and the role of America in the world.*

He could have stopped there and left his audience with an image of a leader railing against all that he saw wrong in the world. But he brought the crowd around to a sense of optimism by presenting a vision of what could be. In full command of the audience, he lifted the room with a wave of repetition.

> *Let's reform the tax code and reduce tax rates across the board.*
>
> *Let's eliminate double taxation by abolishing the taxes on capital gains, on dividends, on interest. And while we're at it, let's eliminate the one on death, too.*
>
> *Let's significantly lower the corporate tax rates so that once again [America is] competitive with the rest of the world.*
>
> *Let's stop big government energy mandates like cap-and-trade, and instead trust the American innovator to make us energy independent.*

If there was any doubt that Marco Rubio had arrived, it was laid to rest by the cheers of the crowd that day. The interruptions told the story too. The crowd kept chanting, "Marco! Marco! Marco!"

The flipside of the adoration in Washington was the body blows Rubio kept having to block back down in Florida. His spending was coming under deeper and deeper scrutiny, and the details were embarrassing. Investigative reporters published allegations that he charged thousands of dollars' worth of what appeared to be personal items on his party-issued credit card, including $1,000 in repairs to the family minivan (Rubio said it was damaged at a political event), more than $750 at Apple's online store, and even small, silly-seeming items like $10.50 at an AMC movie theater, $68 at Happy Wine, a shop near his home, and $134 at a hair salon, that last one drawing mocking comparisons to former presidential candidate John Edwards's expensive grooming habits. Rubio insisted that he paid for any personal items. Newspapers also reported that Rubio had double-billed the state Republican party for airline tickets. When the story came out, he was forced to reimburse the party more than $2,000. And a former ally stated publicly that Rubio had told him about charging $4,000 to the party card for flooring in his West Miami home. "It's all sideshows," Rubio said when asked about the allegation during his campaign. "The bottom line is, the Republican Party has never paid for my personal expenses. To the extent that things ever happened like that, I always paid for it directly to American Express."

Some of the findings were hard to fathom and seemed like an utterly irresponsible commingling of personal and public finances. For instance, more than $6,000 was charged to the state party card of Rubio's chief of staff at the time, Richard Corcoran—who is expected to serve as Florida house speaker in 2017 and 2018—to cover food and lodging for a Rubio family reunion at a plantation resort in Thomasville, Georgia. The charge was brushed off by Rubio's team as another accounting error, payments for a canceled "leadership dinner" that were applied to the Rubio family's bill. His staff also said that Rubio's relatives sent checks to American Express to cover their bills. Ben Wilcox, of the government watchdog group Common Cause Florida, publicly accused Rubio of playing "fast and loose with the rules."

The credit card controversy allowed opponents to dredge

up other money matters that had drawn criticism. For instance, Rubio had scored a $69,000-a-year job to teach political science classes and do research at Florida International University after leaving office. Even though Rubio's staff said he raised much of his salary from private donations, some faculty members complained because the university had been chopping degree programs and cutting jobs at the time. "The Rubio hiring for many was salt in the wound," said Thomas Breslin, chairman of the faculty senate. Then Rubio drew more criticism for hiring his FIU boss, Dario Moreno, to do $12,000 in polling for his Senate race. When the hire was reported by the media, Moreno stopped working for Rubio.

Rubio's personal finances were also questioned because he made a $200,000 profit selling a house he owned to the mother of a chiropractor who was lobbying for a change in state insurance rules. Rubio had been a holdout, but removed a block on the measure shortly after the home sale and voted for it. Rubio was criticized for failing to disclose a home equity loan he received from U.S. Century Bank, whose chairman, Sergio Pino, was a political supporter. The house had been appraised for $185,000 more than the purchase price just thirty-seven days after he bought it. Rubio's staff said the value jumped because he'd locked in a lower preconstruction price and made improvements. U.S. Century Bank—a large recipient of federal bank bailout money—denied making a sweetheart deal.

Crist's supporters pounced on many of the allegations, particularly the credit card spending. "Having expenditures in the tens of thousands of dollars to pay off credit cards, it's clear to me it was being used to live off of," said Mike Fasano, a Republican state senator from New Port Richey, north of Tampa. "The Rubios were living off it."

Rubio's staff fought back aggressively, calling Fasano's suggestion "an absolute, flat-out lie. And Mike Fasano should be ashamed for doing Charlie Crist's dirty work without any regard for the truth." His staff insisted that Rubio kept an accounting of personal expenses charged to the state card and paid those directly to American Express. Oddly enough, some in Tallahassee considered Rubio's handling of the credit card merely a minor issue; their attitude was that Rubio should have practically received a medal for not spending as much as other Republican politicians. For years it had been well known in Tallahassee that raiding party funds was common practice. "One guy bought an engagement ring, and then [his fiancée] broke off the engagement. I don't know what happened with the ring," one Rubio ally told me.

In any case, the impact of the reports was blunted by the troubles building for Crist's hand-chosen Republican Party head, Jim Greer, who would be indicted on charges of using party money for personal expenses in June, while the campaign was in full swing. (Greer has denied the charges, and his case is scheduled for trial in summer 2012.)

By that spring—eight months after Rubio was fighting rumors that he would drop out of the race—Crist's campaign was in so much trouble that he was now facing questions of whether he might bail on the Republican primary. In a Fox News debate, the host Chris Wallace pressed Crist about rumors that he might run as an independent. "Are you ruling out that you will file as an independent by the April 30th deadline?" Wallace asked.

"That's right. That's right," Crist responded. "I'm running as a Republican."

While the Florida papers were questioning Rubio's ethics regarding his credit card spending, the national media was pumping him up and portraying Crist as untrustworthy and disloyal. The popular Fox host Sean Hannity introduced one segment by telling his audience that he considered Rubio "a rock star," then asked Rudy Giuliani about claims that Crist had reneged on a promise to him during the former New York mayor's 2008 presidential campaign. "Charlie Crist told you twice . . . 'You have my endorsement.'. . . He lied to you?" Hannity asked.

"That's right," Giuliani said in the on-air interview. "I mean, he broke—he broke his word, which to me in politics is worth everything."

Crist's campaign was falling apart. He'd gone from a 50-percentage-point lead to a 30-percentage-point deficit, an epic swing. In late April, a month after promising to run as a Republican, Crist dropped out of the Republican primary to run as an independent. His lead advisors—including Stuart Stevens, a top strategist for Mitt Romney's 2012 presidential campaign—left the campaign, and he had to turn to his sister, Margaret Crist Wood, to manage his severely hobbled effort. Big-name endorsers abandoned him and switched to Rubio.

If it had been a boxing match, the referee would have waved his arms and declared a Rubio victory right then and there, a win by technical knockout. There were months to go before the general election, and there was still the matter of getting past the Democrats, who in August would nominate an African American U.S. congressman named Kendrick Meek. But with Rubio's poll numbers so robust, and the prospect of Crist pulling votes away from Democrats rather than Republicans, the race was becoming a foregone conclusion.

Just as Rubio's front-runner status had been impervious to allegations about his use of the Republican Party credit card, he was barely scratched by news in June—five months before the general election—that a bank had initiated foreclosure proceedings against him and political ally David Rivera on a mortgage for a house they co-owned in Tallahassee. Under other circumstances, it might have been a major blemish for a candidate who promised fiscal responsibility in Washington. But Rubio's position at the head of the pack was set in granite. The two men claimed they had stopped paying the mortgage five months earlier in a dispute over the rate, and they quickly came up with $9,000 to settle the debt and stop foreclosure proceedings.

No matter what troubles Rivera encountered or what positions he took, Rubio refused to abandon him. When they were in the legislature together, Rubio had shrugged off Rivera's support of expanding gambling in Miami-Dade County, despite his own frequent public opposition to gambling. Once an ally in the capitol asked Rubio about the seeming disconnect: "He just looked at me like, 'What's your point?'"

"They're like brothers. . . . I think Marco let David be David," the capitol insider said. "He was kind of untouchable."

In years to come Rubio would remain loyal to Rivera amid reports of federal and state investigations into his friend's campaign funds, the accuracy of his financial disclosure reports, questionable loans, and his ties to a former lobbyist and her consulting company. Rivera has consistently maintained he was not involved in any wrongdoing, though he has acknowledged some reporting errors that he says he corrected.

In one investigation, reported extensively by the *Miami Herald* and Associated Press, the FBI and IRS were said to be examining whether Rivera received secret payments totaling between $500,000 and $1 million to help promote an expansion of gambling in Miami-Dade County. The contract for the gambling campaign was given to Millennium Marketing Strategies, run by Rivera's mother and godmother, although it specifically identified Rivera as the chief consultant in galvanizing community support for slot machines. Rivera also initially failed to report loans totaling $132,000 from the company. Later some Florida news reports suggested the investigations were going nowhere.

But Rubio never wavered. In 2010 Rivera was engaged in his own race, a contest for an open seat in the U.S. House of Representatives, and Rubio would sometimes appear with him at campaign events.

As for his own campaign, Rubio stuck to the strategy of courting the right wing of the national party, even though it became increasingly complicated to pull off at times. In April he likened a proposed Arizona law that allowed authorities to stop people and demand their immigration papers to a "police state." Latino activists decried the proposal as racial profiling.

But the measure was popular with the tea party activists and the Republican Party's right wing. Rubio chose the website Human Events, which was influential with the party's most conservative faction, to clarify his remarks in May 2010. The bill had been changed slightly to say that authorities could not "solely consider race" when asking for documents. Latino activists still considered the measure unsavory, but Rubio told Human Events he thought the revised bill "hit the right notes" and suggested he would have voted for it.

Raúl Martinez, the Hialeah power broker who had first opposed Rubio then befriended him, couldn't believe what he was seeing. "This is the new Marco," Martinez thought to himself. "The I-want-to-be-a-senator-at-any-cost Marco." If Martinez had known where Rubio was headed on the immigration issue, he said, they never could have been political allies.

While Rubio was enjoying enthusiastic support from conservative commentators and Republican stars, the national Democratic Party was doing Kendrick Meek few favors, offering him only the most tepid support while stories were being leaked that former president Bill Clinton was urging him to drop out. Meek's mother, Carrie Meek, in 1992 had become one of the first African Americans elected to Congress from Florida since Reconstruction. Her son was a former college football player who was the first African American to serve as a captain in the Florida State Troopers; since 2003 he had represented a U.S. congressional district that straddled Broward and Miami-Dade counties.

During the campaign Meek was once mistaken for a bellboy while checking into a Holiday Inn in northern Florida. Another guest tried to hand Meek his bags. "I can't help you with your bags," Meek told him, according to a staffer who was there. Meek handed the man his card and said, "I'm a U.S. congressman. If you're in town I'll give you a tour."

Meek supporters began to detect a subtle new form of what they believed was racism. It wasn't a sense that he couldn't run because he was black; it was a sense that he couldn't win because he was black. At the time there were no black senators.

On primary night Meek defeated Jeff Greene, a billionaire businessman who had hosted the Hollywood madam, Heidi Fleiss, in his guesthouse after she was released from prison. The erratic boxer Mike Tyson had been the best man at Greene's wedding.

Meek's nomination got little attention amid the headlines about the stunning Republican primary victories by tea party candidates, such as Christine O'Donnell in Delaware and Joe Miller in Alaska, whose thin margin over incumbent senator Lisa Murkowski withstood a furious challenge of the vote total. What little notice Meek got mostly portrayed him as a liability to the Democrats: the argument was made in political circles that Democrats would have been better off with the underqualified Greene as the nominee so they could abandon him and support Crist. Meanwhile Crist was being urged to run as a Democrat. The muddled state of the race both before and after Crist's defection only helped solidify the impression of Rubio as the inevitable victor. And with inevitability came more support and more money. Fanjul hosted a fundraising event for Rubio at his luxurious apartment on New York's Upper East Side. Rubio stood on a sweeping staircase and told the gathered elites about his family story and his vision for America. The guest list was mostly composed of "very cynical, worldly, we-already-know-everything New Yorkers and inside-the-Beltway types," one of the guests told me. "And he moved us. In the environment of a fundraiser, I've never seen it. I was stunned by that."

Opposing strategists marveled at Rubio's ability to stay on message. "It pains me to say this, but I think he legitimately believes the things he says on policy," an opposing strategist said.

The opposition assumed that Rubio's plan was to avoid being

overly aggressive against Meek and to pigeonhole Crist as a liberal. Rubio benefited from Meek's presence in the race because he would siphon moderate votes from Crist, and Democrats failed to make the case to their conservative wing that Crist wasn't one of them. "We screwed it up," one top Democratic strategist told me. "It was the Democrats who failed to pigeonhole Crist as a Republican who really opened the door to be a blowout."

During the three-way debates Crist was easy to torment. He had a tendency to sweat profusely, and opposing strategists sought to rattle him by trying to insert language in debate agreements to block him from placing a fan on the floor beneath him to keep him cool. Video of Crist with a portable fan blowing on him during press interviews circulated on the Internet.

Rubio's team preferred to have their candidate stand either to the left or the right of Meek and Crist, but not between them. Usually candidates like to be at center stage, but placing Rubio to one side would allow him to gesture at both Meek and Crist, as if they were two parts of a contiguous liberal whole. Crist's only hope was to paint Rubio as an extremist, a point he tried to underscore by emphasizing the Miami Republican's popularity with tea party activists. It was a curious approach since the tea party was reaching the zenith of its influence, and strategists involved in the campaign saw it as a desperate attempt to lure liberals away from Meek. "The Republican Party and the right wing of that party went so far right. It's exactly why Marco Rubio stayed there [and] it's exactly the same reason that I left," Crist said.

In September, with his campaign going so well, Rubio went home to Miami for something more important than politics. On a Saturday night he joined his siblings and his mother at Baptist Hospital as his father took his last breaths. Rubio suspended campaign activities to mourn. He issued a poignant letter, reminiscent of the soaring eulogy Vice President Al Gore delivered when his father passed away. "My dad was the one behind the bar," Rubio wrote. "But he worked all his life so his kids could make the symbolic journey from behind the bar to behind the podium. . . . My father mattered. He was not famous, wealthy or influential. But he mattered in a way we too often overlook today. He mattered not because of what he accomplished himself, but because of what his life allowed others to."

Rubio buried his father and returned to a campaign in its final, coronation stage. Rubio's frontrunner status was so solid that he again was easily able to weather a critical newspaper report, this time a story in the *St. Petersburg Times* that said a judge had listed him in an email as one of the "heroes" responsible for securing money to build a palatial, $48 million state courthouse in Tallahassee that was being mocked as the Taj Mahal. Rubio responded that he had never heard of the judge's list and hadn't had anything to do with the courthouse as speaker. His statement was contradicted by Ray Sansom, his former appropriations chairman, who said that Rubio had told him that a $7.9 million budget allotment for the courthouse was, indeed, a priority. Then again, Sansom was under indictment at the time in an unrelated case, so he didn't have the credibility to upend the race. Crist was flailing so badly—and was so eager to appeal to Democrats—that one of his top advisors confirmed rumors that he would caucus with senate Democrats if elected. The race had been over for a long time, so the ploy may not have mattered.

On November 2 Rubio's ascension was complete. The final

vote tally showed him with a resounding margin of victory: 48.9 percent for Rubio, just 29.7 percent for Crist, and 20.2 percent for Meek.

"We make a grave mistake if we believe that these results are somehow an embrace of the Republican Party," he told the jubilant crowd gathered at the Biltmore Hotel in Coral Gables. "What they are is a second chance, a second chance for Republicans to be what they said they were going to be not so long ago."

Chapter Seven

GOD AND COUNTRY

Two affirmations of faith frame Marco Rubio's rise from the state capitol to national acclaim. The first was delivered in a voice quavering with emotion on the floor of the Florida House of Representatives, the second in a voice raised in triumph at the Biltmore Hotel in Coral Gables.

"God is real," Rubio told his colleagues in May 2008 during his farewell speech at the Florida House of Representatives. "God is real. I don't care what courts across this country say, I don't care what laws we pass—God is real."

As Rubio delivered those remarks his political path was unclear; he might have been headed toward Florida attorney general, he might have been headed toward governor, he might have been headed toward the Miami mayor's office, he might have been headed into obscurity.

One and a half years later, in the flush of his Senate win and with his ascension to national stardom assured, Rubio opened his victory speech with another statement of faith: "Let me begin tonight by acknowledging a simple but profound truth. We are all children of a powerful and great God. . . . I bear witness to that tonight as so many of you do in your own lives." These truths, he said, "must always be acknowledged in everything we do and in everywhere we go."

Standing there before a cheering crowd was a man who wanted so much to tell the world about God. But he was also a man who had looked for years for the right place to discover his own spirituality. He was the little boy who went to Catholic Mass. Then the adolescent who embraced Mormonism. He was the teenager who circled back to Catholicism. Then the thirty-something who defined himself as a Baptist. He was the ascendant politician who wanted to be Catholic again.

He was all these things.

Some national politicians shy away from discussions of faith, but Rubio weaves references to it, both large and small, into most of his major addresses. God appears when Rubio discusses energy policy: "We are an energy-rich nation, and conservatism, which is grounded in common sense, says that if you're an energy-rich country, you need to use the energy that God's blessed your nation with." He is there when Rubio discusses the "economic hopes and dreams" of Americans, "that through hard work and sacrifice you can be who God meant you to be." He is there when Rubio discusses foreign policy: "I have the feeling that God has created us and brought us to our present position of power and strength for some great purpose."

A lawyer or a mechanic, a nurse or a teacher, might be able to keep religion a matter of private reflection. But in politics, religious affiliation is a standard line on the list of biographical data points on official websites and public registries.

For four decades Rubio has been in the process of answering that question for himself. Catholic. Mormon. Catholic again. Baptist. Catholic again. "A faith journey," as his staff puts it.

Whether he worshipped in a Mormon chapel, kneeled in a Catholic pew, or gave praise at an evangelical service, it has been clear that faith was a central tenet of Rubio's life, even as he groped for a religious structure that suited him. As a young child, it consumed him. "He's always been into religion," his cousin Michelle Denis says. "Football and religion. Those were his things." The young Rubio seems to have exerted an unusual level of control over his family's religious life. As an adolescent or young teen, he persuaded his mother and younger sister to leave the Mormon church and re-embrace Catholicism. "He really convinced the whole family to switch religions," Michelle Denis said.

As with much of Rubio's family history, there's dispute about the chronology. Rubio says the conversion took place while the family lived in Las Vegas; his cousin Mo Denis says they converted after moving back to Miami. And the Mormon faith may have retained a kind of technical hold on them regardless of their conversion: Rubio and his family members never asked for their names to be removed from LDS rolls, meaning they may still be counted as Mormons by the church.

As an adult, religion remained a source of complexity for the rising young lawmaker. He came to political office as a Catholic, but in his early years in the legislature, he found spiritual kinship with a Baptist, and Rubio eventually came to think of himself as a Baptist too.

Over the years, as he'd done at points during his political career, Rubio sought the counsel of his friend and legislative colleague Dennis Baxley regarding his spiritual life. They prayed
together on the phone, with Baxley calling his younger colleague
and asking, "What's heavy for you?" They shared religious reading material, and Baxley liked to pop into Rubio's speaker's office
to offer, "Can I pray for you?"

In 2004, when both were state legislators, Rubio suggested
that Baxley and members of the devout older legislator's prayer
group see the Mel Gibson film *The Passion of the Christ.* Baxley
liked the idea so much that he rented an entire theater and paid
$1,200 to buy tickets that he offered free of charge to all 120
members of the Florida house. At least one Jewish legislator complained, citing concerns similar to those being voiced in many
synagogues, that the film was anti-Semitic in its portrayal of the
role Jews played in the death of Jesus Christ. When asked about
the concerns Jews were raising, Rubio replied, "You'd have to be
an absolute moron to be anti-Semitic after seeing that film."

During some of those Tallahassee years, Rubio identified
himself in official listings as Catholic and in others as Baptist.
In that time, he was wrestling with where to direct his religious
energies. His wife, Jeanette, and her family had embraced Christ
Fellowship, an evangelical Protestant church affiliated with the
Southern Baptist Convention. Rubio enjoyed the services at
Christ Fellowship, a fast-growing church attended by thousands
of worshippers at six locations in the Miami area. But it was more
complicated than simply driving somewhere new on Sunday
mornings. "We've had talks about that," Baxley, who is a Southern Baptist and served as the head of the Florida Christian Coalition, told me. "He was not comfortable in just making a choice,

severing [his] relationship with one or the other. . . . He's never been comfortable leaving his Catholic roots."

Rather than making a choice between the two, Rubio integrated both into his life. He was baptized, confirmed, and married in the Catholic Church, and he attended Mass on the morning of his election to the U.S. Senate. Once he got to Washington, he identified himself as a Roman Catholic on his web page and in the Congressional Directory for the 112th Congress. And he has said he attends Mass daily at a Catholic church a minute-and-a-half walk from his office in the Hart Building. "One of the great treasures of the Catholic faith is the ability to go to Mass every day," he said. But he also attended Christ Fellowship's services and donated tens of thousands of dollars to the Protestant evangelical church. When reporters asked after his Senate victory if he also donated to the Catholic Church, he declined to say.

Rubio and his friend Baxley shared similar experiences of blending two religions. When Baxley, the son of a Baptist minister, was dating the woman who would become his wife, they attended two religious services each weekend. The couple reserved Saturday nights for Catholic Mass and Sunday mornings to attend Baxley's Baptist services. In straddling two religions, Rubio and Baxley embody a small but not insignificant subset of Americans. Thirty-five percent of Americans attend services outside their own faith, but a much smaller group, just 9 percent, attend services of multiple religions regularly. About the same percentage of Catholics regularly attend services of multiple religions. Latinos are still overwhelmingly Catholic, but the percentage is dropping, and many of those who leave the faith find their way to Protestant Evangelical churches.

The two religions that Rubio participates in, however, have

some major differences with each other: many Southern Baptists practice childhood or adult baptism rather than infant baptism; Evangelical Protestants don't recognize the authority of the pope; and there are major distinctions on the significance of communion, among other things. But they are both Christian faiths.

At the practical level, "the differences are often cultural as much as religious or theological," explains Professor Mark A. Noll of Notre Dame. Converts from Catholicism to Protestant Evangelical faiths are often seeking "a stronger personal sense of God" and more encouragement to study the scriptures themselves instead of having them interpreted. Among converts there's often a desire for a warmer, less formal church atmosphere, Noll said.

Catholics consider the consecrated wafer given at Mass to be the actual body of Christ imbued with an intrinsic power to confer spiritual grace, says the theologian Chad C. Pecknold of Catholic University of America. But in the Rubio family's Evangelical church, communion is considered "a symbolic act of obedience whereby believers, through partaking of the bread and the fruit of the vine, memorialize the death of the Redeemer and anticipate his second coming," according to the church website. "That's a big difference," Pecknold said, and an observant Catholic would thus usually seek permission from a priest or bishop to receive communion at a non-Catholic church.

Not surprisingly, then, Rubio's straddling of the two religions hasn't gone unnoticed, particularly among some Catholics. After Rubio's 2010 Senate victory, Eric Giunta, a Catholic blogger, questioned whether Rubio was "talking out of both sides, the better to court both the Catholic and evangelical votes.

"Rubio's possible newfound Protestantism doesn't offend me, as much as the prospect of Catholics and Baptists having their intelligences insulted by a politician sending mixed messages to two 'religious right' constituencies, the better to garner as many votes from each as possible," wrote Giunta, who at the same time praised Rubio's statesmanship and said he continued to support him politically. "In short: Mr. Rubio doesn't have to be a Catholic to earn my Catholic vote—I just don't appreciate being lied to or misled. And neither should Baptists, if indeed it turns out Rubio is attending and patronizing one of their churches in order to court the Evangelical vote."

Rubio brought his religion to the fore by giving faith such prominence in his speeches, but his staff was irked that Giunta was raising questions about the new senator's religious practices. "If you find that there is a dearth of pertinent material to write about," one Rubio staffer, J. R. Sanchez, wrote in an email that Giunta posted on his site, "perhaps you can focus on the many serious issues facing our nation, and the reasons why the citizens of Florida overwhelmingly elected Mr. Rubio as their next United States Senator. You may wish to highlight Senator-elect Rubio's consistent and conservative social and fiscal policies such as his pro-life stance, his commitment to reducing the national debt, enacting a balanced budget amendment, lowering the tax burden for Americans and maintaining a strong military presence to defend our nation from the various threats abroad. . . . I hope that you find this e-mail helpful, and that you focus your future writings on salient matters that face our nation."

Though Giunta's blogging and similar questions raised in several major publications, including the *New York Times*, generated conversation on the Internet, there is no evidence that Rubio suffered politically. Analysts wrote off any possible political effect, generally concluding that Christians—particularly Hispanic

Christians—weren't drawing distinctions between the two faiths and weren't placing a high level of importance on Rubio's decision to worship at more than one church.

The ho-hum reaction may also have had something to do with broader thawing in relations between Catholics and Southern Baptists that had been under way for years. There was a time when Catholics and Protestant Evangelicals looked at each other from across a substantial divide. "Catholics and Evangelicals tended to not know each other very well, to be in their own subcultures," said Richard Land, president of the Southern Baptist Convention's Ethics & Religious Liberty Commission. But in the past four decades many of those barriers have fallen, in great part because of politics, Land said. Catholics and Southern Baptists formed alliances during that period over social issues, particularly opposition to abortion. Now, Land said, "we're co-belligerents in the culture wars." That alliance was particularly obvious in the reaction to implementing an Obama administration rule requiring employers, including most religious groups, to include contraception in employee health insurance plans. The decision led to a backlash in which Catholics, Southern Baptists, and many other religious organizations once again found common cause. Rubio inserted himself into the center of the battle: he filed a bill to block the rule from going into effect and spoke out against it forcefully at the Conservative Political Action Conference in Washington in early 2012, the scene of his electrically charged introduction to national Republicans in 2010.

The ballroom at the Marriott Wardman Hotel in early February 2012 filled once again, this time to greet a Republican icon in the making rather than a rising young aspirant. Rubio hit on themes that Republicans had been pressing throughout the months before, during a fierce presidential primary: lower taxes, controlling the national debt, liberal judges, Medicare, and, most important, Obama's performance in office. But he pushed two ideas dear to the group: that America is exceptional, and that its government has a constitutional obligation to remain out of religious life.

"We are a blessed nation," Rubio told the crowd. "Think of what God has given us: a nation rich with everything you can imagine. Resources, natural and otherwise. Think of the people God has allowed to come here over 200 and some odd years. The best and brightest the world has to offer. . . . My father, my grandfather—I think they were better men than I was. And yet they never got to accomplish their dreams. Why? What was the difference between them and me? The difference is that I was born with the privilege and the honor of being a citizen of the single greatest nation in all of human history. Being an American is a blessing, and it's also a responsibility."

But it was Rubio's remarks about the Obama insurance mandate that drew some of the loudest ovations. Religious organizations "help families to raise strong people," he said. This was not a social issue, it was a "constitutional issue." His voice rising, Rubio declared, "The federal government does not have the power to force religious organizations to pay for things that that organization doesn't believe in." Before he could finish his sentence most of those filling the huge auditorium were on their feet cheering. In a bank of seats to Rubio's right, a middle-aged man stood and solemnly made the sign of the cross.

The insurance requirement, part of the sweeping Affordable Care Act that had earned Obama such disdain among tea partiers, allowed narrow exemptions for churches but not other faith-based organizations such as universities or hospitals. More than two dozen states have similar laws, and the vast majority of health plans cover birth control. But the issue became a furious election-year fight, and Rubio its most high-profile combatant on Capitol Hill. "This is not about women's rights or contraception, this is about the religious liberties that our country has always cherished," he told Fox's Greta Van Susteren. "At the end of the day, it's about the fact that now the federal government has the power to force a religion to pay for something the religion teaches is wrong." At the top of Rubio's official Senate website his staff posted an "In-Case-You-Missed-It" alert, featuring the opening line from an op-ed he published in the *New York Post*: "Religious freedom is a core American principle, one that our Founding Fathers enshrined in the Constitution and called on our future generations of leaders to preserve and protect." Rubio's legislation, the Religious Freedom Restoration Act of 2012, would expand exemptions for faith-based organizations. "The Obama Administration's obsession with forcing mandates on the American people has now reached a new low by violating the conscience, rights and religious liberties of our people," he said in a video posted on the American Catholic website. Soon after, the Obama administration made small modifications that appeased some Catholic leaders, but fell short of satisfying conservative Republicans.

Just shy of fourteen years since he had canvassed the streets of West Miami for votes to win a city commission seat, Rubio had reached a stage in his career in which he was able to apply his religious convictions on a national scale. As controversy was building over the proposed contraceptive requirement, Rubio spoke favorably—and from personal experience—about the Catholic

Church's teachings that prohibit the use of contraception. "I can tell you that none of my children were planned," the father of four told Politico.

Baxley, his friend from his Tallahassee days, had always known that "at a personal level, Marco's not afraid to embrace the clear understanding that your faith influences your policy. Faith is very important in informing his convictions." Now the entire country knew what his colleagues in the Florida house understood, especially those who were there on that last day to hear his farewell speech. In those remarks, Rubio gave a rousing defense of God's place in public life. "You can't pass a courtroom that is going to keep God out of this building," he told the lawmakers. "You can't because God doesn't care about the Supreme Court of Florida. . . . He cares about them. But he doesn't care about their rulings. And he doesn't care about the Supreme Court of the United States. You can't keep him out."

Rubio's remarks struck Pecknold, the Catholic University professor, as out of step with Catholic thinking. "He was imprudent to say that God doesn't care about laws," Pecknold said after listening to the remarks.

Rubio's discourse on faith wasn't limited to criticism of court rulings. He also wanted to share his notions about God with the men and women he served alongside. "[God] doesn't want you to force him down anyone's throat, by the way—God is not some old man with a big white beard that just kind of hovers over the world, and makes us feel good from time to time," he told his audience in the Florida legislature. "God is a real force of love. Let me tell you what a real force of love is. He loves every human being on Earth, whether you are an embryo or behind bars.

Whether you got here—he doesn't care if you have a visa to be legally in this country. He loves you. He doesn't care. Please don't take this wrong—he doesn't care if you committed the most heinous act that violated the laws of man. He loves you. He doesn't care if you're small and you can't even be seen but with a microscope. You have never met a human being that God doesn't love, and you never ever will. And it's more than that. God doesn't just love every human being. God—you can see it, because I have seen it."

In a sense, he was evangelizing. And they loved him for it. When he finished, the chamber stood in unison to applaud him.

Chapter Eight

THE CENTURY CLUB

The senator was hungry. Ever hungry.

He shed his suit coat and gathered two handfuls of pita chips, piling them onto his plate. Now the salsa. Lots of it.

There were always snacks set out on the long conference table where Senator Jim DeMint, the social conservative conscience of the U.S. Senate, held his weekly afternoon strategy sessions. And Marco Rubio, the new senator from Florida, always went straight for them. As he ate, he tapped his foot at Bugs Bunny speed beneath the table. Aides would steal glances and chuckle to themselves about this new presence in the capitol and his boundless energy. "Looks highly caffeinated," one high-ranking aide noted to himself.

What marveled those who were watching Rubio wasn't so much his antsy feet as his not so antsy approach to the discussions: he seemed more than willing to be a listener. Tom Coburn, the senator who really was an Okie from Muskogee, could grow emotional in debates, lifting his voice to criticize Democrats and his Republican colleagues alike. Rand Paul and Mike Lee, the freshmen tea party heroes from Kentucky and Utah, jumped into the fray on almost every issue. But Rubio hung back, especially in his first months as a senator. He didn't grasp at every issue, didn't offer to fight every fight. He offered insights from time to time but seldom tried to dominate the discussion.

Rubio was at the meetings because DeMint had selected him for the little-known executive committee of the Senate Steering Committee, a group of the most conservative Republican senators that helped establish policy goals and how to achieve them. It was another interior passageway to power opened for Rubio by a more senior lawmaker, not unlike the redistricting committee on which he had impressed Johnnie Byrd in Tallahassee a decade earlier, yet on a much larger scale.

But even during his first year as a senator Rubio was developing a power that transcended the institution of the Senate. It was his nature to move quickly, and the pace of the Senate's seniority system was slow. This was a legislative body that had been filled with members who stayed eternities—men such as West Virginia's Robert C. Byrd, South Carolina's Strom Thurmond, and Massachusetts's Teddy Kennedy, all of whom lasted more than four decades in office.

Not long after Rubio arrived in Washington, a senator explained to him the facts of senatorial life. "You could be here thirty years," the senator said, "and you'd still be the youngest guy." (He was actually the second youngest, born all of six days before Mike Lee.) In the capitol, power came to those who waited. But Rubio was not one to wait, even though his options for making a big splash within the building were limited by his lack of seniority and by the fact that in the Senate his party was the minority.

Just as he had done during his Senate campaign, Rubio projected his message outward, away from the place where he needed support in the form of votes, in this case the U.S. capitol, and benefited from a ricochet effect. Validation outside the building—on blogs, among conservative activists, on Twitter and Facebook—gave him more stroke inside it. More stroke inside the building gave him more validation outside it. The two loops fed on each other. During his Senate campaign he had been active on Twitter, tapping out messages about policy and sharing tidbits of his personal life. Others struggled to find the right tone on this medium, the perfect blend of attitude, insight, and self-promotion. Rubio got it. He displayed the traits and touted the policy positions that made him popular in person: humor, occasional self-deprecation, passion, righteous indignation, and conservative ideas. Little got lost in translation.

Once during his Senate campaign he wore a plaid shirt while trying to fit in at the Strawberry Festival in Johnnie Byrd's hometown of Plant City, Florida. It wasn't quite a Michael Dukakis–in-a-tank-and-helmet moment, but the candidate looked completely out of place dressed that way, like a law school student at a costume party. He defused the mockery by laughing at himself on Twitter: "Went shopping for clothes w/o jeanette."

He could also express his faith in 140 characters or less: "There is great wisdom in resting on the Sabbath. I am amazed how practical/applicable biblical lessons are, even in the age of twitter." And he understood the usefulness of one-on-one exchanges with voters at the speed of DSL. He even conducted press interviews via Twitter. In May 2009 the *National Journal* asked him via Twitter, "Numbers: How many cars do you own? How many houses? How many guns? How many kids in public schools?" He sent back his answers: "Own ford f150 (05), lease an escalade, 2 houses (Miami and Tallahassee), no guns, 3 of 4 kids @ Fl Christian School in Miami."

His advisors boasted that he was the first U.S. Senate candidate to pass 100,000 "likes" on Facebook. His staff uploaded his speeches to YouTube. The Twitter community can often sniff out someone who is paying a flunky to write their tweets, but Rubio fired out photographs of family moments that could only have come from him. The digital investments during his campaign were 100 percent transferable to his new role as a U.S. senator, like an IRA that he was rolling over after changing jobs. Another era's campaign flyers died in landfills or recycling heaps; Rubio's tweets lived on the Internet, and his followers stayed connected to him and multiplied. In mid-February 2012 he counted more than 70,000 followers on Twitter. For comparison, consider that the Massachusetts Democrat John Kerry, who had been the Democratic presidential nominee in 2004 and had served twenty-seven years in the Senate, counted fewer than a third as many followers. Mike Lee, who just beat Rubio for the title of youngest senator, trailed him by nearly 62,000 followers. In just a year in office he was already among the top five most followed senators on Twitter.

The platform Rubio built for himself outside Capitol Hill was being noticed by his elders in Washington. Confirmation of his clout came on July 11, 2011, when Speaker of the House John Boehner, the Ohio Republican, cited Rubio in a news conference at the height of the battle over raising the national debt limit. "As Senator Rubio said last week, we don't need more taxes. What we need are more taxpayers." It was more old saw than new inspiration. The Oklahoma Republican J. C. Watts delivered a nearly identical line during speeches in 2005. And various candidates for local offices had also used it. Yet Rubio had crystallized a Republican talking point at a moment when the debate was becoming muddled. Beyond the strength of his words was the strength of his following. Boehner might have cited the thinking of any number of Republicans on that day, but in his opening remarks he mentioned just one: Marco Rubio. The Florida senator had been in office 190 days.

Rubio had maintained a low profile during his first six months in office, following the approach taken by other savvy first-termers, including former first lady Hillary Clinton when she represented New York in the Senate. In the seniority-bound Senate system, the Old Guard doesn't always take kindly to newcomers being too pushy in the beginning.

Rubio waited until June to deliver his first floor speech. The scuffle over raising the national debt limit offered him an opening for his coming out, and he took it. He had been a frequent guest on conservative networks before, but after this speech there was a new surge in interest. He was invited onto so many programs, shared his thoughts in so many places, that one headline declared, "Marco Rubio is everywhere."

The day after Boehner's shout-out to Rubio, the analyst Dick Morris was so eager to pump the Florida senator's prospects that he cut off Fox host Sean Hannity in midsentence. "Whoever wins the nomination," Hannity began, "should choose him for vice president, no question," Morris chimed in, finishing Hannity's thought.

"This is an arranged marriage," Morris continued. "If the

bride is chosen, the groom [is] to be named later. We need to carry the Latino vote. We need to carry Florida. And Marco Rubio is a superstar."

A few days later, speaking on Bill O'Reilly's top-rated show, the longtime journalist and commentator Bernard Goldberg went a step further. "If the Republicans don't put Marco Rubio on the ticket, they need to get their heads examined," he said.

For Rubio, building himself into a senator whose national influence far exceeded his seniority came naturally. It was the same trajectory his career had taken in Florida when he leaped into the leadership ranks at the statehouse when he was barely thirty.

But adjusting to living in Washington didn't come as easily. As the end of his first year approached he was wrestling with the demands of a fractional life: work in Washington, family in Florida. His wife and children—ages four, six, nine, and eleven—remained in Miami. "It's been tough. It's been hard," he admitted. "It's hard to realize that you're not around on Tuesdays or Wednesdays. It's difficult on the kids on Sundays. It's difficult on me. . . . I still believe and, you know, I'm not sure I'll always get this right, but my number one job is still husband and father. I've got to get those right. And it's hard to do that when you're not there. So it's an ongoing struggle. . . . We've got to figure that out."

In Washington Rubio struck some capitol insiders as detached from the social scene. Lindsey Graham, the senior senator from South Carolina, is often described by his colleagues as "a cruise director, like Julie from *Love Boat*," always organizing social get-togethers. "I almost never hear Rubio's name associated with those evenings," a senior Republican aide told me.

Washington, though, was changing, becoming less chummy. "Imagine freshman year of college if the entire student body left every Thursday afternoon and didn't come back until Monday night. This is more of a commuter college than a traditional four-year university," said Chris Coons, a freshman senator from Delaware.

Making friends with money had been effective for Rubio in Tallahassee, and he went back to that strategy in Washington, forming a political action committee in October 2011 called Reclaim America PAC. The intent was to support conservative Republican candidates. It was patterned on a PAC formed by De-Mint that had supported Rubio in the Florida politician's senate race. In the House, Eric Cantor, a Virginia Republican, had formed a group called the Young Guns to raise money for Republican candidates. It had been so effective that Cantor became majority leader. Like Rubio, Cantor is a young lawmaker who is being touted as a potential future president or vice president.

In a building where everyone is watching and every utterance or gesture is parsed for deeper meaning, some of Rubio's fellow senators and their aides formed a picture of the new Florida senator that was framed by his ambition. "There is a prism through which everything he does is seen," a top Republican aide told me. "The presidential prism." Senators and aides took note that Rubio often appeared at events with an outside political consultant rather than solely with his Senate staff. Considering the fact that senators have six-year terms and Rubio wouldn't be running for reelection until 2016, the presence of a political consultant was interpreted by some as an obvious telegraphing of intentions. It reminded some people of Senator Evan Bayh, the Indiana Democrat who left office in 2011 but until then often seemed to be openly putting together a presidential-style outside political operation. President Obama and Secretary of State Hillary Clinton also put together formidable political operations with eyes toward grander things while they were in the Senate.

Rubio, who had been so good at shaping his image during his rise, had lost some control of the narrative as his first year in the Senate ended. Investigations of his finances, his religious history, and his family background often put him on the defensive. While Washington was atwitter about the movie *Game Change*—an HBO feature about the botched vetting of Republican vice presidential nominee Sarah Palin—political writers were chronicling the thousands of dollars that Rubio was paying a California company to do opposition research on himself.

During the Senate campaign Rubio and his staff had deftly shaped a story line of an outsider with tea party backing who was challenging the establishment. But once he was in office they began steering journalists away from the tea party theme.

The tea party presented something of a conundrum for Rubio. He enjoyed the support of voters who associated themselves with the movement, but he didn't want to be pigeonholed. Getting boxed in to a tea party stereotype could limit how far he could go politically. The tea party was also an amorphous group whose influence was hard to manage. He seemed to understand implicitly that the tea party was more a state of mind than a tangible entity, and that harnessing it to Washington-based institutions could weaken whatever effectiveness it had. "My fear has always been that if you start creating these little clubs or organizations in Washington run by politicians, the movement starts to lose its energy," Rubio explained. "I don't think it'll ever become an organization. If it does, it'll end up quickly falling apart. I think it draws its strength from the fact that it's a legitimate grassroots movement of everybody, people from all over the country who share [a] difference of opinion on a bunch of issues, but ultimately on the core of what the role of government should be, find commonality, and are able to express it now in ways that weren't available to us 20 years ago." He declined to participate in the tea party caucus formed by his fellow freshman Rand Paul. The move irked a few tea party supporters. "He wants to have it both ways," said George Fuller, a tea party activist from Sarasota. "We're going to be zeroing in on him like a laser." But, by and large, the decision had minimal effect. "He feels the tea party is a grassroots thing and should not be tied to D.C.," said Everett Wilkinson, whose South Florida tea party issued press releases supporting Rubio's decision. Tom Tillison, cofounder of the Central Florida Tea Party Council, didn't care about Rubio's arm's-length approach to the tea party: "I see these caucuses as more a politician's thing."

Still, Rubio wanted to cultivate his image as a nontraditional politician. He would be in Washington but not *of* Washington. One month after taking office he traveled to Naples, Florida, for a town hall meeting and said, "I think it's a lot more fun to be a bartender than a U.S. senator some days."

He spoke to the audience as if reporting back from a space mission. "It's as crazy as you thought it was," he said. "There is a significant disconnect between the planet you live on and the planet they live on. . . . What I don't want is to get Washingtonized."

His talk in Naples addressed an elemental riddle for candidates who ran on anti-Washington platforms, a difficulty that isn't exclusive to tea party favorites, but is also a challenge for President Obama, who had run on the promise of hope and change. It's usually a great idea to run against Washington, to criticize all that it stands for: dysfunction, disconnection, waste, inefficiency, greed. But once you're elected, whether you want to be defined by it or not, you are a part of Washington. Welcome to town. Once you could talk of "them"; now "them" is *you*.

On the long list of characteristics that the so-called real American despised about Washington, partisan bickering was near the top. And Rubio, who had attempted a kind of détente in Florida with Democrats with varying degrees of success, tried that approach in his first year in Washington. His most significant foray into playing well with others started one Thursday afternoon, getaway day for commuter-class senators. Rubio was watching the clock, and so was Chris Coons, his fellow freshman from Delaware. Debates over the president's jobs proposal had been dragging on, a continuous loop of finger-pointing and partisan sniping that showed no sign of ceasing. "I said to him, 'What do you think it's going to take for this to get better?' " Coons, a Democrat, recalled in an interview. Rubio, who moved so quickly on so many things in his career, didn't see a rapid solution. For once, he would have to be patient. "The next election will sort this all out," Coons remembers Rubio telling him.

Coons pushed back; he wasn't buying it, and he challenged his Republican colleague. "Have you ever read the president's job plan?" Coons asked. "He kind of looked at me and said, 'Yeah, I'm familiar with it.' I said, 'No, the whole thing. Have you really looked at it?' " Rubio conceded that he hadn't, but he parried by asking Coons whether he had read the proposals being put forth by Mitt Romney, the former Massachusetts governor and Republican presidential frontrunner. Coons hadn't. They had talked themselves to a draw.

Coons had been hoping to meet up with Rubio for some time. His friend, the wealthy philanthropist Adrienne Arsht, had been raving about the Florida senator. Arsht, who grew up in Delaware, also had strong connections in Florida. She donated millions for a performing arts center in downtown Miami that bore her family's name. "You can work with [Rubio]," she kept telling Coons. She was so intent on matching up the lawmakers from competing parties that she offered to host a dinner for the two of them at her home, but they got to know each other on their own through chance encounters in the gym and at prayer breakfasts.

The conversations built to the point that they decided to collaborate on a bill that ended up having more symbolic value in the divided capitol than legislative success. They called it the AGREE Act, choosing an acronym that left little doubt about the statement they wanted to make about what was happening in Washington. At that time Rubio's career was racing ahead, and sometimes when you're in a hurry you don't do your homework. On the morning that he was set to unveil the proposal—which had been heavily hyped—he appeared for an interview streamed live over the Internet with Mike Allen, whose Politico Playbook arrived via email to thousands of readers each morning.

"I don't want to induce a Rick Perry moment," Allen said, referring to the Texas governor who had helped to sink his presidential campaign during a debate by forgetting one of three federal departments he wanted to abolish. "But do you know what AGREE stands for?"

"No," Rubio said. "The actual acronym? No I don't."

Rubio's tone was so light, his demeanor so unflustered, that empathetic chuckles rippled through the live audience at the Newseum, a journalism museum on Pennsylvania Avenue, just a few blocks from the capitol.

Perry had smiled awkwardly and infamously said, "Oops." Rubio just moved on. "But I also didn't come up with it. So I—and I didn't come up with the AGREE acronym."

He described what really mattered—not an acronym in a city awash in them, but a concept: bipartisan cooperation. "What's important is what's in the bill, and that I know pretty well. . . . We went through everything Republicans have proposed, Democrats have proposed, the president had proposed, the jobs council has proposed, and we tried to identify things that were in all of the plans. And we put those in one bill. . . . What it's going to do is two things. One is actually pass things we agree on. But I think secondly and more importantly, send a message which is that we can still get things done here in Washington."

Rubio didn't just say he knew what was in the bill, he got into the details, rattling off something called "the 179 provision." "I don't want to get too technical," he said, before getting technical about the provision, which he explained would extend the ability of small businesses to write off the costs of capital purchases. "That's really important for businesses that are looking to next year's tax uncertainty and saying, well maybe next year's not the right time to invest in our business because we're going to have to pay taxes on this. So I think everybody will like that."

But in the hypercharged partisan atmosphere of Washington in the run-up to a presidential campaign there is often more profit in attacking the other side than in finding common ground. Attacks get headlines, and Rubio's knack for the sharply worded barb is tailor-made for a 140-character world.

In July, barely half a year into his first term, he took the floor of the Senate and began by saying, "I do not enjoy nor relish the partisan role of attack dog. I've never found any fun in that. I don't think it's constructive. I don't intend to become that in the Senate." He then went on to scorch Obama over the president's request to raise the nation's debt limit. The United States was spending roughly $300 billion a month, he said. It was taking in $180 billion through taxes and other revenue, so it had to borrow $120 billion a month. That was unacceptable and it was hurting the country. Raising the debt limit should no longer be a routine vote, he argued.

John Kerry, the Massachusetts senator, tried to argue that Democrats and Republicans should reason with each other. But the new senator didn't back down. He pushed harder. "Compromise, that's not a solution, is a waste of time," Rubio said. "If my house was on fire, I can't compromise about which part of the house I'm going to save. You save the whole house or it will all burn down!"

In a YouTube headline the message was shaved to its most defiant essence: "Save the whole house or it will all burn down." By early 2012 the video had been linked and relinked, cited over and over, and viewed more than 730,000 times on the free video-sharing website.

Rubio's notoriety increased to the point that almost any statement he made was instantly news, allowing him to leverage his prominence on almost any issue. In January 2012 he sent an open letter to Obama, criticizing the president's expected request for an increase in the debt limit. Now keep in mind, Washington sags under the weight of letters written by members of Congress complaining about one thing or another, even those written directly to the president. Most get launched into the ether and evaporate. But in January, at the height of the GOP presidential primary season, the strength of Rubio's national profile fused with the sharpness of his rhetoric to create a letter that actually got noticed. The Drudge Report, the venerable Internet aggregator, ran a headline about the letter in its coveted centerpiece spot, the ne plus ultra of conservative media: "Rubio to Obama: You're turning America into a deadbeat nation." Other Republicans were complaining too, but Rubio had distilled his party's rage into two words.

And when he made mistakes, as all young senators do, Rubio proved nimble at reversing them. The same month that he chided Obama, Rubio risked alienating conservatives because of his cosponsorship of a bill to combat Internet piracy and preserve intellectual property, known as PIPA, short for the Protect IP Act. The legislation seemed to be just the kind of intrusive government regulation that Rubio would naturally oppose. Wikipedia, the ubiquitous Internet encyclopedia, went black on January 18 to protest PIPA and another Internet piracy measure. Conservatives were beginning to talk about mounting primary challenges against Republicans, including Rubio, who supported the measures.

It was too much for Rubio. The senator, smartly, took to the Internet to announce that he was pulling his support for PIPA. He made his announcement on his Facebook page. What could have been a political disaster turned into a political coup. Once again, as on the day he saved Nancy Reagan from falling, he was hailed as a hero. "He listened," Julia Wrightstone, a retired banker from Pittsburgh, told me at the February 2012 Conservative Political Action Conference. "He's one of the few who listened to his constituents."

During his first year Rubio was beginning to have real influence in several arenas. His political identity had always been defined by his Cuban heritage, and in Washington he sought to position himself as a defender of the Cuban embargo, a cold war–era holdover that had failed for half a century to topple the Castro regime. He also castigated diplomats who weren't deemed sufficiently confrontational with the Cuban government.

Just months into his first term, Rubio angered moderate Republicans by working—first behind the scenes, then in public—to scuttle the nomination of Jonathan D. Farrar as ambassador to Nicaragua. Farrar had been chief of the U.S. Interests Section in Havana, an office a notch below embassy status because the United States did not maintain full diplomatic relations with Cuba. Rubio raised concerns because he said he had received complaints from dissidents and human rights activists who had wanted more aggressiveness against the Castro regime during Farrar's two-year tenure in Havana, and because some visiting State Department officials had stayed at the government-owned Hotel Nacional—which had been expropriated by Castro—rather than occupying guest rooms at the large official residence of the chief of mission in Havana. Rubio also noted that Farrar had removed a large electronic ticker that was affixed to the side of the building that the U.S. Interests Section shares with the Swiss Embassy along the Malecón, Havana's stone seawall. The ticker was symbolic of the schoolyard antagonism between the U.S. and Cuban governments. It scrolled a mix of anti-Castro propaganda, human rights messages—such as quotes by Martin Luther King, Jr.—and news reports intended to rile Castro. One evening when I was in Havana, the ticker reported that Jose Contreras, a Cuban baseball star who defected to the United States in 2002, had won his thirteenth consecutive game for the world champion Chicago White Sox. Then it repeated a report from *Forbes* magazine that named

Fidel Castro the world's seventh-wealthiest head of state, with a fortune estimated at $900 million.

The problem with the ticker was that hardly anyone could see it. Castro's government had installed 148 flagpoles in the state-owned Anti-Imperialism Park in front of the building, blocking the view of anyone who wasn't standing directly across the street. As Farrar explained, the Obama administration had removed the ticker because it wanted to concentrate instead on what it considered more savvy ways to undermine the Cuban government, such as offering blogging classes to Cubans so they could send their uncensored thoughts out to the world. But Farrar's argument didn't neutralize his opponents, and in the end the State Department withdrew his name. Rubio had succeeded in keeping Farrar from becoming an ambassador—for now.

As the end of his first year approached, Rubio was expressing frustrations, just as he'd done after leaving Tallahassee. "I can't think of a single real high point," he said. But this time an entire country was listening.

Chapter Nine

GREAT EXPECTATIONS

It wasn't easy to find a seat that bright morning in February 2012. The ballroom at the Marriott Wardman Park in Washington swelled with conservative fans. A line formed at the entrance.

Two twenty-somethings in red-white-and-blue ties broke through. They scanned the space. "We didn't miss him—did we?"

On stage, Al Cardenas—a Marco Rubio believer, turned Marco Rubio doubter, turned Marco Rubio believer again—was introducing his former protégé. If there were any doubts about his fealty to the Republican rock star he was about to introduce, Cardenas seemed intent on putting them to rest. One day, Cardenas predicted, I'll be saying "hello to [Rubio] at 1600 Pennsylvania Avenue."

Cardenas, who had once underestimated Rubio, was late to the lovefest. By then, the act of predicting that Marco Rubio would become president of the United States someday had risen to the level of cliché. Back in Florida, Ken Pruitt, the Republican senate president, had opened the Florida legislative session in 2007 by flashing a sign that read "Rubio for President '08" from the dais.

The chamber erupted in laughter.

The Florida senate and the house, despite both being controlled by Republicans, were frequently at odds. The poster was a signal of friendship, but it would also be portrayed as a chummy, good-natured jab at Rubio, who was then still two months shy of his thirty-sixth birthday. The tenor of the young legislator's political discourse, his habit of reaching for larger truths even amid the mundane business of the legislature, had made his national ambitions clear. And his *100 Ideas* book had gotten notice outside Florida's borders, raising his national profile. Rubio's grander intentions weren't only detected by the senate president, who was a decade and a half Rubio's senior; they were obvious to anyone who met Rubio. Projecting him out of Tallahassee and into the Oval Office, or at least into the vice president's residence at the Naval Observatory, was becoming de rigueur.

The previous March, Pruitt—apparently not a master of electoral calendar math—had forecast a Marco Rubio presidency in 2022. Rubio's legislative ally Dennis Baxley, the Christian conservative lawmaker from Ocala, had also mused about a Rubio presidency, and the Florida papers were taking note of the high aspirations of the ascendant lawmaker from Miami. Even Democrats got into the prediction game. "He's good, and that's what makes me nervous," Susan Bucher, a Democratic state lawmaker from West Palm Beach, said the month before Pruitt's poster moment. "I tease him about when he's going to open his campaign in Iowa." Steven Geller, a Democratic senator from Hallandale

Beach, later said, "It's no secret he wants to be the first Cuban-American president."

Politicians have a spotty record predicting political futures, and their motives are always open to question, leaving their listeners to wonder whether they are trying to raise up or push down expectations. But Hollywood, well, that town's scriptwriters often get it right. By 2010 they had already gone ahead and elected a Cuban American president, Elias Martinez, the fictional head of state on a short-lived NBC drama called *The Event*. The show combined the nonlinear narrative style of the popular drama *Lost* with the pounding rhythm of the conspiracy hit *24*. *The Event's* Cuban American president was not an exact match for Marco Rubio—Martinez was black—and there has never been any public hint that Rubio was the character's inspiration. But the idea of an American president born to Cuban immigrants in Miami was clearly no stretch for the creators of the show. The question was whether it would be for the electorate.

Once a political figure gets launched into the category of future president, it follows that reporters are going to crawl all over his record, analyzing his statements, flipping through his documents, craning to spot discrepancies or blunders. Some of this is the product of enterprising, public interest reporting. Some of it is the product of enterprising, self-interested opposition research and leaking by rivals. The process amounts to a public form of vetting that can be as thorough and as important as the private scrutiny that candidates hire expensive, white-shoe law firms to conduct.

Another thing certain to happen—at least when the candidate's family roots trail off the continental United States—is that the so-called birthers are going to challenge the aspirant's qualifications to lead the nation. In the 2008 presidential campaign birthers chased nominees from both parties: the Democrat, Barack Obama, and the Republican, John McCain. They continued to question Obama's eligibility through the first few years of his presidency.

In 2011, in a perverse nod to his status as a risen star, Marco Rubio experienced both. Birthers made a wobbly case that the Constitution prevented him from joining a national ticket, and the unearthing of discrepancies in his life history and a long-forgotten family blemish caused him to tangle at various times with the *St. Petersburg Times*, the *Washington Post*, National Public Radio, and the Spanish-language powerhouse network Univision.

The birthers launched their assault in the spring of 2011, firing a shot heard almost nowhere. On May 22 Charles Kerchner, a retired U.S. Navy commander, wrote a provocative post on his WordPress website, CDR Kerchner's Blog. "Senator Marco Rubio's father was not a naturalized citizen when Marco was born in May 1971 per National Archives data," Kerchner declared. "His father applied for naturalization in Sep 1975. Marco Rubio [is] not constitutionally eligible to run for President or VP. . . . A natural born Citizen of the United States is a child born with sole allegiance to the United States, a person born without Citizenship in any other country other than the USA at the time of their birth. A natural born Citizen has no foreign influence or claim on them by another country at the time of their birth under U.S. law and the Law of Nations."

Kerchner based his argument against Rubio's eligibility primarily on one sentence in the U.S. Constitution and on a dog's breakfast of legal writings and court rulings. His most important reference point, which he emphasized when he updated his post five days later, was Article II, Section 1 of the Constitution: "No Person except a natural born Citizen or a Citizen of the United States, at the time of the adoption of this Constitution, shall be eligible to the Office of President." In various writings about Rubio's eligibility, Kerchner would also reference *The Law of Nations*, a work by the Swiss philosopher Emer de Vattel published in 1758, sometimes cited as an influence on the founding fathers. "The natives, or natural-born citizens, are those born in the country, of parents who are citizens," Vattel wrote. Kerchner also relied on a U.S. Supreme Court case of 1875, *Minor v. Happersett*, that used the term "natural born citizen" to refer to children born in the United States of U.S. citizens.

In his post Kerchner said that he had made many attempts to contact Rubio via letters and phone calls. Rubio, or perhaps it was his staff, opted to ignore the entreaties, which seems like a logical response. Kerchner's legal arguments were weak, and for months his posting and his arguments attracted little attention. But by the fall his claim started to get a bit of traction. Other bloggers were picking up the string and writing their own birther pieces. In September Alan Keyes, a former Republican presidential candidate, sided with the birthers on a radio talk show. "The other shoe has dropped," said Keyes. "Now you've got Republicans talking about Marco Rubio for president when it's obviously clear that he does not qualify. Regardless of party label, they don't care about the Constitution. It's all just empty, lying lip service."

That same month the *Fort Myers News-Press* was sufficiently intrigued to look into the claims. "There's no serious question because he was born in the USA. Any contrary argument is birther-like silliness," Daniel Takaji, a law professor at Ohio State

University, told the paper. "His parents' immigration status is ir-relevant to his U.S. citizenship under the 14th [Amendment]."

Yet the chatter had grown loud enough that the next month the *St. Petersburg Times*, an award-winning newspaper that boasts Florida's highest daily circulation and has since changed its name to the *Tampa Bay Times*, gave the controversy front-page treat-ment. The 1,200-word article is a sober, clear-eyed, and balanced analysis of the birther claims. Among others, it cites a George-town professor, Lawrence Solum, who wasn't buying the birthers' reasoning, but at least allowed that "the arguments aren't crazy."

Deep in the *Times* piece is a mention of another claim made by Kerchner, this one dealing with Rubio's depiction of his fam-ily's migration to the United States. In short order that claim was going to consume the considerable bandwidth allotted to Rubio by the mainstream media. But in the days leading up to the pub-lication of the article the matter at hand was the birther assertion.

As the birther claim about Rubio drew more attention it was frequently compared to the Obama birther controversy. A vari-ety of suspicions had been raised about Obama, ranging from an assertion that he was a British citizen through his Kenyan-born father to a claim that his Hawaiian birth certificate either didn't exist or was a forgery. One of the loudest proponents of birtherism was Donald Trump, who made so much noise about the issue that Obama eventually bent to pressure and released his long-form birth certificate. While Trump was on his crusade, Rubio was asked what he thought about the controversy. Rubio responded with a zinger. Rubio was "more concerned with issues that are happening back here on planet Earth," said Rubio.

The Rubio birther folderol bears less resemblance to the Obama silliness than to the fight over McCain's eligibility. Mc-

Cain, some had argued, was not a "natural born citizen" and therefore not eligible to run for the White House because he was born in the Panama Canal Zone. I contacted the two most prominent legal scholars on each side of the McCain debate: Harvard University's Laurence H. Tribe and Gabriel "Jack" Chin, a University of Arizona law professor who later took a post at the University of California at Davis. Tribe had argued that McCain was unquestionably eligible, and Chin had written a widely cited and deeply researched legal brief arguing that the Arizona senator was not. I asked them both what they thought of the Rubio case. Tribe responded by email, writing, "Once we start distinguishing among natural-born citizens to decide which have the requisite pedigree for the presidency, there is no stopping point. Why not say that citizens born in the U.S.A. whose grandparents or great-grandparents weren't U.S. citizens at the time of their birth are ineligible to become President? Where will this craziness stop?"

Chin concurred in a phone interview. Without hesitation he said Rubio "clearly" was "born a citizen" and that his parents' lack of citizenship at the time was irrelevant because Rubio was born on U.S. soil. "My view, and I'm pretty comfortable that this would be the mainstream view, is that he's a natural born citizen," Chin said. But he allowed that it's not particularly surprising that there would be debate about the natural-born-citizen requirement. "This is a provision of the Constitution that when legal scholars get together and talk about the dumbest provisions of the Constitution . . . is always in the top tier."

The birther debate fizzled. But by the summer of 2011 Rubio was already accustomed to the media sifting through his personal life. His 2010 campaign was speckled with hard-hitting investigative pieces about his mortgages, his credit card spending, and the like. But what happened in July 2011 represented another level of scrutiny, one that would provoke a national discussion about how far and how wide the press should go in probing a public figure's family life and shed light on how Rubio handles public controversy. Rubio's pursuer was Univision, a network better known for steamy soap operas, *telenovelas*, than investigative reporting. The senator's battle with Univision would ripple into the presidential campaign and further affirm how extraordinarily important this first-term senator had become in national Republican politics.

It began in early July 2011, when the phone rang at the West Miami house where Rubio's sister and brother-in-law, Barbara and Orlando Cicilia, lived with Rubio's eighty-year-old mother. On the other end of the line was Gerardo Reyes, a seasoned investigative reporter who had spent more than twenty years at the *Miami Herald* and *El Nuevo Herald* before leaving newspapers a few months earlier to become the head of the investigative unit at Univision.

Barbara Cicilia took the call. Reyes, a respected investigative reporter, asked for comment about Orlando's 1987 drug arrest and his 1989 conviction. Barbara denied that they had taken place. Then she hung up the phone.

The denial did not dissuade Reyes in the least. He had the story down cold. He and his staff had spent hours looking through court records, and there was no doubt about what had happened back in the '80s. They gathered documents that clearly showed Cicilia had been convicted in 1989 and sentenced to a long prison term. The documents also showed that the federal government had confiscated Cicilia's home and another property he owned because investigators were unable to locate $15 million in drug profits that the jury concluded he had received. By the time

Univision was looking into the case it was nearly a quarter century old, and Cicilia, who had been released early, had been a free man for more than a decade.

Less than an hour after Reyes's call, Rubio's communications director, Alex Burgos, who had honed his skills as a spokesman for Mitt Romney's 2008 presidential campaign, called the Univision newsroom. Rubio had stocked his staff with experienced political operatives who were adept at responding aggressively when the media challenged their boss. Theirs was an in-your-face, rapid-response approach, a style that struck some political veterans and reporters as disproportionate and unnecessarily hostile. At the same time they did battle with reporters who crossed them, they had also cultivated strong allies at conservative publications and on activist websites that produced news-like reports. When negative stories were written or aired about Rubio, these sites would often hit back as hard as or harder than the senator's own staff. They served as Rubio's surrogates in an increasingly fuzzy media landscape, where the lines between journalism and partisan advocacy were blurring almost beyond recognition.

The veteran Univision producer and reporter Maria Martinez-Henao took the call from Burgos. The conversation was brief. Burgos thought the call to Cicilia might have been "a prank." Martinez-Henao hadn't been working on the Cicilia investigation, so she sought out Reyes to see what was going on. "It's not a prank," he told her.

The next move by Rubio's staff was to try to apply pressure at the corporate level. An email the following day complaining about a Univision television crew staking out the Cicilias' home was sent to Randy Falco, Univision's chief executive officer. Falco is a former executive at NBC and was once the chairman of the board and chief executive officer of AOL. He didn't want to handle the complaint himself; it was a matter for the newsroom, not the executive suite. So he bounced the problem back down to Miami and Isaac Lee, his new president for news. Lee is a bear of a man with a dark beard and stylish glasses. He speaks with a Colombian accent and can be found many afternoons lunching at the Ritz Carlton in Coconut Grove, where the waiters greet him like an old pal. Lee is a veteran journalist, and he'd made friends with many U.S. foreign correspondents during the height of the Colombian cocaine wars. Having taken the job just seven months earlier, he was eager to burnish the network's news credentials, and Reyes's investigative unit was a big part of that strategy. The network was also looking to increase its visibility and influence by angling to host a Republican presidential debate.

The arrival of Lee and Reyes marked a pronounced shift in the power structure at the network. The network's news division had once been controlled, in great part, by Cuban Americans. "For many years, Univision was seen through the lens of the hard right Cuban American community," a top Univision executive said. But Lee, Reyes, and Daniel Coronell, Univision vice president, were all of Colombian descent, and they were filling an upper-management tier at the newsroom that was being vacated by several Cuban Americans. The importance, both symbolically and practically, of this shift cannot be underestimated.

In American politics, there are deep divisions among Latinos. Cuban Americans often find themselves on the opposite sides in arguments with non-Cuban Latinos on issues such as immigration. Florida is the perfect example: its large Cuban American population skews Republican, and its large Puerto Rican population bends Democratic. Univision was positioned to reach millions of Hispanics—not just in Florida, but throughout the country. In 2010 it aired forty-six of the fifty most watched television shows among Hispanics age eighteen to forty-nine. And 70 percent of those viewers watched no other network, compared to less than 10 percent who watched only Fox, NBC, ABC, or CBS. In many markets Univision routinely topped the big three English-language networks; and nationally, it sometimes beat all networks—regardless of language—as it did in mid-February when it notched the highest rated 10 P.M. program among eighteen- to thirty-four-year-olds.

Univision is unapologetic about presenting information from a Latino point of view. Its star anchor, Jorge Ramos, is a vocal supporter of comprehensive immigration reform and of the Dream Act, a proposal that would offer a path to citizenship to youths who entered the United States before the age of sixteen, had lived in the country for five consecutive years, and graduated from high school or were accepted to a college. Ramos is one of the most respected and best known Hispanics in the United States. But his political advocacy contrasts with the efforts of major English-language network television anchors to maintain an air of impartiality.

Univision's news bosses arranged an off-the-record conference call with Rubio's representatives to discuss the Cicilia report. Three Univision news staffers—Reyes, Martinez-Henao, and Coronell—joined Lee in Miami, and two of the network's lawyers listened in by phone. Lee needed a room large enough to accommodate his staff, so they gathered around a desk in the office of Cesar Conde, the thirty-something president of Univision

Networks, who was away at the time. (Cesar Conde should not be confused with Cesar Conda, a former top advisor to Vice President Dick Cheney who serves as Rubio's chief of staff.) Rubio was represented in the conference call by Burgos and the political consultant Todd Harris.

What happened during that forty-five-minute call would become the subject of debate and recriminations. There are two versions: Univision's and the Rubio staff's. The two accounts are similar in many ways, but they differ on a key point. Harris and Burgos claim that Univision offered a deal, a quid pro quo: if Rubio appeared on the Sunday-morning talk show *Al Punto*, Univision would either kill or soften its report about Cicilia. Univision denies that a deal was offered.

During the call Rubio's staff argued that Univision should back down because Cicilia was a private citizen, not an elected official. Harris, who had helped catapult Rubio from Miami to Washington, posed a hypothetical: "What you're saying is we can poke into the private life of Jorge Ramos?" The Univision staffers heard the question as a threat. For a consultant who represents a senator who sits on committees with subpoena power to make such a suggestion made the journalists uncomfortable. As a rule, Rubio's staff was not above attacking the personal credibility of journalists as well as attacking the veracity of their reports. Applied effectively, such an approach could have a chilling effect on journalists; members of the Rubio camp would boast about freezing out those who crossed them. "Ramos is a private citizen, not elected, not paid by the taxpayers," Lee responded to the suggestion of someone investigating his anchor.

Lee, who took the lead in the call, argued that Rubio had turned Cicilia into a public figure by bringing him on stage during political events. Lee also pointed out that Rubio's campaign had hired Cicilia's son as a paid traveling aide.

Rubio's staff argued that it was unfair and outrageous to dredge up the old case. They also considered it ridiculous to dedicate an entire report to the case. Lee took that as an opening to other possibilities. "This is about substance, not format," he told them. "You want us to do an interview, we'll do an interview. If you want us to do a profile, we'll do a profile." Later, Lee said in an interview, "To me it was completely irrelevant if you do it through an interview or whatever."

That discussion would later be portrayed as a quid pro quo. Burgos's notes from the meeting, which were analyzed by *The New Yorker*'s Ken Auletta, paint a mushier picture, however. One line says that Univision would "abandon this piece in favor of 'Al Punto.'" But that line is contradicted by the next, which has Lee saying "No promises." The notes also say Univision offered "no guarantees."

Changing the format would not necessarily have softened the piece. Even if the Cicilia story was included in a larger report, an on-screen comment from Rubio would have considerably increased the report's visibility and forced him to address a family trauma for the first time. In the end, the Rubio staff never committed to the senator's giving an interview, and the call wrapped up inconclusively. Whether or not a deal was offered, none was struck. When Rubio's staff hung up, Coronell says, the Univision attorneys on the call applauded.

The next day Burgos sent off another letter of complaint, outlining the parameters of the conference call. He chided Univision for taking the position that "any life aspect of any public official's relatives is 'fair game'—no matter how dated." He continued, "We interact on a daily basis with virtually every major news outlet in America, and I assure you that Univision stands alone in adopting such a policy."

Conspicuously missing from that correspondence is any mention of a quid pro quo. Because the letter provides such a detailed recounting of the conference call and an in-depth analysis by Rubio's staff of Univision's news judgment, it seems unlikely that it would not have included at least a passing mention of the alleged deal.

The Univision news executives saw no reason to kill the story, and four days later they led the evening newscast with the Cicilia report. Rather than opening the story with their discovery, they chose to start by laying out their justification for doing the piece. The report pointed out that Rubio had "provided generous details about his family, expressing time and again during his successful U.S. Senate campaign that he was proud of his parents' efforts to build a better future for their four children in this country." It went on to say that Rubio's sister had been "caught up in the year's most significant anti-narcotics operation in South Florida." That statement was a stretch because Barbara Cicilia was never charged in the case and there was no indication that she was involved in the drug ring in any way.

The three-minute report also included an excerpt from Burgos's letter, read on air: "Quite simply, the pursuit of this story and the targeting of the Senator's relatives, who are private citizens, is outrageous," Burgos wrote. "When Senator Rubio's sister's husband was a younger man 25 years ago, it is a fact that he made many mistakes. He and his family have paid the price for them. . . . This is not news. This is tabloid journalism."

The Univision report bothered Rubio deeply. "He was very

upset about this because it pained his elderly mother, who sits down and watches Univision every night," said Ana Navarro, a close friend of Rubio's. "His sister works in a public school. She probably had friends and colleagues who did not know how this happened."

But for all that worry, the story generated almost no buzz. The mainstream media mostly ignored it, and in the few places where it was mentioned it was usually derided. There was so little attention that it was almost as if the report had never aired.

Two and a half months later an email from a *Miami Herald* reporter showed up in Lee's inbox. The note said that the *Herald* had spoken to senior Rubio staffers and some of Lee's own employees, all of whom were saying that he had offered "what sounded like a quid pro quo" to "soften or spike" the drug bust story. "Some in the newsroom have suggested to us as well," the email went on, "that the direction of Univision is changing under your leadership in which you've brought a flashier style of reporting that is more akin to journalism in Colombia than in Miami."

Lee was offended by the suggestion that journalism in Colombia was somehow different than it is in Miami. At various times Colombia has been one of the most dangerous places in the world to practice journalism, a country where journalists who challenged drug cartels sometimes paid with their lives. The Committee to Protect Journalists has confirmed forty-three cases of journalists killed in Colombia between 1992 and 2011 because of their work. Among those killed was Jaime Garzón, a Colombian political satirist and a friend of Lee's, who was shot repeatedly in the head and chest.

Lee responded to the *Herald's* inquiry by denying that he had offered a quid pro quo to Rubio's staff, drawing another email from the *Herald* explaining the Rubio position: "Of course the Rubio family simply calls it agenda-based 'trash,' considering the substance of the story, the targeting of a brother-in-law, the quarter-century age of the arrest, the circumstances arising from the aforementioned call, the two days of play you gave the story, the twitter hash tag '#rubio #drugs,' etc."

Once the *Herald* started pursuing the quid-pro-quo story, Univision committed what would be a major blunder. Rather than defend itself, it pulled back. The handling of the inquiries was shifted away from the newsroom and into the hands of a corporate public relations executive named Monica Talán. Talán, whose résumé includes a PR stint for the Latin American operation of the doomed Enron firm, effectively placed a gag order on the newsroom. Lee and the others were forbidden to speak to the *Herald* on the record. She boasted, "I've killed stories before," Univision staffers told me.

———

If the *Herald* and *El Neuvo Herald* reporters had been allowed to interview some of the participants and review their correspondence, as several news organizations did months later, they might have encountered the same unified front that some reporters who followed up on the imbroglio found. All six Univision participants were in agreement that there was no quid pro quo offer. However, the ineffective Talán responded to the *Herald* by merely sending the reporters a statement attributed to Lee denying the allegation. At that point the scales were tipped in favor of Rubio. On one side, the *Herald* reporters had Rubio's staff clearly stating their version of events, a version supported by unnamed newsroom sources. On the other side was an uncooperative news organization.

The *Herald* and *El Nuevo Herald* reporters would later say they got onto the story after receiving tips from "friends of Rubio" and from unnamed Univision staffers. After some initial reluctance, Rubio's staff confirmed the story, they said. This is a key point. It's hard to imagine the *Herald* publishing such an authoritative-sounding piece without the confirmation of Burgos and Harris. By cooperating, Rubio's staffers did what Univision had been incapable of doing: they made Orlando Cicilia's shame a national story, one that penetrated an English-speaking audience that reached far beyond Univision's Spanish-speaking viewership. In the parlance of political campaigns, they effectively threw Orlando Cicilia—a man who had paid his debt to society—under the bus.

The *Herald* and *El Nuevo Herald* published their pieces on October 1. The articles include the statement from Isaac Lee, but mostly present a version of events that aligns with the Burgos and Harris account: "Days before Univision aired a controversial story this summer about the decades-old drug bust of Marco Rubio's brother-in-law, top staff with the Spanish-language media power-house offered what sounded like a deal to the U.S. senator's staff."

The drug bust story may have been mostly ignored, but the allegations in the *Herald*'s story erupted into a national scandal. Erik Fresen, a young Cuban American lawmaker who had filled the Florida house seat vacated by Rubio, says he was furious when he read the *Herald*'s allegations about Univision. On October 3 he and two other Florida politicians, Rubio's close friend, the U.S. Congressman David Rivera and Florida house majority leader Carlos Lopez-Cantera, sent an outraged letter to Reince Priebus, the chairman of the Republican National Committee, demanding an apology and the dismissal of Lee. All three signed the letter, but its distribution was handled by Rivera, Fresen said. The letter noted that Univision was angling to host a presidential debate on January 29, two days before the Florida Republican primary. "Given the reprehensible nature of Univision Television Network's news division, we are advising all of the Republican presidential candidates not to participate in Univision Television Network's planned debate."

The letter went on to say that the three men would exact a political toll on any candidate who didn't take their advice: "Furthermore, when voters go to the polls during the January 31st Florida presidential primary, it is our intention to inform Hispanic voters, particularly Cuban American voters, as to which presidential candidates chose to ignore our concerns." They even suggested an alternative, the much smaller Spanish-language network Telemundo, whose star anchor was José Diaz-Balart, the brother of the Republican congressman Mario Diaz-Balart and the former congressman Lincoln Diaz-Balart.

The threat seemed to hit home with top Republicans. "Obviously we don't want to do anything to alienate Rubio or his constituents," the veteran Republican strategist Ed Rollins said. The leading Republican candidates then said they would not participate in the proposed Univision debate.

But the sequence of events seemed to some observers to be almost too neat to be coincidental. On Friday, September 30, the Florida Republican Party moved up its presidential primary, a decision that forced other early-primary and caucus states to move up their dates. The next day the *Herald's* Univision article appeared. Two days after the article Rivera and the other Florida lawmakers released their letter to the RNC, followed quickly by the presidential candidates pulling out of the proposed debate.

A possible motive—denied by Republicans—would be to spare their candidates the discomfort of facing a barrage of questions from Ramos about immigration. Both parties were eager to attract Hispanic votes in the 2012 election, and some analysts were describing Hispanic voters as possible difference-makers if the balloting between the Republican candidate and President Obama was particularly close. But immigration was a delicate subject for Republicans to talk about in the primary because of the harder line GOP candidates had been taking on enforcement and border security.

The quid-pro-quo allegations were shredding Univision's reputation. Despite the network's denials, the general impression was that it had acted unethically. And as the furor rose the network continued to bungle its management of public perception. The newsroom brought in Rick Altabef, an attorney who had done work for the CBS news magazine *60 Minutes*, to conduct an internal review. But the potential impact of the review was blunted because he hadn't interviewed all the Univision participants on the call, and it received little notice.

At this point Rubio clearly had the upper hand. He had become an object of sympathy, and Univision the embodiment of all that was bad about the media. But that winter, other interpretations began to circulate. First *The New Yorker* magazine and then the *Columbia Journalism Review*, a respected industry publication, raised questions about the tone of the *Herald* story, its sourcing, and the role Rubio's staff and friends played in making it happen. "There are some things about the *Herald*'s story that don't add up," Erika Fry wrote in the *Columbia Journalism Review*. "Its sources, for instance. Beyond Rubio's people, the story hinges on anonymous 'Univision insiders' who are at an ambiguous distance from the quid-pro-quo allegation. One is described as a 'Univision executive'; others are said to 'have knowledge of the discussion.' It is not clear . . . whether these 'insiders' work for the network or the Miami affiliate, a question that has relevance given that the two entities have very different relationships with Rubio's camp. Most problematic, though, is the fact that none of the 'insiders' are said to have been on the phone call in which the quid pro quo was allegedly made."

In response the *Herald* vigorously defended its story and the way it was reported. "We felt very comfortable with what we had," Aminda Marques, the *Herald*'s executive editor, told me. "We do have our sources."

Marques was irked by the implication in some assessments of the controversy that "we were used" and that the *Herald* may have gone soft on Rubio. The newspaper had published tough investigative pieces about him during the campaign, writing about his use of the state Republican Party credit card and his personal finances. One of its writers—the investigative reporter Beth Reinhard—was actually banned from Rubio's campaign press vehicle. "I can tell you, it was a difficult relationship with the candidate," Marques said.

Univision was also criticized by the two publications, but for different reasons. *The New Yorker* and *CJR* questioned whether the original report about Cicilia was worthy of the attention and resources the network had given it. Marques said the Cicilia story "was not a story that the *Miami Herald* was going to publish," in part because the arrest had taken place so long in the past and because Rubio was just a teenager when it occurred. "For us, I will say, that it didn't meet our bar."

An oddity about the saga was that the *Herald* reporters had not called Gerardo Reyes, a former colleague. On the night before the story ran, Reyes called Marques, the editor of the *Miami Herald*, at her home to warn her that she was about to publish a false story. Marques said the reporters did not contact Reyes because "he was not really in a position to be a neutral arbiter."

Even as the Univision version of the story was starting to get wider play, the network was still doing damage to itself. Its chairman, Haim Saban, a big contributor to the Democratic Party and one of America's wealthiest people, emphasized his political leanings by making a comment to *The New Yorker* that no news organization striving for balance would want its chairman to make. "The fact that Rubio and some Republican Presidential candidates have an anti-Hispanic stand that they don't want to share with our community is understandable but despicable. So 'boycotting' Univision, the largest Spanish-language media company in the U.S., is disingenuous at best and foolish at worst," Saban said.

Saban was trashed for that remark by Republicans, including Rubio's one-time mentor and the chairman of the American Conservative Union, Al Cardenas. "Who is he to determine what the points of view of all Americans are?" Cardenas asked. "[Suggesting Hispanics] are monolithic in their thought process is insulting to us and more of a plantation mentality." Lee defended Saban, saying "he doesn't get involved in the newsroom. I have never received a call from him on an editorial matter. Yet from the moment Saban's words entered the public domain, Republicans were handed a powerful weapon to argue that Univision is biased against them.

In the end, Univision never got its debate. The network had to settle for a modest candidate forum, in which Ramos interviewed Republican hopefuls separately. It was a major missed opportunity for the network, especially in a campaign whose debates were drawing large audiences and playing an outsize role in determining the fortunes of the candidates. It was also a missed opportunity for Hispanic voters in the United States.

If the goal of the Univision contretemps was to kill the Republican debate, Rubio and the Republicans won. If the goal wasn't to kill the debate, they still won something. But at what cost?

Chapter Ten

THE GOLDEN DOOR

The men and women who came to see Marco Rubio speak that day in the early 2000s had calloused hands and countless worries. The vans that shuttled them and their friends—and their sisters and brothers, wives and husbands—to work in the fields weren't safe. When the vehicles skidded, workers would be thrown to the asphalt, dead or injured before they even got to the job. Their lungs filled up with pesticides once they reached the farms. And even after a hard day under the sun, their employers sometimes refused to pay them the federally guaranteed minimum wage, knowing that an undocumented migrant would have little recourse to fight them.

Yet there was something about the energetic politician who came to talk to them that day at the migrant-laborer housing complex that gave them hope. It wasn't just that he understood Spanish and spoke to them in their language; it was that they felt like he understood *them*. "My heart goes out to the workers in this industry," he had once said. "Like a lot of my constituents, they come over to this country and work hard and try to get ahead and they should be treated fairly."

Rubio was still a rising state legislator, and there was only so much he could promise to the fifty or so Latinos who turned out to meet him. But "he gave a good speech, expressed his support of farmworker issues," said Tirso Moreno, a labor organizer who heads the Farmworker Association of Florida. "They were happy." They applauded.

Rubio's ability to make Latinos happy—not just Cuban Americans, but voters with roots in places such as Mexico and Guatemala and El Salvador—forms one of the central questions of his political future. Is he one of them or not one of them? A child of exiles or of immigrants? Or both? An answer to Republican hopes to attract Latino votes or a liability?

The paradox is, in great part, Rubio's creation, the result of the emphasis he places on his Cuban roots and the tough enforcement positions on the volatile immigration issue. As he says, "I talk about my family legacy and my family history as a core part of my political identity because it is the source of my political identity." But the Rubio paradox also speaks to a larger truth about ethnic politics in the United States: Latino political figures are often expected to reflexively favor a lenient path to immigration generally and a generous system for accepting immigrants who are already here illegally. The Latino vote has grown increasingly influential in American politics. More than 21 million Hispanics were eligible to vote in the United States in 2012. Hispanics represented 7.4 percent of the electorate in the 2008 presidential election, more than twice the percentage in 1988. Hispanics were the second largest minority group in 2008, trailing African Americans, who accounted for 12.1 percent. And all the trend lines point toward Hispanics growing exponentially in national importance. The Hispanic population is projected to rise from the current 16 percent to 29 percent in 2050, according to the Pew Hispanic Center. Between 2005 and 2050 Latinos are expected to compose 60 percent of all population growth in the United States.

Strategists generally agree that to win the White House a Republican nominee needs to secure 40 percent of the Latino vote, the portion George W. Bush won in 2004. Four years later Republican John McCain got only 33 percent when he lost to Democrat Barack Obama.

But for Republicans seeking their party's nomination, the calculation can be different: it is more important to gain white working-class votes by staking out the position of being the toughest candidate on illegal immigrants than it is to court the ascending bloc of Latinos, whose influence registers mainly in the general election. So in the 2012 primary the former Massachusetts governor Mitt Romney promoted the idea of a high-tech fence stretching the entire length of the U.S.-Mexico border, nearly two thousand miles long, and Congresswoman Michele Bachmann of Minnesota called for double fencing. Not to be outdone, Herman Cain, a former pizza parlor executive whose campaign caught fire and briefly enjoyed front-runner status before he dropped out, endorsed an electrified fence and added in a moat and alligators for good measure.

Moderation on immigration in late 2011 did not help win primary votes, as Rick Perry and Newt Gingrich discovered. Perry, the governor of Texas, came under sharp attack for allowing in-state tuition for the children of some undocumented immigrants. Gingrich early on endorsed the idea of a guest worker program and suggested there ought to be a route for some of the nation's 11 million undocumented immigrants to stay legally, but he was quickly labeled soft on the issue and pounded by conservative activists, who accused him of nudging the country toward amnesty.

Two months later, as the primary contest moved to Florida, a state with the nation's third largest Latino population of 4.2 million, Rubio and his former mentor Jeb Bush both chastised their fellow Republicans for alienating Latinos with anti-immigrant rhetoric. "In the 15 states that are likely to decide who controls the White House and the Senate in 2013, Hispanic voters will represent the margin of victory," Bush wrote in an op-ed for the *Washington Post*. "For the Republican Party, the stakes could not be greater. Just eight years after the party's successful effort to woo Hispanic voters in 2004, this community—the fastest-growing group in the United States, according to census data—has drifted away."

At the same time that Republicans seemed to be pushing away Latinos, Democrats weren't doing themselves any favors either. The Obama administration reported a record number of deportations in its first three years. Democrats argued that the increase was reflective of a renewed focus on pushing criminals out of the country, while it still left a bad impression with many Latinos. And the president was also being criticized for expending political capital on sweeping measures, such as health care reform and the stimulus, but not putting much energy into comprehensive immigration reform.

Neither Democrats nor Republicans were striking all the right notes with migrant communities.

And Latinos were there for the taking, if only someone could figure out how to reach them.

——

Nearly 200,000 men and women work the fields in Florida, a state that produced a large majority of the U.S. orange and grapefruit crops and where two out of every five fresh market tomatoes in the country is grown.

No one knows exactly how many of the Florida farmworkers entered the country illegally, but it is well understood that most are undocumented. "Upwards of three-quarters," said Greg Schell, the managing attorney for the Migrant Farmworker Justice Project, an organization that provides legal services to laborers. Implicit in any effort to help farmworkers is an understanding that undocumented migrants would be the main beneficiaries. "It's no secret," Schell said. "Everybody knows who we're talking about."

Schell and his colleagues took a liking to Marco Rubio when he was in the Florida house. In meetings with the group's advocates, Rubio would interrupt enthusiastically as they talked about their wish lists. "That's only fair!" he would exclaim.

"We had great hopes that he was going to be a champion of farmworkers," Schell said.

In the early years of the century Rubio affirmed those hopes by lending his growing stature to their cause. Rubio formed an unlikely alliance for a young South Florida Republican hoping to burnish his conservative credentials, teaming with Frank Peterman, a liberal African American Democrat from St. Petersburg who was pressing a variety of farmworker protection proposals. With Peterman, Rubio cosponsored a measure that banned labor contractors from forcing workers to pay for transportation and basic equipment needed to do their jobs. This was a way of combating the fact that unscrupulous labor contractors increased their own profits by withholding the cost of tools and transportation from workers' salaries. Rubio and Peterman also cosponsored a much more far-reaching proposal that granted workers the right to sue labor contractors who did not pay the minimum wage. Neither proposal became law, but activists were impressed that Rubio, a lawmaker with such great promise, had at least tried.

Rubio also supported giving in-state tuition discounts to the children of undocumented immigrants who had lived in Florida for at least three consecutive years before graduating from high school. Other states with large immigrant populations, including Texas and California, had enacted similar measures, but the Florida proposals that Rubio backed stalled two years in a row during his ascent to the state house speakership.

The coronation of Rubio as speaker was accompanied by renewed attention to his compelling family history. When he accepted the speakership in September 2005 before the Florida legislature, he positioned himself as a son of the generation of political refugees who had found freedom and opportunity in America.

Rubio is a sophisticated speaker and on that day he delivered a sophisticated address. In it, he deftly included himself with the sons and grandsons of Cubans forced off the island of Cuba by Castro. The suggestion, however, was in conflict with the facts of his family history. Immigration documents for his father, mother, and brother showed clearly that they arrived in the United States in May 1956—two and a half years before Castro took power. But that discrepancy wouldn't surface until months after Rubio was elected to the U.S. Senate. "In January of 1959," he said during his speech accepting the speakership, "a thug named Fidel Castro took power in Cuba and countless Cubans were forced to flee and come here, many—most—here to America."

When they arrived, they were welcomed by the most compassionate people on all the Earth. And they were told in America if you worked hard and you play by all the rules you can get ahead in life, and so that's precisely what they did. They took work anywhere they could find it and they weren't always good jobs. But they worked hard and played by the rules, and as she had done for countless others before, America kept her promise to them. In time they became the managers, the owners and the entrepreneurs themselves.

They bought their first homes here and became involved in civic life. They sent their sons and daughters off to fight and sometimes die in the jungles of Vietnam and the deserts of Iraq. They watched their children grow up, go to college and start their own life, a life better than their own. A significant number of the men and women I represent are members of that generation and so I wanted to take just a moment to speak to them, especially those who join us here today. I know that when you were young you too had dreams. When you were young you had dreams of being doctors or lawyers, engineers or journalists. But when you lost your homeland most of you also lost the opportunity to realize those dreams. Today I speak to you on behalf of a grateful generation that is the generation of your children and grandchildren.

Although you suffered great hardships, you never made

us into victims. You never instilled in us bitterness. Instead you instilled in us the deeply held belief that our only limit was our willingness to work. And now as you reflect back on your lives, you need to know this: your dreams did not die. You passed them on to us.

Today your children and grandchildren live the dreams of your youth. Today those dreams find fulfillment in our lives. Today we live the dreams you once had for yourselves.

Today your children and grandchildren are the secretary of commerce of the United States and multiple members of Congress, they are the CEO of Fortune 500 companies and successful entrepreneurs, they are Grammy winning artists and they are renowned journalists, they are a United States Senator and soon, even Speaker of the Florida House.

The speech was met with cheers and no small amount of tears. But there were also sneers. Something about the speech rang phony to some of the Cuban Americans in the audience, though they never would have said so publicly. These Cubans knew, without a doubt, that their own parents had been forced off the island and somehow felt Rubio was making too much of his parents' experiences. Rubio's parents "were not the only ones who had to sacrifice," one said.

In his remarks, Rubio had mentioned only the generation that was forced to flee and the generations composed of their children and grandchildren. There is no mention of pre-Castro immigrants or a larger community of exiles.

When he said "Today I speak to you on behalf of a grateful generation that is the generation of your children and grandchildren" he was assuming the role of spokesman for the children and grandchildren of the generation of Cubans who fled. He included himself in that generation by saying, "You never made us into victims . . . never instilled in us bitterness."

The message of his speech was clear to the state's largest newspaper and to the nation's largest wire service, both of which reported that Rubio's parents had fled Castro. "Rubio was born in Miami to Cuban American parents, and he spoke of how they escaped a 'thug,' Fidel Castro, to make a better life for their children in America," read the *St. Petersburg Times* account. "The 34-year-old Miami lawyer described Cuban President Fidel Castro as a 'thug' who forced his parents to flee their homeland before he was born," the Associated Press dispatch said. The *Palm Beach Post* published a similar report about Rubio's parents being forced off the island. And later Human Events online, a site that often describes Rubio in glowing terms, wrote that the outgoing house speaker had "denounced Castro as a thug who forced Rubio's parents to flee Cuba before he was born."

In years to come Rubio would be far more explicit. The false claim that his parents came to the United States after Castro took over would be featured prominently in the biographies on his Senate campaign website and his official Senate website after he was elected. During the 2010 Senate race, the *Miami Herald*'s Beth Reinhard took note that his "standard stump speech packages his campaign as the next chapter of a classic American success story. 'I am the son of Cuban exiles,' he began in Navarre, telling the story of his parents meeting in Havana and moving to the U.S. in 1959 [in] search of a better life." His campaign advertising presented the image of a family that left Cuba against its will. "My parents lost everything—their home, their families, friends, even their country." In fact, much of their family was already in the United States or on its way, according to immigration documents. Many Cubans had truly lost homes and farms seized by the Castro regime and were pushed off the island as political enemies; Rubio's came voluntarily.

Rubio further spread the post-Castro exodus tale by saying his parents arrived in 1959 during interviews on Tampa's Fox 13 television station, on NPR, and on *America's Nightly Scoreboard*, a program on the Fox News network. "I think that the direction we're going in Washington, D.C.," Rubio told the host, David Asman, "would make us more like the rest of the world, and not like the exceptional nation that my parents found when they came here from Cuba in 1959, and the nation they worked in so hard so that I could inherit." And Rubio, who was developing a large Twitter following, also transmitted the post-Castro story digitally, tweeting in July 2009: "Thank you USA for welcoming my parents 50 years ago. I am so blessed to be an American."

The narrative was so deeply entrenched that at least fifty different print and broadcast outlets published stories referencing the flight of Rubio's family from post-Castro Cuba. They included nearly every major newspaper in Florida, as well as national and international publications and television programs, such as the *New York Times*, the *Washington Post*, the *Weekly Standard*, the *American Spectator*, Agence France-Presse, and ABC's *Nightline*. The false flight from Castro also showed up in books written by the conservative pundit and former U.S. education secretary William J. Bennett and by the well-known pollsters Scott Rasmussen and Doug Schoen.

The narrative was exposed as false in October 2011 in reports published by the *St. Petersburg Times* and the *Washington Post*. The evidence was irrefutable, and not particularly hidden. I first stumbled across it while doing some routine background research for this book. "Petitions for naturalization" filed by Rubio's mother, father, and older brother in the 1970s show they arrived in the United States on May 27, 1956.

Rubio and Republican allies reacted with outrage at the *Post's* report. Mitt Romney, then the runaway favorite for the Republican presidential nomination, called the *Post* piece "a smear." Rubio responded with an op-ed on the well-read website Politico.com, writing, "The Washington Post on Friday accused me of seeking political advantage by embellishing the story of how my parents arrived in the United States. That is an outrageous allegation that is not only incorrect, but an insult to the sacrifices my parents made to provide a better life for their children." In interviews he argued that he was relying on "family lore," though when pressed later about whether anyone in his family ever specifically told him they came in 1959, he said, "Ultimately, look, that's not the way it was discussed in our family or by many people in the exile community. It's more about a loss of their home country, and the inability to go back to it or be part of it. . . . That was a deep part of our upbringing, growing up in this community surrounded by people who had lost everything, who had been sent here as young children while their parents stayed behind."

———

In writing his defense on Politico, Rubio only extended the controversy. He stated that his mother had returned to Cuba in February 1961 with his older siblings "with the intention of moving back," while his father remained in Miami "wrapping up family matters." They decided not to stay after realizing Cuba was becoming a communist state, he wrote.

The same day Rubio's op-ed ran, NPR broadcast previously unaired tape of an interview conducted with him in 2009. In the interview Rubio stated that his parents came from Cuba in 1959, but he also gave other details that are not supported by documents and were at odds with his explanation. He told the interviewer, Robert Siegel, that his mother returned to Cuba in 1960 to care for his grandfather after he was "hit by a bus." "When the time came to come home, the Cuban government wouldn't let her," Rubio said. "They would let my sister come because she was a U.S. citizen, but they wouldn't let my brother and my mom come. And they would go to the airport every day for nine months waiting to be let go, and then finally were able to come. So, it was very frightening. And I think that's when they knew for sure that that's not the place they wanted to be."

It was a dramatic story, but it wasn't supported by the documents. The Cuban passport of Rubio's mother showed that she was never in the country for a nine-month period in the 1960s. The year of her return was also different—1960 instead of 1961. Rubio's spokesman tried to argue the two accounts weren't in conflict, though they clearly were.

The episode was an early test of how Rubio and his team handled crises at the national level, one that several prominent national Republicans said raised concerns about his temperament and experience. "A little bit more experience and he wouldn't have had such an overreaction," a seasoned and influential Republican kingmaker told me. "It's important to separate what's really critical to your principles from what may be a media test."

Paul Gigot, a *Wall Street Journal* columnist who has written that Rubio may benefit from an early national vetting, observed that "Team Rubio didn't handle [the revelations about his family migration] well." Still, the tenaciousness of Rubio's response may have won him some support among conservative Republicans who were rushing to his defense. Fighting with the mainstream media is almost always a popular move.

———

Some Rubio allies and Miami Cubans argued that there was no difference between Cubans who came to the United States before Castro and those who came afterward. Andy S. Gomez, a University of Miami professor, was so exercised that he took the unusual step of issuing a press release to say there was no distinction: "They all share the painful heritage of not being able to return home."

But others pointed out that there were clear political advantages for Rubio in portraying himself as the son of parents who fled Castro. Raul Martinez, the Hialeah mayor who had once supported Rubio, suggested Rubio was motivated by "political expediency" and an attempt to win acceptance with post-Castro exiles, otherwise "they look at you like, 'Wait, you're not one of us.' It's more important to get elected than to, I guess, to tell the truth," said Martinez, whose family was pushed out of Cuba after Castro's takeover.

"If [Rubio] had been honest or truthful that they came pre-revolution Cuba, I don't think he would have had the same political career," said George Gonzalez, a University of Miami political science professor whose father was rescued from Cuba by the Pedro Pan program after his grandmother was imprisoned for possessing counterrevolutionary documents. "That's part of the Cuban exile experience, the political and psychological trauma of it. So the idea that he was murky on those does not cut ice . . . To my father and grandparents, if you came before the revolution, it puts you in a different category.

"Every Cuban-American knows when their parents arrived and the circumstances under which they arrived."

Frank Gonzalez, a Miamian whose father was a Bay of Pigs veteran, lived the intensity of the exile divide. His father received death threats after suggesting dialogue with the Castro regime to free political prisoners. The senior Gonzalez was blackballed from exile groups, and was branded as a kind of traitor to the cause despite his service in the botched invasion, Frank Gonzalez said. "You have to say [you were pushed out by Castro] because if you're not, you're not part of the clique," Gonzalez said. And Ralph Fernandez, a leader of the Cuban exile community in Tampa, remembered clear lines being drawn: "They even had different clubs" for pre-Castro and post-Castro Cubans. Pre-Castro immigrants were known as *verduleros*, or vegetable street vendors, pigeonholing them as economic migrants. And the pre-Castro migrants "had equally unpleasant names for us," said Fernandez, who came to the United States after Castro took power.

Whether Rubio did not know his family history or intentionally misled voters and colleagues is a question that has followed him. On two occasions, he has made statements that indicated he might have known it was possible they came before Castro's 1959 takeover: Once in a February 2010 *Fox News* interview, he said, " '58, '59" in reference to their arrival and once in a September 2011 *Miami Herald* interview he said " '57 or '58 or '59," then, when pressed, that they had come before the Revolution. The paper reported that his parents came "just before the 1959 Revolution."

But he was unequivocal that they came after Castro took

power on his official campaign and senate websites, in two television interviews, in a radio interview, and on his Twitter account. Though he was a close reader of articles about himself, he has never attempted to correct the dozens of news reports that stated his parents came in 1959. The one date that does not appear in a database search of his statements is the correct one: 1956.

What is clear is that during his rise he placed great emphasis on his family's narrative, and he was eager to identify himself as the son of exiles. Even after the real story came to light, he argued that he was justified in calling himself an exile because his parents could not return. But that argument ignores the fact that he'd been describing them not as exiles because they could not return, but as exiles because they were forced to leave.

———

In the months after Rubio's high-profile speech to the Florida legislature, lawmakers there pressed him to make immigration enforcement part of his agenda as speaker. "I was saying it was a big deal," one of his advisors said. "Marco did not want anything to do with it."

Once he ascended to the speaker post, he continued to keep immigration legislation from becoming central to his speakership. Employing a series of maneuvers, he assured that six immigration measures would be buried in the legislative equivalent of the basement rather than coming up for debate. The measures were mild compared to later laws in Arizona and Alabama that made it easier for authorities to request immigration documents and round up undocumented migrants. But the substance of the measures wasn't the problem. It was the potential that they could be amended to add more draconian components. And it was the ferocious and potentially divisive debates that could ensue that Rubio wanted to avoid.

"Marco told me that he didn't want those immigration bills to come up because they could become very ugly," a former associate said. "One of his jobs was to manage the house and help keep things civilized."

Rubio did so at the risk of alienating the right wing of his party. "A lot of us are mad at him because he did block those bills," said David Caulkett, a founder of Floridians for Immigration Enforcement. "Rubio claims to be anti-amnesty, but the question is, 'Do we trust him?' "

The decision to keep immigration out of the spotlight, though, also accrued a political benefit for Rubio. Because the proposals weren't getting any oxygen, he wasn't being forced to talk about an issue that was perilous for any conservative. So what was good for Rubio politically turned out, in the short term at least, to be good for undocumented immigrants too.

———

Marco Rubio's U.S. Senate campaign wasn't going to be about farmworker rights and tuition breaks for the children of undocumented migrants. His campaign was about defining Charlie Crist as a liberal, and it was about Barack Obama—how Rubio would stand up to the president, oppose measures such as the federal stimulus, defend the free enterprise system, and affirm America's exceptionalism.

Yet Rubio wasn't just a candidate; he was a Hispanic candidate. That meant his record on immigration would undergo scrutiny beyond what a non-Hispanic candidate would face. And suddenly the way he talked about the issue was noticeably different. "His tone has changed on the subject, and to me it's very obvious that it's for political reasons," Juan Zapata, the Miami state legislator, said a year before the U.S. Senate election. Zapata, who served on the executive committee of the National Hispanic Caucus of State Legislators, an organization that pressed for immigration reform and fair treatment of migrants, had worked with Rubio on the tuition bill, but in the 2010 race he was backing Crist.

Rubio was all too aware of the dilemma he faced. After months of questions about his opposition to Obama's nomination of Sonia Sotomayor, a *puertorriqueña* who would become the first Hispanic justice on the U.S. Supreme Court, Rubio wrote an op-ed column that sought to address the expectations many placed on Hispanic politicians. Sotomayor had said that the experiences of a "wise Latina" could lead to better judicial decisions. "Some have said my opposition to Sotomayor's confirmation and that of Republican senators would incense Hispanic-American voters. Right on cue, many are now attempting to brand Republicans as anti-Hispanic," Rubio wrote on Politico.com. "It should be clear, however, that our opposition to her judicial philosophy is in no way a wholesale opposition to Hispanics. I believe the greatest disservice we could offer the Hispanic community and the nation as a whole is to avoid a serious, principled discussion about the role of the judiciary."

Rubio said he opposed her nomination because of her case history and testimony on "the so-called right to privacy" that resulted in the Roe v. Wade abortion rights decision and a concern that she "would bring an activist approach" to the court.

The Arizona legislation that allowed authorities greater latitude to ask individuals for immigration documents placed Rubio in an even more difficult position. By first criticizing the measure, then embracing it after only slight modifications, he opened himself to charges of political gamesmanship on an issue that was central to his national appeal. In going after the Senate seat, he also staked out a position against the Dream Act, a measure that would provide a path to citizenship for youth who met a range of criteria, including coming to the United States before they were sixteen, living in the country for more than five years, and graduating from high school. In opposing the proposal, he was veering farther to the right than a host of prominent Florida Republicans including Congresswoman Ileana Ros-Lehtinen, whom Rubio had interned for, and Jeb Bush, who had mentored him. It was hard for some to reconcile the Marco Rubio who had met with farmworkers in Homestead and had kept potentially divisive immigration bills from coming to the Florida house floor with the Marco Rubio of the campaign trail. Schell, the migrant rights attorney, detected a clear turn to the right. J. C. Planas, a former Republican colleague in the Florida legislature, said, "His rhetoric does not reflect his actions as speaker."

In appealing to the party's right flank, Rubio also drew distinctions between his immigration story and those of others, seeming to suggest that the Cuban exile experience put him above other migrants. This was a way of reconciling his tough positions on immigration—making it hard for illegals to gain easy entry—and his defense of Cubans and their special status. In so doing he was segregating Cubans, who represent 3.5 percent of Hispanics in the United States, from the other 97 percent, who come primarily from Mexico and Central America. "Nothing against immigrants, but my parents are exiles," he says in a speech that was posted on YouTube by a supporter during his Senate campaign. "The exile experience is different from the immigrant experience. It's similar in many ways. But different in the sense that folks that are exiles are people that have lost their country—who basically are from somewhere and would still be living there if not for some political reason."

Cubans have long received preferential treatment through a series of U.S. government initiatives, including the "wet-foot, dry-foot" policy that almost guaranteed admission to any Cuban who made it to American soil. The refugee programs instituted to help them are the "longest lasting in American history and the most generous in terms of support," wrote Roger Daniels, a leading authority on immigration, in his fascinating book *Guarding the Golden Door: American Immigration Policy and Immigrants since 1882.*

Mario H. Lopez, president of the conservative-leaning Hispanic Leadership Fund, would later say, "I think [Rubio] unwittingly brought up some of that old tension that exists with older generations within the Hispanic community of, well, they have a special status and they don't want it for anyone else."

And though he won an overwhelming victory in the Senate campaign, there were indications that he might have some work to do in the future repairing relations with non-Cubans. Just before the November 2010 election a poll by the Latino Decisions firm showed that Rubio's support among Cuban Americans was strong: 78 percent said they were going to vote for him. But his support among non-Cuban Latinos—a segment of the Florida electorate that is growing in both size and influence—was just 40 percent.

———

In his first months in the Senate Rubio continued to aggravate immigration reform advocates. After the reintroduction of the

Dream Act—which was supported by a majority of Americans in polls—Rubio reiterated his opposition to it: "I've said repeatedly I want to help these kids. I think these were kids who were brought to this country by their parents when they were very young; they were high academic achievers and want to go to college and contribute to America's future or serve in the armed forces. And I think helping them would be good for America. I do want to help them; I just don't think the Dream Act is the right or best way to do it." He argued that the measure could be part of a "broader effort to grant blanket amnesty." Any suggestion of amnesty for the estimated 11 to 12 million undocumented immigrants in the United States was strongly opposed by Republican Party stalwarts, and the mere suggestion of proposals that appeared to resemble amnesty—even if they weren't actually amnesty—could sink careers.

In June 2011 Rubio signed on as cosponsor of a controversial measure that would make e-Verify, an Internet-based system for verifying immigration status, mandatory for all employers. "I know firsthand the great things that immigration has meant for America," he said in a statement. "But we can't be the only nation in the world that does not enforce its immigration laws. Consistently, I have stated that a modernization of the legal immigration system is impossible unless we must first secure the border and implement an E-Verify system that will help prevent the hiring and exploitation of undocumented workers."

The proposal was hotly opposed by migrant activists and by many farmers, including those in Rubio's home state, who were warning that crops would rot in the fields if the requirement was imposed on them. "I gotta say, some of our members—on immigration specifically—have expressed some frustration with what they believe to be his intransigence on this issue," Mario Lopez said. And there were moments when that frustration was expressed directly. During Rubio's speech at a Hispanic Leadership Network conference on January 27, 2012, just two days before the Republican presidential primary, two young men held up a sign that said "Rubio: Latino or Tea Partino." Rubio, who has a gift for spontaneity at the dais and an ability to transmit empathy, turned what might have been a more embarrassing episode into an affirmation of American values. "These young people are very brave to be here today," he said into the microphone. "I ask you to let them stay. . . . I don't want them to leave. They have the bravery and the courage to raise their voices. I thank God that I'm in a country where they can do that.

"I'm not who they think I am," he said. "I don't stand for what they claim I stand for."

In spring 2012, Rubio revealed that he was developing a different version of the Dream Act that would grant legal status— but not citizenship—to migrants who were brought to the United States as children and later enrolled in college or joined the military. Talking about the idea once again positioned Rubio as a leading Hispanic voice in the United States. "I think the vast majority of Americans understand that if you were four years old when you were brought here—you grew up in this country your whole life, and you're now a valedictorian of a high school or are a high-achieving academic person, and have much to contribute to our future—I think most Americans, the vast majority of Americans, find that compelling and want to accommodate that."

Ruben Navarette Jr., a widely read columnist who had sometimes criticized Rubio, hailed the idea as a "commonsense solution" that "could break a stalemate and improve millions of lives." Democrats were scathing in their criticism. Without mentioning Rubio by name Senate Majority Leader Harry Reid, of Nevada, wrote in the *Miami Herald* that the "Republican plan to relegate hundreds of thousands of young people to a permanent underclass is unprecedented in American law or history, and goes against the basic American value of equal opportunity."

Rubio has said he opposes the original Dream Act proposal in part because he believes it would cause "chain migration," with people who gain citizenship through the act turning around and sponsoring other family members. "That could be three, four million people," Rubio said. "I support the idea behind the Dream Act, which is to help these young kids. I don't support the Dream Act as currently drafted because it allows for chain migration, because it creates a pathway to citizenship that could potentially encourage illegal immigration in the future. I do support and I have consistently supported, even during my campaign, the notion that we need to help accommodate these kids who through no fault of their own find themselves in this legal limbo. But we have to do it the right way."

Yet a migratory chain runs through Rubio's own family history. His aunt and uncle—Irma and Luis Lastres—filed paperwork in November 1956 saying that they would "receive, maintain and support" Rubio's grandfather, Pedro Víctor García, if he was allowed to come to the United States from Cuba. In May 1956, the Lastreses had also filed an "affidavit of support" for Rubio's grandmother—Dominga García Rodriguez—and his aunts, Adria García Rodriguez and Magdalena García Rodriguez. And that same month, Rubio's parents applied for an immigrant visa and alien registration, noting that they were "destined to" his aunt, Dolores Denis.

Many conservative leaders dismissed the idea that Rubio's positions on immigration would somehow dampen his national appeal in general and among Latinos. Alfonso Aguilar, who served as chief of the U.S. Citizenship Office under President George W. Bush and now heads the Latino Partnership for Conservative Principles advocacy group, argued that immigration was overemphasized in the assessment of Rubio. "Most importantly, he espouses values that Hispanics believe in—family, faith, entrepreneurship. All this talk that Republicans are not paying attention to Latinos—all that argument is based on immigration." It would be "very naïve" to think that immigration was all Latinos were worried about, he said. Aguilar praised Rubio for including a provision in his AGREE Act that would end per-country limits on employment visas and increase the number of visas granted for family members. They're small steps. But Aguilar liked the approach. By not asking for too much now, he argued, Rubio might be able to ask for more later.

Afterword

In 2012, as his personal history continued to be questioned, Marco Rubio—the politician who built a political identity on his family story—spent campaign donations to hire a California firm to study him, to conduct a vetting process not unlike the examinations of possible running mates conducted by presidential nominees.

The revelation that he had told a story that didn't fit the facts was "a blessing in disguise," he told a Florida audience. "It made me do something that we don't do enough, and that's go back and discover who our parents were when they were our age. What were their hopes and dreams? What did they want out of life? . . . From the tattered pages of passports and the yellowed papers of old documents, across five decades, I clearly heard the voice of people I never met."

He learned, he said, that his father, Mario Rubio, had struggled. He learned about his grandfather too, the *abuelo* who loved to talk about history with his grandson while they sat on his front porch, the air rich and sweet with cigar smoke. Pedro Víctor García had once prospered, Rubio said, but fell on hard times after losing his job running a railroad station in Cuba. He had to walk for hours looking for work, coming home with bloodied knees because polio had stripped him of the use of one leg. He couldn't always keep his balance and would crash to the ground. No one was there to catch him.

In that moment of political tenuousness, Rubio once again became the professional apprentice, the student eager to share what he had learned. In two decades of ascension he had learned to slide quickly on the issues, tailoring messages on immigration and spending that got him where he needed to go, even if they sometimes raised questions about his political core. He had absorbed the lessons of street-wise political brawlers in Hialeah, of savvy mentors in West Miami, of ideologists in Tallahassee, and of wise men in the national Republican elite. Now he was taking a pedagogical cue from the sting of a public embarrassment.

His tone was not defiant and angry, as it once had been. The politician who could be so thin-skinned in Tallahassee, so brittle and brutish when he was challenged in Washington, struck notes of warmth and empathy.

His gifts, both innate and learned, were fully on display.

Rubio had reached a position of influence with remarkable speed. But in politics, just as on the football fields of his youth, speed alone doesn't guarantee that you'll react in time to get you to the right place at the right time. You need to be prepared to execute the right move when you get there. Now, with an eye on the national stage, Rubio needs all the diligence, tenacity, and patience of his ancestors to reach the goal line.

Acknowledgments

A book, it seems to me, is an idea transferred onto paper (or pixels). And the idea for this one came from Jonathan Karp and Priscilla Painton at Simon & Schuster, who both recognized early on that Marco Rubio is one of the more fascinating figures in present-day American politics.

I couldn't have asked for a better editor than Priscilla, who took time to chew over even the most minute details of this book with me, even if it meant delaying getting started cooking Valentine's Day dinner or straining to be heard over New York traffic. I'm grateful for her guidance and friendship and for the help of her colleague, associate editor Michael Szczerban.

Dozens of people—Republicans and Democrats, football coaches and teachers, insiders and outsiders—gave generously of their time. Whether I was in Washington, Miami, Tallahassee or elsewhere, people sat patiently for long interviews, answering my questions about documents, campaigns, legislation, and ideas. Politics can be a delicate profession and many of these people— some named and some not named—spoke frankly even though there can be consequences for candor.

I'm fortunate to have great friends who also happen to be world experts in all things Florida. Peter Wallsten, a colleague at the *Washington Post* who was a Miami Beach neighbor of mine when he worked at the *Herald* and I was the *Post*'s Miami bureau chief, helped me enormously by reading the manuscript and by giving of his Rolodex. Michael Grunwald, a former *Post* colleague who was also a Miami Beach neighbor, shared insights *and* shared his home. "Dance party music breakfasts" with Michael, his wife, Cristina Dominguez, and their children, Max and Lina, were the best way to start a Florida morning. My friend and colleague at the *Post*, Ian Shapira, also read portions of the manuscript and added useful perspective. Peter Baker, Robert Draper, and Mark Leibovich offered lessons learned from their book writing experiences.

Melissa Maltby helped locate interesting photographs for the insert. It's nice to count Pulitzer Prize–winning photographers among your friends—the *Post*'s Michel duCille gave advice about selecting photos and the amazing Nikki Kahn was kind enough to take an author photo.

Marcus Brauchli, the executive editor of the *Post*, was an enthusiastic supporter of this project from the outset. My editors Frances Sellers, Christine Ledbetter, Sydney Trent, and Kevin Sullivan gave me time away from the newspaper to report and write. Editors Kevin Merida, Marilyn Thompson, and Steven Ginsberg paved the way for publication of material gleaned from my early research in the *Post*. I'm also appreciative that the *Post* maintains a commitment to foreign journalism, which allowed me to travel Cuba on reporting trips and get a deeper sense of the island when I was a foreign correspondent based in Mexico City.

I owe a special debt of gratitude to Alice Crites, a researcher extraordinaire at the *Post*, a finder of things large and small. Her excitement at discovery is infectious. And I was fortunate that Maria Helena Carey stepped in at a crucial moment in the research to provide valuable assistance and friendship. I also encountered professional and helpful researchers and records custodians at the U.S. Citizenship and Immigration Services and the National Archives. And Alan Cooperman at the Pew Forum on Religion & Public Life steered me toward enlightening data.

The articles produced by numerous Florida reporters helped inform my thinking and bolster my research. I found it especially helpful to read pieces by Alex Leary and Adam C. Smith in the *St. Petersburg* (now *Tampa Bay*) *Times*, Gary Fineout in the *New York Times* regional newspapers, Zac Anderson in the *Sarasota Herald-Tribune* and Beth Reinhard and Mary Ellen Klas in the *Miami Herald.* Tim Elfrink of the *Miami New-Times* was generous with advice and help. My brother Carlos Roig aided me in navigating the world of technology. And I'm thankful to literary agent Andrew Wylie and his associate Adam Eaglin for their guidance and support.

I thought a lot about two cigar-smoking gentlemen while working on this project: Senator Rubio's grandfather Pedro Víctor García and my own abuelo, Manuel Roig Meca, to whom the Spanish-language edition of this book is dedicated. Each shared wisdom with their grandsons through a cloud of fragrant smoke. My abuelo, now in his nineties, called from Spain every Sunday following his afternoon Montecristo and was always interested to hear what I was learning about the other abuelo I was getting to know. I think the abuelos would have liked each other.

But the person I owe the most thanks to is Ceci Connolly, the love of my life. Ceci, to whom this book is dedicated, lives through every up and down of every project I undertake. She is my most tireless editor and my most important guiding light.

Notes

INTRODUCTION: THE HEIR

1 *He wasn't fast:* James Colzie, interview by author, Nov. 16, 2011.

2 *A Los Angeles Times blog:* Andrew Malcolm, "Marco Rubio to the Rescue! Freshman Senator Saves a Falling Nancy Reagan," *Los Angeles Times* blogs, Aug. 24, 2011.

3 *Watching the video:* Ron Reagan, interviewed by author, Dec. 16, 2011.

3 *"We joked in the office:* Author interview with confidential source, 2011.

5 *Gerald Parsky, a trustee:* Gerald Parsky, interview by author, Dec. 21, 2011.

5 *"Mrs. Reagan," he:* Remarks by Marco Rubio at Politico Playbook breakfast, Washington, D.C., Nov. 16, 2011.

7 *"It is a startling place:* Remarks by Marco Rubio at the Reagan Presidential Library, Simi Valley, California, Aug. 23, 2011.

8 *The senator from:* Report of Medicare state enrollment, 2010, Centers for Medicare and Medicaid Services, Department of Health and Human Services, http://www.cms.gov/MedicareEnRpts/Downloads/10All.pdf.

9 *For Marco Rubio:* Transcript of *The Ed Show* with Ed Schultz, MSNBC, Aug. 25, 2011.

9 *"What, would he:* Transcript of *The Rachel Maddow Show*, MSNBC, Aug. 25, 2011.

10 *"The speech drove extreme:* Alex Leary, "Reagan Speech 'Drove Extreme Liberals Crazy,' and He Turns It into Fundraising Pitch," *St. Petersburg Times* blogs, Aug. 31, 2011.

10 *"I think that:* Parsky, interview by author, Dec. 21, 2011.

11 *Two weeks after:* Alex Leary, "Rush Limbaugh Goes Nuclear on the

Anti-purists and Brings Up Crist vs. Rubio," *St. Petersburg Times* blogs, Sept. 7, 2011.

CHAPTER ONE: THE ISLAND

13 *In a village:* Record of birth of Pedro Víctor García, Civil Registry of City of Santo Domingo, Las Villas, folio 170, volume 24, dated July 7, 1899, provided by U.S. National Archives.

13 *The infant gulped:* Jacobo de la Pezuela, *Diccionario geográfico, estadístico, histórico, de la isla de Cuba* (Madrid: Imprenta del Establecimiento de Mellado, 1863), 45, 215.

13 *In 1492 the explorer: The Journal of Christopher Columbus (during his first voyage, 1492–93)* (Cambridge: Cambridge University Press, 1893), 61.

13 *After four centuries:* U.S. War Dept., Cuban Census Office, *Report on the Census of Cuba, 1899* (Washington, D.C.: Government Printing Office, 1900), 625.

14 *village called Jicotea:* Esteban Pichardo, *Diccionario provincial casi-razonado de voces cubanas* (Havana: Soler, 1849), 150.

14 *The landscape flattens out:* Description of Santo Domingo area geography in *Lippincott's New Gazetteer* (London: J. P. Lippincott, 1906), 1651.

15 *On May 25:* Baptismal certificate of Pedro Víctor García, Our Lady of Hope Church, Las Villas Province, book 40, folio 50, provided by U.S. National Archives.

15 *During the uprising:* Louis A. Pérez Jr., *Cuban Studies,* vol. 38 (Pittsburgh: University of Pittsburgh Press, 2007), 52.

15 *Santa Clara:* Ibid., 52.

16 *The rebels took:* Gillian McGillivray, *Blazing Cane: Sugar Communities, Class and State Formation in Cuba, 1868–1959* (Durham: Duke University Press, 2009), 60.

16 *The rebels called:* David C. Carlson, *In the Fist of Earlier Revolutions* (Chapel Hill: University of North Carolina Press, 2007).

16 *Revolutionary leaders such:* Gillian McGillivray, *Blazing Cane,* 38.

16 *"destroying a social . . . system":* Ibid., 38.

17 *At 9:40 on the night:* James Rankin Young and Joseph Hampton Moore, *History of Our War with Spain including Battles on Sea and Land* (Washington, D.C.: National Publishing Company, 1898), 59.

17 *The death toll:* Louis Fisher, *The Destruction of the Maine (1898)*, The Law Library of Congress publication, August 24, 2009.

18 *On January 1, 1899, John P. Wade:* George Washington Cullum, *Biographical Register of the Officers and Graduates of the U.S. Military Academy at West Point, N.Y.* (Saginaw, Mich.: Seemann & Peters, 1920), 762.

18 *He refused to attend:* Leslie Bethell, ed., *The Cambridge History of Latin America*, vol. 5 (Cambridge, U.K.: Cambridge University Press, 1986), 246.

18 *In Santo Domingo:* U.S. War Dept., Cuban Census Office, *Report on the Census of Cuba, 1899* (Washington D.C.: Government Printing Office, 1900).

18 *When U.S. forces:* John R. Brooke, *Civil Report of Major-General John R. Brooke* (Washington, D.C.: Government Printing Office, 1900), 9.

19 *As a youth:* Class "B" Medical Certificate of Pedro Víctor García, Miami Florida Station, Dec. 18, 1956, provided by the National Archives of the United States.

19 *"He couldn't work:* Remarks by Marco Rubio at the Reagan Presidential Library, Simi Valley, California, Aug. 23, 2011.

21 *Prío later quipped:* Joan Didion, *Miami* (New York: Simon & Schuster, 1987), 12.

21 *It's no wonder that:* Application for immigrant visa and alien registration, Pedro Víctor García, American vice consul at Havana, Cuba, provided by U.S. National Archives.

CHAPTER TWO: A PATH TO CITIZENSHIP

23 *National Airlines Flight:* Mario Rubio, United States of America immigrant visa and alien registration at Port of Miami, May 27, 1956, provided by U.S. Citizenship and Immigration Services, U.S. Department of Homeland Security, National Records Center.

23 *For a time:* Louis A. Pérez, *On Becoming Cuban: Identity, Nationality and Culture* (Chapel Hill: The University of North Carolina Press, 1999), 435.

24 *Nine days earlier:* Mario Rubio, application for immigrant visa and alien registration, Foreign Service of the United States of America, American vice consul, Havana, Cuba, May 18, 1956, provided by U.S.

Citizenship and Immigration Services, U.S. Department of Homeland Security, National Records Center.

24 *The lineups in:* Baseball-reference.com, Box Score, Indians vs White Sox, May 27, 1956, http://www.baseball-reference.com/boxes/CHA/CHA195605271.shtml.

24 *At Fenway Park:* Baseball-reference.com, Box Score, Senators vs Red Sox, May 27, 1956, http://www.baseball-reference.com/boxes/BOS/BOS195605272.shtml.

25 *By the time:* Peter C. Bjarkman website, http://www.baseballdecuba.com/NewsContainer.asp?id=2558.

25 *In the reductive:* Mario Rubio, Application for immigrant visa and alien registration, May 18, 1956.

25 *No more than:* Annual Report of the Immigration and Naturalization Service for 1956, Department of Justice, 42.

25 *The Cuban National:* Affidavit by Mario Rubio, National Police, Cuban Ministry of Defense, Apr. 10, 1956.

26 *A prison archivist:* Certificate issued by Arsenio Fariñas Moreno, archives manager of the Vivac prison in Havana, Apr. 10, 1956.

26 *The head of:* Certificate issued by the Havana Local Recruiting Commission of the Republic of Cuba, Folio Number 64, Volume 20 of the Registry Book of military inscriptions, Jan. 26, 1956.

26 *On Mario's visa:* Mario Rubio, Application for immigrant visa, May 18, 1956.

26 *Mario was either:* Marco Rubio, letter written upon the death of his father, Sept. 4, 2010.

26 *On the same:* Remarks by Marco Rubio at the Conservative Political Action Conference, Washington, D.C., Feb. 18, 2010.

26 *As a teenager:* Marco Rubio, letter upon the death of his father, Sept. 4, 2010, http://saintpetersblog.com/2010/09/heartbreaking-inspiring-and-a-must-read-a-letter-from-marco-rubio-about-the-passing-of-his-father/.

26 *Senator Rubio has:* Sen. Marco Rubio, interview by author, Oct. 20, 2011.

26 *In 2012, Marco Rubio:* Marc Caputo, "Three things you didn't know about Marco Rubio," *Miami Herald*, Feb. 23, 2012.

27 *It had the region's:* Cuba Transition Project, "Socioeconomic Conditions in Pre-Castro Cuba," Cuba Facts, Institute for Cuban & Cuban-American Studies, University of Miami, Issue 43, Dec. 2008.

27 *30 percent of:* 1956–57 study cited in Jaime Suchliki, *Cuba: From Columbus to Castro* (New York: Scribner, 1974), 152.

27 *Then in April, 1956:* Patricia Sullivan, "Ramon M. Barquin, 93; Led failed '56 coup in Cuba," *Washington Post*, Mar. 6, 2008.

27 *Earlier migration patterns:* Lisándro Pérez, "Cubans in the United States," http://latinamericanstudies.org/exile/cubans.pdf.

27 *Migration spiked:* Lisándro Pérez, "Cubans in the United States," *AAPSS Annals*, Sept. 1986, 127.

28 *In 1953 the average:* Remarks by John F. Kennedy at Democratic Dinner, Cincinnati, Ohio, Oct. 6, 1960, http://www.jfklibrary.org/Research/Ready-Reference/JFK-Speeches/Remarks-of-Senator-John-F-Kennedy-at-Democratic-Dinner-Cincinnati-Ohio-October-6-1960.aspx.

28 *and in 1956:* Jaime Suchliki, *Cuba: From Columbus to Castro and Beyond* (Washington, D.C.: Potomac Books, 2002), 119.

28 *Two years later:* Tad Szulc, *Fidel: A Critical Portrait* (New York: Avon, 1987), 20.

29 *Oriales's sister and:* Luís Enrique Lastres and Irma García Rodriguez de Lastres, Affidavit of Support, United States Immigration and Naturalization Services, May 26, 1956, provided by National Archives of the United States.

29 *Irma was making:* J. Enolff, Tama Sportswear Inc., Letter regarding character reference and salary information, New York, Nov. 7, 1956.

29 *Luís Enrique was:* George Goldberg, Jollé Jewelers International Inc. Letter confirming salary and employment, New York, Nov. 7, 1956.

29 *On the day before:* Luís Enrique Lastres and Irma García Rodriguez de Lastres, Affidavit of Support, May 26, 1956.

30 *The Lastreses had:* Ibid.

30 *Six months later:* Luís Enrique Lastres and Irma García Rodriguez de Lastres, Affidavit of Support, United States Immigration and Naturalization Services, Nov. 10, 1956.

30 *Pedro Víctor followed:* Class "B" Medical Certificate of Pedro Víctor García, Miami Florida Station, Dec. 18, 1956, provided by the National Archives of the United States.

30 *The report, reflecting:* Ibid.

30 *His spine was:* Ibid.

30 *"We are willing:* Luís Enrique Lastres and Irma García Rodriguez de Lastres, Affidavit of Support, Nov. 10, 1956.

31 *For the meantime:* Exclusion hearing worksheet and memorandum, U.S. Department of Justice Immigration and Naturalization Service, Oct. 4, 1962.

31 *For a time:* William J. Bennett, *The Book of Man: Readings on the Path to Manhood* (Nashville, Tenn.: Thomas Nelson, 2011).

31 *It appears that:* Polk's *Miami Beach (Dade County, Fla.) City Directory, 1958* (Miami: R.L. Polk & Co., Publishers, 1958), 433.

31 *The Roney was a:* Patricia Kennedy, *Miami Beach in Vintage Postcards* (Charleston, SC: Acadia Publishing, 2000).

31 *Celebrities flocked to:* Larry Shupnick, interview by author, Nov. 18, 2011.

32 *It was not uncommon:* Ibid.

32 *Bartenders at the:* Ibid.

32 *Frequent flights in:* Alejandro Portes and Alex Stepick, *City on the Edge: The Transformation of Miami* (Los Angeles: University of California Press, 1993), 100.

33 *In 1958, as:* Robert M. Levine and Moises Asis, *Cuban Miami* (Piscataway, NJ: Rutgers University Press, 2000), 21.

33 *Reflecting the prevailing:* Helen Muir, *Miami U.S.A.* (Gainesville: University Press of Florida, 2000), 240.

33 *Police supervisors were:* Ibid.

34 *"His primary concern:* Richard Nixon, Confidential Memorandum of Vice President Nixon, conversation with Fidel Castro, Apr. 25, 1959, http://www.gwu.edu/~nsarchiv/bayofpigs/19590425.pdf.

35 *Pedro Víctor lived:* Pedro Víctor García, audio recording of Exclusion Hearing, U.S. Department of Justice Immigration and Naturalization Service, Miami, Oct. 4, 1962.

35 *He repaired shoes:* Ibid.

35 *"I had to:* Ibid.

35 *On Jan. 15, 1959:* Ibid.

35 *He had left behind:* Ibid.

35 *For the first three:* Ibid.

35 *The job was with:* Ibid.

36 *Years later:* Ibid.

36 *He rented an apartment:* Ibid.

37 *Rents for the:* Mark Falcoff, *Cuba the Morning After: Confronting Castro's Legacy* (Jackson, TN: American Enterprise Institute Press, 2003).

37 *Six days later:* Pedro Víctor García, audio recording of Exclusion Hearing, Oct. 4, 1962.

37 *"How could I have:* Peter Wyden, *Bay of Pigs: The Untold Story* (New York: Simon & Schuster, 1979), 8.

37 *The United States eventually:* Report on the Bay of Pigs, John F. Kennedy Presidential Library and Museum, http://www.jfklibrary.org/JFK/JFK-in-History/The-Bay-of-Pigs.aspx.

38 *As the band:* Michael Dobbs, *One Minute to Midnight: Kennedy, Khrushchev, and Castro on the Brink of Nuclear War* (New York: Vintage Books, 2009), 149.

38 *The block committees:* Manuel Roig-Franzia, "Cuba's Waning System of Block-Watchers; Raúl Castro May Push to Revitalize a Legacy, and Enforcement Tool, of the Revolution," *Washington Post*, Oct. 30, 2007.

38 *"The CDRs paralyzed:* Ibid.

39 *He boarded:* Memorandum of Special Inquiry Officer to Immigration Officer, United States Department of Justice, Immigration and Naturalization Service, Miami, Aug. 31, 1962.

39 *A U.S. immigration:* Notice to Applicant for Admission Detained for Hearing before Special Inquiry Officer, Form I-122, United States Department of Justice, Immigration and Naturalization Service, Miami, Aug. 31, 1962.

41 *On October 4, 1962:* Exclusion hearing worksheet and memorandum, Oct. 4, 1962. Milich would be involved in a series of high-profile proceedings in the years to come, including the strange Vietnam-era case of a draft dodger who had fled to Canada and formally renounced his U.S. citizenship without becoming a citizen of any other country. Milich ordered that man deported from the United States.

41 *Pedro Víctor's hearing was:* Ibid.

42 *And before getting:* Pedro Víctor García, audio recording of Exclusion Hearing, Oct. 4, 1962.

42 *"Señor, levante su mano:* Ibid.

47 *"Within the past week:* Televised remarks by President John F. Kennedy, Nov. 12, 1962.

48 *Pedro Víctor's legal:* Pedro Víctor García, audio recording of Exclusion Hearing, Oct. 4, 1962.

48 *The next summer:* Pedro Víctor García, Application by Cuban Refugee for Permanent Residence, United States Department of Justice, Immigration and Naturalization Service, Miami, Aug. 2, 1967.

48 *Refugee status may:* Bill Yates, interview by author, Nov. 12, 2011.

CHAPTER THREE: THE MIAMI SON

51 *In the first two:* Mario Rubio, Application to file petition for naturalization, U.S. Department of Justice, Immigration and Naturalization Service, Mar. 4, 1975.

51 *On game day:* Statement of official colors of the Miami Dolphins at NFLshop.com, available at http://www.nflshop.com/category/index .jsp?categoryId=716624.

52 *The cheers would:* Mario Rubio, Application to file petition for naturalization, Mar. 4, 1975.

52 *The Rubio family:* Ibid.

52 *Their house sat:* Joan Didion, *Miami* (New York: Simon & Schuster, 1987), 11.

53 *"As a young child:* Marco Rubio, letter written upon the death of his father, Sept. 4, 2010, http://saintpetersblog.com/2010/09/heartbreaking -inspiring-and-a-must-read-a-letter-from-marco-rubio-about-the-passing -of-his-father/.

53 *Kennedy took the:* John F. Kennedy, address on the return of Bay of Pigs prisoners, Miami, Dec. 29, 1962, http://www.youtube.com/watch?v=bg WRxNUR494.

53 *But the memory:* Alejandro Portes and Alex Stepick, *City on the Edge* (Los Angeles: University of California Press, 1993), 142.

54 *During the ceremony:* John F. Kennedy Presidential Library and Museum, article on the Bay of Pigs, http://www.jfklibrary.org/JFK/JFK-in -History/The-Bay-of-Pigs.aspx.

54 *By 1980, Cuban:* "The Cuban Refugee Problem in Perspective, 1959– 1980," Heritage Foundation Reports, July 18, 1980.

54 *On average Cubans:* Ibid.

Notes

54 *The sociologist Juan M. Clark:* Ibid.

54 *Just two decades:* Ibid.

54 *Years later, Marco:* Marco Rubio, letter written upon the death of his father, Sept. 4, 2010.

55 *On March 4:* United States Department of Justice, Immigration and Naturalization Service, application to file petition for naturalization, Mario Rubio, Mar. 4, 1975.

55 *During the 227:* Ibid.

55 *A handwritten note:* United States Department of Justice, order to appear for a hearing on petition of naturalization, Mario Rubio, Oct. 22, 1975.

55 *He was an:* United States Department of Justice, certificate of naturalization number 10196055, Mario Rubio, Nov. 5, 1975.

55 *For at least five and a half years prior to becoming a citizen, until:* Ibid.

55 *The famed architect:* Jeffrey Limerick, *America's Grand Resort Hotels* (New York: Pantheon, 1979), 44.

56 *In frothier times:* Gypsy Rose Lee, *Gypsy: Memoirs of America's Most Celebrated Stripper* (New York: Harper, 1957), 347.

56 *the hotel once painted:* "The Shah by the Seashore," *Life*, Feb. 14, 1955.

56 *By 1977:* Patrick Riordan, "Miami Beach Tourist Development Authority," *Miami Herald*, July 7, 1977.

56 *He took them:* Marco Rubio, letter upon the death of his father, Sept. 4, 2010.

57 *The six years:* Ibid.

57 *In the 1970s:* Eugene P. Moehring, *Resort City in the Sunbelt, Second edition* (Reno and Las Vegas: University of Nevada Press, 2000), 264.

57 *In 1980, the:* Ibid., 265.

57 *And even though:* Mary Manning and Andy Samuelson, "A Gamble in the Sand: How Las Vegas Transformed Itself from a Railroad Watering Hole to the 'Entertainment Capital of the World,'" *Las Vegas Sun*, May 15, 2008.

57 *It had been built:* Website of Boyd Gaming, www.boydgaming.com/about-boyd/mission-and-history.

57 *Despite twenty years:* Marco Rubio, letter upon the death of his father, Sept. 4, 2010.

57 *They set up:* Ibid.

Notes

57 *"He would write:* Alex Leary, "A Speaker of Intrigue and Ambition," *St. Petersburg Times,* Mar. 4, 2007.

58 *"I remember when:* Ibid.

58 *In neighborhood games:* Ibid.

58 *Armando Denis:* Mo Denis for Assembly, official website, http://www .modenis.com/biography.htm.

58 *Dolores and Armando:* Obituary of Dolores Denis, *Las Vegas Review-Journal,* Mar. 4, 2008.

58 *"[Marco] has much:* Ray Hagar and Anjeanette Damon, "Capital Notes," *Reno Gazette-Journal,* Apr. 17, 2005.

58 *Like his parents:* Ibid.

59 *Mario, who had:* McKay Coppins, "Marco Rubio's Mormon Roots," BuzzFeed.com, Feb. 23, 2012, http://www.buzzfeed.com/mckaycop pins/exclusive-marco-rubios-mormon-roots.

59 *"When they lived:* Mo Denis interview with Univision, Nov. 2011, provided by Univision.

59 *"He was totally:* McKay Coppins, "Marco Rubio's Mormon Roots," BuzzFeed.com, Feb. 23, 2012.

59 *Marco attended LDS:* Ibid.

60 *"It was just:* Ibid.

60 *"When he was a kid:* Author interview with confidential source, 2011.

60 *The grandfather's loquaciousness:* Tim Elfrink, "Marco Rubio, Tea Party Pretty Boy," *Miami New Times,* July 22, 2010.

61 *"My parents feared:* Marco Rubio, letter upon the death of his father, Sept. 4, 2010.

61 *Marco has said:* McKay Coppins, "Marco Rubio's Mormon Roots," BuzzFeed.com, Feb. 23, 2012.

61 *"When they returned:* Mo Denis interview with Univision, Nov. 2011.

61 *"He really convinced:* McKay Coppins, "Marco Rubio's Mormon Roots," BuzzFeed.com, Feb. 23, 2012.

61 *There were so many:* Joseph Davis quoted in *Cocaine Cowboys,* film released in 2006, directed by Billy Corben.

62 *"What I see:* Ibid.

62 *"For Fidel Castro:* Ralph Renick quoted in *Cocaine Cowboys.*

63 *"Mariel was very:* Alfonso Chardy, "Mariel Boatlift Tested Miami's Strength, Then Made It Stronger," *Miami Herald,* Apr. 25, 2010.

Notes

63 *Mario found a:* Marco Rubio, letter upon the death of his father, Sept. 4, 2010.

63 *The* Herald *called:* Fred Tasker, "Hold the Hype for a Few Little Details," *Miami Herald*, Aug. 7, 1985.

63 *One review that:* Tom O'Toole and Joanne O'Toole, "Things Looking Up for Boom-and-Bust Miami," *Globe and Mail (Toronto)*, Nov. 30, 1985.

63 *The hotel manager:* Fred Tasker, "Hold the Hype for a Few Little Details," Aug. 7, 1985.

64 *"It was an Hispanic:* Fran Cosgrove, interview by author, Nov. 2011.

65 *James Colzie, who:* James Colzie, interview by author, Nov. 16, 2011.

65 *"One of the best-:* Sam Miller, interview by author, Nov. 16, 2011.

65 *"He wasn't the most:* Otis Collier, interview by author, Nov. 17, 2011.

65 *Marco played in:* Otis Collier, interview by author, Nov. 17, 2011.

65 *"He was not fast:* James Colzie, interview by author, Nov. 16, 2011.

66 *"He pushes himself:* Elfrink, "Marco Rubio, Tea Party Pretty Boy," July 22, 2010.

66 *"You could always:* Ibid.

66 *"We played it:* Otis Collier, interview by author, Nov. 17, 2011.

67 *Kenneth Dodd, who:* Kenneth Dodd, interview by author, Nov. 20, 2011.

67 *"That type of:* Ibid.

68 *Players shed tears in:* Mike Phillips, "Season Ends One Point Too Soon for South Miami," *Miami Herald*, Dec. 5, 1987.

68 *On December 16:* Jeff Leen, "Miami Cops Tied to Another Drug Ring," *Miami Herald*, Dec. 17, 1987.

68 *The indictment paints:* Indictment of Orlando Cicilia.

68 *the gang orbited:* Ibid.

69 *The other Tabraue:* Frank Cerabino, "Trial of Alleged Jewelry-Store Drug Ring Begins," *Miami Herald*, Nov. 4, 1988.

69 *He had been a:* David Lyons, "Jeweler Tabraue Gets 5-year Sentence, Fine," *Miami Herald*, May 25, 1989.

70 *There were only:* Mike Phillips, "S. Miami Beats Gables in a Game without Fans," *Miami Herald*, Sept. 23, 1988.

70 *"Marco Rubio was:* Elfrink, "Marco Rubio, Tea Party Pretty Boy," July 22, 2010.

70 *On October 27:* Mike Phillips, "Homestead Holds off S. Miami," *Miami Herald*, Oct. 28, 1988.

70 *"We should have:* John J. Miller, "Rubio Rising—The Florida GOP Has a New Star," *National Review,* Sept. 7, 2009.

71 *But Kellner stepped:* Richard Cole, "U.S. Attorney Who Indicted Noriega Resigns," Associated Press, June 18, 1988.

71 *Dexter was a:* Bob Minzesheimer, "New Woman of the House," *USA Today,* Sept. 7, 1989.

71 *If it had been:* Frank Cerabino, "Trial of Alleged Jewelry-Store Drug Ring Begins," *Miami Herald,* Nov. 4, 1988.

71 *Mario Tabraue's attorney:* Ibid.

71 *The case went:* Frank Cerabino, "Tabraue Drug Trial Now in Jury's Hands," *Miami Herald,* Jan. 27, 1989.

71 *The ringleader:* "Key Figure in Drug-Smuggling Ring Draws 100 Years," Associated Press, Apr. 13, 1989.

71 *Cicilia received the:* Ibid.

72 *The government seized:* United States of America vs. Orlando Cicilia, Final Judgment of Forfeiture, Jun. 15, 1989.

72 *The other alleged:* Associated Press, "Key Figure in Drug-Smuggling Ring Draws 100 Years."

72 *They later got:* David Lyons, "Jeweler Tabraue Gets 5-Year Sentence, Fine," May 25, 1989.

73 *Tim Elfrink of:* Tim Elfrink, "Tea Party Pretty Boy," July 22, 2010.

73 *also added a:* South Miami high school yearbook.

73 *"We sent out:* Sam Miller, interview by author, Nov. 16, 2011.

73 *In those days:* Mike Muxo, interview by author, Dec. 14, 2011.

74 *"I explained to:* Mike Muxo, interview by author, Dec. 14, 2011.

74 *Tarkio did not:* Doyle Slayton, interview by author, Dec. 7, 2011.

74 *Marco showed up:* interview by author, Northwest Missouri State University registrar's office (custodian of Tarkio College records), October 2011.

74 *When placekickers booted:* Mike Muxo, interview by author, Dec. 14, 2011.

75 *The population of:* 1990 U.S. Census data.

75 *"If you blink:* Doyle Slayton, interview by author, Dec. 7, 2011.

75 *The nearest McDonald's:* Mike Muxo, interview by author, Dec. 14, 2011.

75 *The football players:* Ibid.

75 *Tarkio played in:* Heart of America conference list, published in *St. Louis Post-Dispatch*, Dec. 20, 1989.

75 *At Tarkio, which:* Doyle Slayton, interview by author, Dec. 7, 2011.

75 *One afternoon he:* Ibid.

76 *The month before:* Jo Ann Tooley, Marianna I. Knight, and Joannie M. Schrof, "A Class of Deadbeats," *U.S. News & World Report*, July 3, 1989.

76 *The school had:* Associated Press, "Tarkio College Gets Probation," *St. Louis Post-Dispatch*, Nov. 10, 1989.

76 *His wife, Catherine:* Catherine Slayton, interview by author, Dec. 7, 2011.

76 *The Slaytons and:* Doyle Slayton, interview by author, Dec. 7, 2011.

76 *Most were poor:* Anthony DePalma, "A College Acts in Desperation and Dies Playing the Lender," *New York Times*, Apr. 17, 1991.

77 *"Basically what you:* Ibid.

77 *He lived on:* Marco Rubio, letter upon the death of his father, Sept. 4, 2010.

78 *"He would always:* Zac Anderson, "Money Matters Follow Candidate Rubio," *Herald Tribune*, Sept. 20, 2010.

78 *"If this election:* Andrew Phillips, "Battle in the Sun: To Dole and Clinton, as Florida Goes, So Goes the Presidency," *Maclean's*, Oct. 21, 1996.

78 *"It kind of:* Leary, "A Speaker of Intrigue and Ambition."

CHAPTER FOUR: THE APPRENTICE

82 *Excluding the island:* 2000 U.S. Census data, analyzed by ePodunk, http://www.epodunk.com/ancestry/Cuban.html.

82 *Back in the 1940s:* Miami-Dade Transportation and Community Mapping, Community History Report, Florida International University GIS-RS Center and Metropolitan Center, http://mpoportal.fiu.edu/community_history_view.cfm?hist_id=25.

82 *Soldiers returning from:* Ibid.

82 *"But the place:* Cecile Betancourt, "West Miami Begins Beautification with Live Oaks; 50 Young Trees to Be Planted," *Miami Herald*, Jul. 15, 1998.

83 *"Its real estate:* Cesar Carasa, interview by author, Nov. 1, 2011.

83 *It became a haven:* Tania Rozio, interview by author, Nov. 5, 2011.

83 *"A small town:* Ibid.

83 *Now, when:* Website of the West Miami Police Department, "House Checks," http://westmiamipolice.org/.

83 *"How many nights:* Remarks by Marco Rubio at the Conservative Political Action Conference, Washington, D.C., Feb. 18, 2010, http://www.youtube.com/watch?v=8XY0pX5xBGE.

84 *"She has kind:* Cristina Silva, "To Love, Honor and Campaign for, Ladies," *St. Petersburg Times,* Aug. 1, 2010.

84 *At first glance:* Tim Elfrink, "Marco Rubio, Tea Party Pretty Boy," *Miami New Times,* July 22, 2010.

84 *"He started talking:* Elfrink, "Marco Rubio, Tea Party Pretty Boy."

85 *Now a member:* Cesar Carasa, interview by author, Nov. 1, 2011.

85 *On January 13, 1998:* Marco Rubio, Florida Department of State Division of Elections, Campaign Treasurer's Report Summary, Jan. 1–Mar. 20, 1998.

85 *Cardenas tossed in:* Ibid.

85 *Rubio also got $200:* Jake Bernstein, "Florida Bank, Used as ATM by Insiders, Won TARP Loan But Now Teeters," ProPublica, Oct. 22, 2011.

85 *In March Rubio:* Marco Rubio, Campaign Treasurer's Report Summary, Florida Department of State Division of Elections, Mar. 27, 1998.

86 *[Rubio] had a lot:* Tonia Rozio, interview by author, Nov. 5, 2011.

86 *He always wanted:* Danny Ruiz, interview by author, Dec. 15, 2011.

86 *"I'd like our: Herald* Staff, "Meet the Candidates," *Miami Herald,* Apr. 5, 1998.

86 *When Rozio first:* Tonia Rozio, interview by author, Nov. 5, 2011.

87 *"Nobody was out:* Danny Ruiz, interview by author, Dec. 15, 2011.

87 *"It was Jeb Bush:* Elfrink, "Marco Rubio, Tea Party Pretty Boy."

87 *On June 12, 1998:* Frank Davies, "Sen. Gutman Indicted on Fraud Counts, Lawmaker Says He'll Fight Charges," *Miami Herald,* June 13, 1998.

88 *U.S. Attorney Thomas:* Jay Weaver, "Gutman's Career on the Line; State Senator Faces Medicare Fraud Charges, Says He's Innocent," *Sun-Sentinel,* Jun. 13, 1998.

88 *"This would never:* Will Lester, "Court: Carollo Is Mayor of Miami," Associated Press, Mar. 11, 1998.

88 *A Florida newspaperman Robert:* Robert Andrew Powell, "Miami Vice:

A New Golden Era of Government Corruption," *Newsday*, Jul. 5, 1998.

89 *Valdes had been*: Website of Carlos Valdes, http://www.carlosvaldes .com/, accessed Mar. 12, 2012.

90 *"In the Florida*: Dan Gelber, interview by author, Oct. 28, 2011.

90 *A poll taken*: Karen Branch, "Eight Contend for House Seats," *Miami Herald*, Dec. 1, 1999.

90 *Rodriguez-Chomat had earlier*: Adam C. Smith, "Lawmakers Engage in Roughhousing," *St. Petersburg Times*, Apr. 10, 1998.

90 *By the third*: Ibid.

91 *Ponce, who was recovering*: Joan Fleischman, "Miami Nice Personi-fied," *Miami Herald*, Oct. 12, 1998.

91 *Just a few days*: Mike Bryant and Rosy Pastrana, Miami-Dade Elections Department, email correspondence with author, Jan. 25, 2012.

91 *Three out of*: Branch, "Eight Contend for House Seats."

91 *"Everybody's a carpetbagger*: Jose Fuentes, interview by author, Dec. 15, 2011.

92 *He called it*: Cecile Betancourt, "City's First Bike Officer Takes Road Less Traveled," *Miami Herald*, Jun. 28, 1998.

92 *"Now I know why*: Cecile Betancourt, "W. Miami Debates Commis-sioner's 'Free Ride,' " *Miami Herald*, June 21, 1998.

93 *The message Rubio*: Cesar Carasa, interview by author, Nov. 1, 2011.

93 *In the days*: Ivette M. Yee and Charles Savage, "Primary Candidates Rake in the Contributions," *Miami Herald*, Dec. 14, 1999.

93 *"He can turn*: "The Herald Recommends for Florida House District 111," editorial, *Miami Herald*, Dec. 10, 1999.

93 *"Thirty percent of*: Ivette M. Yee, "House District 111 Voters to Choose Rep. on Tuesday," *Miami Herald*, Jan. 20, 2000.

94 *"The thought process*: Danny Ruiz, interview by author, Dec. 15, 2011.

94 *During the race*: Author interview with confidential source, 2011.

94 *For a time*: Ibid.

95 *Lehtinen would have*: James Rowley, "Justice investigating Miami US Attorney for Misconduct," Associated Press, Apr. 28, 1990.

95 *Rubio's mentor from*: Modesto Pérez, interview by author, Nov. 1, 2011.

96 *Rodriguez served in*: Regino Rodriguez, interview by author, Nov. 1, 2011.

97 *"It was a:* Modesto Pérez, interview by author, Nov. 1, 2011.

98 *"I did not:* Raul L. Martinez, interview by author, Mar. 6, 2012.

98 *"He knows how:* Regino Rodriguez, interview by author, Nov. 1, 2011.

98 *Pérez told the:* Modesto Pérez, interview by author, Nov. 1, 2011.

99 *"[Rubio] came over:* Ibid.

99 *Alex Penelas, the:* Ivette M. Lee, "District 111 Candidate's War Chest Tops $99,000," *Miami Herald,* Jan. 22, 2000.

99 *Rubio amassed more:* Ibid.

CHAPTER FIVE: THE ALCHEMIST

101 *Pickens was amazed:* Joe Pickens, interview by author, Dec. 6, 2011.

102 *He recalled, "Half:* Lloyd Dunkelberger and Gary Fineout, "Battle over 2006 Speaker Shaping Up," *Lakeland Ledger,* Aug. 3, 2003.

102 *But sitting there:* Ibid.

103 *Years later Byrd:* Johnnie Byrd, interview by author, Dec. 5, 2011.

103 *At the time:* Lesley Clark, "Marco Rubio Makes Mark as GOP Wonder Boy," *Miami Herald,* Mar. 9, 2003.

104 *"They may take:* Dan Gelber, interview by author, Oct. 28, 2011.

104 *He liked the younger:* Johnnie Byrd, interview by author, Dec. 5, 2011.

105 *"I know Ralph:* Jim Ash, "Fla. House Speaker Byrd Serious about His Spanish," *Palm Beach Post,* Nov. 24, 2002.

105 *But by the time:* Fred Barnes, "Demolition Derby in Florida, Can Marco Rubio Prevail?," *Weekly Standard,* Aug. 9, 2010.

106 *"I spent a lot:* Johnnie Byrd, interview by author, Dec. 5, 2011.

106 *And the club:* Federal Election Commission campaign data, analyzed by OpenSecrets.org, http://www.opensecrets.org/politicians/summary .php?cid=N00030612&cycle=2012.

106 *During his early years:* PolitiFact, "Marco Rubio Wasn't Always against Earmarks," Nov. 16, 2010.

107 *Later, Rubio would:* Jim DeMint, *The Great American Awakening* (Nashville: B & H Publishing Group, 2011).

107 *But the comparison:* Janny Scott, "In Illinois, Obama Proved Pragmatic and Shrewd," *New York Times,* July 30, 2007.

108 *"All those deals:* Author interview with confidential source, Nov. 2011.

108 *Byrd could be:* Jim Ash, "House Speaker Stirs Budget Pot," *Palm Beach Post,* Apr. 7, 2003.

Notes

108 *Once he said:* Steve Bousquet, "Byrd's 'Sheep' Analogy Riles Colleagues," *St. Petersburg Times*, Feb. 26, 2004.

108 *When Byrd's style:* Ash, "Fla. House Speaker Byrd Serious about His Spanish."

109 *if Republicans weren't:* Peter Wallsten, "Drug Plan a Cure for What Ails GOP," *Miami Herald*, Feb. 23, 2003.

109 *But when the budgets:* Jim Ash, "House Speaker Stirs Budget Pot," *Palm Beach Post*, Apr. 7, 2003.

110 *"Their constituents would:* Jim Saunders, "Bush Calls Special Session May 12," *Daytona Beach News-Journal*, May 3, 2003.

110 *But Rubio's eyes:* Author interview with confidential source, Feb. 2011.

110 *Once, Florida's lieutenant:* Nancy Cook Lauer, " 'New Democrats to Watch' List Includes Ausley," *Tallahassee Democrat*, May 18, 2003.

111 *"It was the:* Jeff Kottkamp, interview with author, Mar. 13, 2012.

112 *That practice continued:* Gary Fineout, "Thanks to a Campaign Finance Loophole Many Lawmakers Are Raising SECRET MONEY," *Sarasota Herald-Tribune*, Sept. 28, 2003.

112 *Rubio initially defended:* Steve Bousquet, "Lawmakers Secretly Raise Big Bucks," *St. Petersburg Times*, Sept. 28, 2003.

112 *When the names:* Adam C. Smith, Beth Reinhard, and Scott Hiaasen, "Marco Rubio's Lavish Rise to the Top," *St. Petersburg Times* and *Miami Herald*, Mar. 12, 2010.

113 *"I am proud:* Ibid.

113 *"The bookkeeping:* Ibid.

113 *"He's not the:* Author interview with confidential source, 2012.

114 *Most felt they:* Author interview with confidential sources.

114 *"Marco actually:* Joe Pickens, interview by author, Dec. 6, 2011.

115 *"We kind of:* Author interview with confidential source.

117 *"There were a lot:* J. C. Planas, interview by author, Oct. 11, 2011.

117 *When I asked:* Dennis Baxley, interview by author, Dec. 6, 2011.

118 *Later Rubio gave:* Jan Pudlow, "Rubio to Lead House: Lawyer-Legislator Takes Center Stage in 2006," *Florida Bar News*, Apr. 1, 2005.

119 *"There are people:* "Some Opt for Baseball over Legislative Vote," Associated Press, Oct. 28, 2003.

119 *Looking back:* Fred Brummer, interview by author, Dec. 15, 2011.

119 *"There wasn't any:* Ibid.

119 *A chartered Falcon:* Mary Ellen Klas and Lesley Clark, "Rubio Sets Goals Issues Challenge," *Miami Herald*, Sept. 14, 2005.

120 *Years later Modesto:* Modesto Pérez, interview by author, Nov. 1, 2011.

120 *And he was given:* Bousquet, "House Makes History with Choice of Speaker."

122 *The nickname was:* Adam Smith, "Marco Rubio Is the Messiah," *St. Petersburg Times*, The Buzz blog, Mar. 23, 2010.

122 *"That was a:* Author interview with confidential source.

122 *"One of the:* Dennis Baxley, interview by author, Dec. 6, 2011.

123 *The Miami-Dade:* Rebecca Wakefield, "Miami Dade County Days: Welcome to Fabulous Tallahassee Where Your Humble State Legislators Work Hard by Day and Play Hard by Night," *Miami New Times*, Apr. 22, 2004.

123 *An analysis by:* Amy Keller, "Cheap Labor: Fla. Lawmakers," *Florida Trend*, Oct. 1, 2009.

123 *Rubio's income, however:* Marco Rubio, "Full and Public Disclosure of Financial Interests," Florida Commission on Ethics, Aug. 8, 2003; and "Final Full and Public Disclosure of Financial Interests," Commission on Ethics, Feb. 9, 2009. Available from Florida Commission on Ethics.

123 *Starting in 2004:* Marco Rubio, "Full and Public Disclosure of Financial Interests," Florida Commission on Ethics, 2006, 2007, 2008. Available from Florida Commission on Ethics.

123 *The firm did:* Zac Anderson, "Money Matters Follow Candidate Rubio," *Herald Tribune*, Sept. 20, 2010.

124 *"Rubio's approach came:* Carol E. Lee, "Rubio, Hotly Wooed, Plays Cool," *Wall Street Journal*, Jan. 28, 2012.

124 *"They really hit it:* Ibid.

124 *"This is as smart:* Mary Ellen Klas, "Rubio on GOP Mission," *Miami Herald*, Mar. 20, 2006.

124 *"I think they:* Ibid.

124 *The ideas range:* Marco Rubio, *100 Innovative Ideas for Florida's Future* (Washington, D.C.: Regnery, 2006), 136, 57, 70, 168.

125 *In April 2006:* Jim Ash, "Agency Woes Not Helping Gay-Adoption Advocates," *Tallahassee Democrat*, Apr. 6, 2006.

125 *"Some of these kids:* Ibid.

125 *"Documentary stamp tax:* Fred Brummer, interview by author, Dec. 15, 2011.

126 *"You deal the cards:* Dan Gelber, interview by author, Oct. 28, 2011.

126 *"A bully,"* *Brummer:* Fred Brummer, interview by author, Dec. 15, 2011.

126 *"One of the most:* Author interview with confidential source, 2012.

127 *"He punted on:* Carol Marbin Miller and Marc Caputo, "Arza Won't Heed Calls to Resign," *Miami Herald*, Oct. 25, 2006.

127 *"When you have:* Mary Ellen Klas, "Arza Scandal Puts Incoming Speaker Rubio in Tough Spot," *Miami Herald*, Nov. 6, 2006.

128 *Six months later:* Susannah A. Nesmith, "Ex Rep. Arza gets Probation in Voice Mail Case," *Miami Herald*, May 25, 2007.

128 *He hired a:* Alex Leary and Steve Bousquet, "New House Speaker Paying New Aides Hefty Wages," *St. Petersburg Times*, Dec. 1, 2006.

129 *"The joke was:* Fred Brummer, interview by author, Dec. 15, 2011.

129 *Three of the previous:* Alex Leary, "Rubio Already Changes House," *St. Petersburg Times*, Aug. 31, 2006.

129 *He argued, "There's:* J. Taylor Rushing, "Speaker's Spending Draws Scrutiny," *Florida Times-Union*, Dec. 8, 2006.

129 *He did it so often:* Author interview with confidential source.

129 *"For some people:* Dennis Baxley, interview by author, Dec. 6, 2011.

130 *During his apprenticeship:* Johnnie Byrd, interview by author, Dec. 5, 2011.

131 *At the back:* Dan Gelber, interview by author, Oct. 28, 2011.

131 *Rubio was still:* Marco Rubio tweet, Oct. 25, 2009. Video available at http://www.youtube.com/watch?v=ptxVK4xWr8g#tcot.

131 *"He's practically Cuban:* Peter Wallsten, "Bush Brothers, Exiles Renew Their Support," *Miami Herald*, May 21, 2002.

131 *"He was all:* Fred Brummer, interview by author, Dec. 15, 2011.

132 *Bush was alternately dubbed:* Steve Bousquet, "The Bush Legacy; Part I: The Office," *St. Petersburg Times*, Dec. 29, 2006.

133 *"The Bushes know:* Johnnie Byrd, interview by author, Dec. 5, 2011.

133 *"I wonder if:* J. C. Planas, interview by author, Oct. 11, 2011.

133 *He'd been a:* J. Taylor Rushing, "Despite Apparent Dismissals, Crist Campaign Seems Likely," *Florida Times-Union*, Apr. 21, 2004.

133 *Writing in the:* Adam C. Smith, "It's All New GOP Day," *St. Petersburg Times*, Mar. 30, 2007.

134 *"He was cloyingly:* Author interview with confidential source, 2011.

135 *In April, while:* Marc Caputo and Mary Ellen Klas, "House Speaker Rips Compromise Tax-Cut Plan," *Miami Herald*, Apr. 27, 2007.

135 *"That was a:* J. C. Planas, interview by author, Oct. 11, 2011.

135 *In April 2008:* Gary Fineout, "Rubio Helps Political Ally in Budget," *Miami Herald*, Apr. 7, 2008.

136 *He'd done so:* Author interview with confidential sources.

136 *Editorialists ripped Rubio:* "A Favoritism Fill-Up," *Palm Beach Post*, April 14, 2008.

136 *Rubio had tried to:* Marc Caputo, "Rubio Defends Adding Wording," *Miami Herald*, Apr. 8, 2008.

136 *"Just because a:* Linda Kleindienst and John Kennedy, "Budget Full of 'Turkeys'—Even in Lean Times, House Leaders Steered $350 million in Pork-barrel Spending into the State Budget, Critics Said," *Orlando Sentinel*, Apr. 15, 2003.

136 *"He's very good:* Jill Chamberlin, interview with author, Dec. 12, 2011.

137 *The award-winning:* Aaron Sharockman, "PolitiFact: Rubio's Claim of Spurring 57 Laws Proves High," *Tampa Bay Times* and *Miami Herald*, Feb. 28, 2010.

137 *"He talked the:* Adam C. Smith and Alex Leary, "Rubio Record Diverges from Campaign Rhetoric," *St. Petersburg Times*, Nov. 6, 2009.

137 *He left office:* Gary Fineout and Marc Caputo, "Rubio Leaves Mixed Record; Florida's First Cuban-American House Speaker Ends His Two Years in Office with a Record of Highs and Lows," *Miami Herald*, May 4, 2008.

138 *The greatness of:* Remarks by House Speaker Marco Rubio, Florida House of Representatives, May 2, 2008.

CHAPTER SIX: A HIGHER CALLING

139 *Baxley, who describes:* Dennis Baxley, interview by author, Dec. 6, 2011.

139 *Rubio was contemplating:* Ibid.

140 *And getting past:* Jose K. Fuentes, interview by author, Dec. 15, 2011.

140 *Rubio would be:* "Rubio's Rise: Tax Returns Show How Income, Influence Rose," *Miami Herald*, May 22, 2010.

140 *"It's not very:* Dennis Baxley, interview by author, Dec. 6, 2011.

140 *"There was a:* Ibid.

Notes

140 *"She doesn't get:* Ibid.

141 *"He had that:* Ibid.

142 *Crist skipped a:* Frank Cerabino, "What Hug? Governor Just Doing His Duty," *Palm Beach Post*, Nov. 10, 2008.

142 *The Crist-Obama:* Adam C. Smith, "Crist, Obama Go Bipartisan," *St. Petersburg Times*, Feb. 11, 2009.

143 *Rubio's plans finally:* Beth Reinhard, "Marco Rubio Quietly Registers to Run for U.S. Senate," *Miami Herald*, Mar. 5, 2009.

143 *The month before:* Paula McMahon and Peter Franceschina, "Ex-Power Broker: 4 Years in Prison," *Sun-Sentinel*, June 2, 2011.

143 *He was later:* Ibid.

143 *A Quinnipiac poll:* Quinnipiac University, "Florida's Crist Has Pick of Gov. or Senate Race, Quinnipiac University Poll Finds; Voters Back Seminole Casino Plan," Feb. 18, 2009, http://www.quinnipiac.edu/institutes-and-centers/polling-institute.

143 *Rubio's sister Veronica:* Veronica Ponce blog, "Six Months Is a Long Time," Mar. 8, 2011, http://veronicaponce.typepad.com/v_photography/.

145 *He dashed off:* Adam C. Smith, "Rubio's Boldness Beat All the Odds," *St. Petersburg Times*, Nov. 14, 2010.

145 *All of fourteen minutes:* Beth Reinhard, "Gov. Charlie Crist Announces Bid for U.S. Senate," *Miami Herald*, May 12, 2009.

146 *He had what:* Stephen F. Hayes, "It Was Rubio's Tuesday; The Most Important Freshman Senator," *Weekly Standard*, Nov. 15, 2010.

146 *As he'd done:* Fred Barnes, "Demolition Derby in Florida, Can Marco Rubio Prevail?," *Weekly Standard*, Aug. 9, 2010.

146 *"I remember my:* Stephen F. Hayes, "It Was Rubio's Tuesday; The Most Important Freshman Senator," *Weekly Standard*, Nov. 15, 2010.

147 *Even though his:* Tom Tillison, interview by researcher, Feb. 7, 2012.

147 *On April 15, 2009:* Marco Rubio address to tea party activists, West Palm Beach, Florida, April 15, 2009, http://www.youtube.com/watch?v=5CHFJgqCv0c.

148 *"People loved what:* Everett Wilkinson, interview by researcher, Feb. 7, 2012.

148 *Looking back, Rubio:* Remarks by Marco Rubio at Politico Playbook Breakfast, Nov. 16, 2011.

148 *One night his:* Remarks by Marco Rubio on his election to the U.S.

Senate, Coral Gables, Florida, Nov. 2, 2010, http://rncnyc2004.blog
spot.com/2010/11/marco-rubio-marco-rubio-acceptance.html.

148 *"Our nation is:* Bill Thompson, "Fla. Christian Coalition Head Baxley
Quits to Endorse Rubio," *Gainesville Sun,* June 8, 2009.

148 *The two traveled:* Dennis Baxley, interview by author, Dec. 6, 2011.

149 *"My colleagues literally:* Jim DeMint, *The Great American Awakening*
(Nashville: B & H Publishing Group, 2011), 9.

149 *Crist's report was:* John McArdle, "Crist Far Outpaces Rubio in Second-
Quarter Fundraising," *Roll Call,* July 7, 2009.

149 *Rubio's advisors gave:* Smith, "Rubio's Boldness Beat All the Odds."

150 *"One of the:* Author interview with confidential source, 2011.

150 *"You do not:* Smith, "Rubio's Boldness Beat All the Odds."

150 *Rubio's young campaign:* Adam C. Smith, "Two Leave Rubio's Campaign Staff," *St. Petersburg Times,* July 24, 2009.

150 *Rubio brought in:* William March, "Rubio Draws Crowds; Coffers
Slow to Fill," *Tampa Tribune,* July 25, 2009.

150 *Shortridge argued:* Smith, "Rubio's Boldness Beat All the Odds."

151 *"He can spit:* Author interview with confidential source, 2011.

151 *"You know, I:* Remarks by Marco Rubio at Politico Playbook Breakfast,
Nov. 16, 2011.

151 *"I have strong:* Smith, "Rubio's Boldness Beat All the Odds."

152 *Rubio's advisors were:* Author interview with confidential source, 2011.

152 *It calls Crist:* John J. Miller, "Rubio Rising—The Florida GOP Has a
New Star," *National Review,* Sept. 7, 2000.

152 *It was the turning:* Dennis Baxley, interview by author, Dec. 6, 2011.

153 *He was spending:* Smith, "Rubio's Boldness Beat All the Odds."

153 *A December 2009:* Rasmussen Reports, 2010 Florida Republican
Senate Primary, Dec. 4, 2009, http://www.rasmussenreports.com/
public_content/politics/elections/election_2010_senate_elections/
florida/questions/toplines_2010_florida_senate_republican_primary_
december_14_2009.

153 *The embrace was:* Author interview with confidential source, 2011.

154 *In January, he:* Marco Rubio tweet, Jan. 27, 2010.

154 *"A lot of:* Dennis Baxley, interview by author, Dec. 6, 2011.

154 *José "Pepe" Fanjul:* Author interview with confidential source, 2012.

154 *Two things came:* Author interview with confidential source, 2012.

155 *Rubio and his:* Ibid.

155 *"A week ago:* Remarks by Marco Rubio to the Conservative Political Action Committee, Washington, D.C., Feb. 18, 2010, http://www.you tube.com/watch?v=8XY0pX5xBGE.

157 *Investigative reporters:* Beth Reinhard, Scott Hiaasen, and Adam C. Smith, "Rubio Credit Flap Grows," *St. Petersburg Times,* Feb. 26, 2010.

158 *"It's all sideshows:* George Bennett, "Rubio Casts Race as Battle for America," *Palm Beach Post,* Oct. 23, 2010.

158 *For instance, Rubio's:* Adam C. Smith and Beth Reinhard, "Rubio's Aide Spent Lavishly like His Boss," *St. Petersburg Times,* Mar. 23, 2010.

158 *Ben Wilcox, of:* Adam C. Smith, Beth Reinhard, and Scott Hiaasen, "A Lavish Rise for Rubio," *St. Petersburg Times,* Mar. 13, 2010.

159 *"The Rubio hiring:* Zac Anderson, "Money Matters Follow Candidate Rubio," *Sarasota Herald Tribune,* Sept. 20, 2010.

159 *Rubio had been:* Ibid.

159 *Rubio's staff said:* Jake Bernstein, "Florida Bank, Used as ATM by Insiders, Won TARP Loan But Now Teeters," ProPublica, Oct. 22, 2011.

159 *"Having expenditures in:* Ibid.

160 *Rubio's staff fought back:* Ibid.

160 *"One guy bought:* Author interview with confidential source, 2011.

160 *In a Fox News: Fox News Sunday,* Mar. 28, 2010, http://www.politics daily.com/2010/03/28/transcript-of-charlie-crist-marco-rubio-debate-on -fox-news-sund/.

161 *The popular Fox:* Transcript of Sean Hannity program on Fox News, Apr. 6, 2010, http://www.foxnews.com/on-air/hannity/2010/04/07/giu liani-backing-rubio-fiery-fla-senate-race.

161 *His lead advisors:* William March, "It's Farewell to the GOP," *Tampa Tribune,* Apr. 30, 2010.

162 *Once an ally:* Author interview with confidential source, 2012.

163 *In one investigation:* Scott Hiaasen and David Ovalle, "FDLE Team Takes Lead of David Rivera Probe," *Miami Herald,* Jan. 29, 2011.

163 *Rivera also initially:* Laura Wides-Munoz, "Fla. Probe Finances of New U.S. Rep. David Rivera," Associated Press, Jan. 20, 2011.

163 *In April he:* Beth Reinhard, "3-Way Senate Race Would Change Old Script," *Miami Herald,* Apr. 28, 2010.

164 *Rubio told Human Events:* Jason Mattera, "Exclusive: Rubio Clarifies Critique of Arizona Law," Humanevents.com, May 6, 2010.

164 *During the campaign:* Author interview with confidential source, 2011.

165 *Fanjul hosted a:* Author interview with confidential source, 2012.

165 *The guest list:* Ibid.

165 *"It pains me:* Author interview with confidential source, 2011.

166 *"We screwed it up:* Ibid.

166 *Video of Crist:* http://www.youtube.com/watch?v=9hG1PsA_ltE.

166 *Rubio's team preferred:* Author interview with confidential source, 2011.

166 *"The Republican Party:* CNN Florida Senate debate, Oct. 24, 2010, http://transcripts.cnn.com/TRANSCRIPTS/1010/24/sotu.01.html.

167 *"My dad was:* Marco Rubio, letter upon the death of his father, Sept. 4, 2010, http://saintpetersblog.com/2010/09/heartbreaking-inspiring-and-a-must-read-a-letter-from-marco-rubio-about-the-passing-of-his-father/.

167 *Rubio's frontrunner status:* Lucy Morgan, "Rubio Listed as 'Hero' to the Court," *St. Petersburg Times,* Sept. 23, 2010.

168 *"We make a grave:* Remarks by Marco Rubio on his election to the U.S. Senate, Coral Gables, Florida, Nov. 2, 2010, http://rncnyc2004.blogspot.com/2010/11/marco-rubio-marco-rubio-acceptance.html.

CHAPTER SEVEN: GOD AND COUNTRY

169 *"God is real:* Remarks by Marco Rubio to the Florida House of Representatives, Tallahassee, May 2, 2008, http://www.youtube.com/watch?v=z5uugXEZY58.

169 *One and a half:* Remarks by Marco Rubio on his election to the U.S. Senate, Coral Gables, Florida, Nov. 2, 2010, http://rncnyc2004.blogspot.com/2010/11/marco-rubio-marco-rubi o-acceptance.html.

170 *God appears when:* Remarks by Marco Rubio at the Conservative Political Action Conference, Washington, D.C., Feb. 9, 2012.

170 *He is there when Rubio discusses:* Remarks by Marco Rubio at the Reagan Presidential Library, Simi Valley, California, Aug. 23, 2011.

171 *"He's always been:* McKay Coppins, "Marco Rubio's Mormon Roots," BuzzFeed.com.

171 *"He really convinced:* Ibid.

171 *And the Mormon:* Ibid.

Notes

172 *Over the years:* Dennis Baxley, interview by author, Dec. 6, 2011.

172 *In 2004, when:* Gary Fineout, "Lawmakers Invited to See 'Passion,' " *Miami Herald*, Mar. 10, 2004.

172 *When asked about:* Ibid.

172 *"We've had talks:* Ibid.

172 *He was:* Damian Thompson, "Marco Rubio Tries to Still Debate over His Religion," *Daily Telegraph (London)*, Nov. 12, 2010.

173 *he identified himself:* Marco Rubio, official biography, Florida House of Representatives website, http://www.myfloridahouse.gov/Sections/Representatives/details.aspx?MemberId=4180.

173 *in the Congressional:* Marco Rubio, official biography, Congressional Directory for the 112th Congress.

173 *"One of the:* Remarks by Marco Rubio at Politico Playbook Breakfast, Nov. 16, 2011.

173 *But he also:* Ibid.

173 *Rubio and his friend Baxley shared:* Ibid.

173 *Thirty-five percent:* Pew Research Center, Forum on Religion and Public Life, poll, "Many Americans Mix Multiple Faiths," Dec. 2009.

173 *Latinos are still:* "U.S. Latino Religious Identification 1990–2008: Growth, Diversity and Transformation. A Report Based on the American Religious Identification Survey 2008," Trinity College, Hartford, Connecticut.

173 *Rubio's two religions:* Mark Noll, interview by author, Feb. 1, 2012.

174 *"At the practical:* Ibid.

174 *Catholics consider the:* Chad C. Pecknold, interview by author, Feb. 9, 2012.

174 *But in the:* Website of Christ Fellowship church, "Our Beliefs," http://cfmiami.org/im-new/our-beliefs/.

174 *"That's a big:* Chad C. Pecknold, interview by author, Feb. 9, 2012.

174 *After Rubio's 2010 Senate:* Eric Giunta, "Marco Rubio: Catholic or Southern Baptist? Voters Deserve to Know," RenewAmerica.com, Nov. 4, 2010, http://www.renewamerica.com/columns/giunta/101104.

175 *"If you find:* Eric Giunta, "Rubio Campaign to Catholic Voters: 'Screw You; Get a Life!,' " RenewAmerica.com, Nov. 11, 2010, http://www.renewamerica.com/columns/giunta/101111.

175 *Analysts wrote off:* Mark Oppenheimer, "Catholic or Protestant? Few Seem Troubled," *New York Times*, Nov. 26, 2010.

176 *"Catholics and evangelicals:* Richard Land, interview by author, Feb. 9, 2012.

177 *"We are a blessed:* Remarks by Marco Rubio at the Conservative Political Action Conference, Washington, D.C., Feb. 9, 2012.

178 *"This is not: On the Record with Greta Van Susteren,* Fox News, Feb. 8, 2012.

178 *"Religious freedom is:* Marco Rubio, "Religious Liberty Can Still Trump ObamaCare," *New York Post,* Feb. 2, 2012.

179 *"I can tell:* Glenn Thrush, "Marco Rubio's Unplanned Parenthood," Politico 44 blog, Feb. 2, 2012.

179 *Baxley, his friend:* Dennis Baxley, interview by author, Dec. 6, 2011.

179 *In those remarks:* Remarks by Marco Rubio to the Florida House of Representatives, Tallahassee, May 2, 2008.

179 *Rubio's remarks struck:* Chad C. Pecknold, interview by author, Feb. 9, 2012.

179 *"[God] doesn't want:* Remarks by Marco Rubio to the Florida House of Representatives, Tallahassee, May 2, 2008.

CHAPTER EIGHT: THE CENTURY CLUB

181 *"Looks highly caffeinated:* Author interview with confidential source, 2011.

182 *"You could be here:* Marco Rubio, Town Hall, Naples, Florida, http://www.youtube.com/watch?v=Oh93MAjeDT4.

182 *He was actually:* Jennifer E. Manning, "Membership of the 112th Congress: A Profile," Mar. 1, 2011. Available at: http://www.senate.gov/reference/resources/pdf/R41647.pdf.

183 *He defused the:* Marco Rubio Twitter account.

183 *"There is great:* Marco Rubio Twitter account, March 29, 2009.

184 *In May 2009:* Marco Rubio Twitter account, May 21, 2009.

184 *"As Senator Rubio:* "Media Availability with House Speaker John Boehner, (R-Oh.), Subject: Budget," Federal News Service, July 11, 2011.

185 *It was more:* Andrew Price, "Watts Brings Message of Diversity, Opportunity," *Richmond Times-Dispatch* (Virginia), Sept. 30, 2005.

185 *"Marco Rubio is:* Jeremy Wallace, "Marco Rubio Is Everywhere," HT politics.com, July 14, 2011, http://htpolitics.com/2011/07/14/marco-rubio-is-everywhere/.

185 *"Whoever wins the:* "Analysis with Dick Morris," *The Sean Hannity Show,* Fox News, July 11, 2011.

186 *A few days:* "Talking Points Memo," *The O'Reilly Factor,* Fox News, July 18, 2011.

186 *His wife and:* Remarks by Marco Rubio at Politico Playbook breakfast, Washington, D.C., Nov. 16, 2011.

187 *"This is more:* Chris Coons, interview by author, Nov. 21, 2011.

187 *"There is a prism:* Author interview with confidential source, 2012.

188 *"My fear has:* Marco Rubio at Politico Playbook breakfast.

189 *"He wants to:* Alex Leary, "Marco Rubio Faces an Immigration Issue," *St. Petersburg Times,* May 29, 2011.

189 *"He feels the:* Everett Wilkinson, interview by researcher, Feb. 7, 2012.

189 *Tom Tillison, cofounder:* Tom Tillison, interview by researcher, Feb. 7, 2012.

189 *One month after:* Marco Rubio, Town Hall, Naples, Florida.

190 *"I said to him:* Chris Coons, interview by author, Nov. 21, 2011.

191 *"I don't want:* Remarks by Marco Rubio at Politico Playbook breakfast, Washington, D.C., Nov. 16, 2011.

192 *"I do not enjoy:* Senator Rubio's YouTube channel, Dec. 16, 2011, http://www.youtube.com/user/SenatorMarcoRubio.

194 *"He listened:* Julia Wrightstone, interview by author, Feb. 5, 2012.

195 *Rubio raised concerns:* "Senator Rubio Challenges Farrar on His Record on Cuba," June 8, 2011, http://www.youtube.com/watch?v=U1n8 GufRsuA.

195 *One evening when:* Manuel Roig-Franzia, "Havana's 148 Flags Prove Mightier Than the Billboard," *Washington Post,* May 13, 2006.

196 *"I can't think:* William E. Gibson, "Rubio's First Year in Senate Filled with Frustration," *Fort Lauderdale Sun-Sentinel,* Dec. 18, 2011.

CHAPTER NINE: GREAT EXPECTATIONS

197 *One day Cardenas:* Remarks by Al Cardenas at the Conservative Political Action Conference, Washington, D.C., Feb. 9, 2012.

197 *Back in Florida:* Alex Leary, "Rubio for Prez," *St. Petersburg Times* blog, Mar. 6, 2007.

198 *The previous March:* Mary Ellen Klas, "Rubio on GOP Mission," *Miami Herald,* Mar. 20, 2006.

Notes

198 *He's good, and:* Michael C. Bender, "Son of Immigrants Trumpets People's Agenda," *Palm Beach Post*, Feb. 26, 2007.

198 *Steven Geller, a:* Tim Elfrink, "Marco Rubio, Tea Party Pretty Boy," *Miami New Times*, July 22, 2010.

199 *By 2010 they: The Event*, NBC, http://www.nbc.com/the-event/about/president-martinez/.

200 *On May 22:* CDR Kerchner blog, "Senator Marco Rubio's Father Was Not a Naturalized Citizen When Marco Was Born in May 1971 per National Archives Data," May 22, 2011, http://cdrkerchner.wordpress.com/2011/05/22/senator-marco-rubios-father-was-not-a-naturalized-citizen-when-marco-was-born-in-may-1971-per-national-archives-data-his-father-applied-for-naturalization-in-sep-1975/.

201 *In various writings:* Ibid.

201 *"The natives, or:* Emer de Vattel, *The Law of Nations or Principles of the Law of Nature Applied to Conduct and Nature of Nations and Sovereigns* (London: G. G. and J. Robinson, 1797).

201 *In September Alan Keyes:* Alex Leary, "Birthers Call Out Rubio," *St. Petersburg Times*, Oct. 20, 2011.

201 *That same month:* Bob Rathgeber, "Exclusive: Now, 'Birthers' Have Eye on Marco Rubio, Is He 'Natural Born?' A Debate Has Begun," News-press.com, Sept. 20, 2011.

202 *The 1,200-word:* Leary, "Birthers Call Out Rubio."

202 *Rubio responded with:* Jim Puzzanghera, "Leading Republicans Take Shots at Trump," *Sun-Sentinel*, May 2, 2011.

203 *Tribe responded by:* Laurence H. Tribe, email correspondence with author, Oct. 17, 2011.

203 *Without hesitation he:* Gabriel Chin, interview by author, Oct. 17, 2011.

204 *It began in:* Isaac Lee, interview by author, Oct. 31, 2011.

204 *Barbara Cicilia took:* Gerardo Reyes, interview by author, Nov. 28, 2011.

205 *Less than an:* Maria Martinez-Henao, interview by author, Dec. 2, 2011.

205 *Burgos thought the:* Ibid.

205 *An email the:* Alex Burgos, email correspondence to Randy Falco, July 6, 2011.

Notes

206 *"For many years:* Interview by author with confidential source, Oct. 31, 2011.

207 *In 2010 it:* Univision statistical analysis.

207 *Three Univision news:* Isaac Lee, interview by author, Oct. 31, 2011.

209 *Burgos's notes from:* Ken Auletta, "War of Choice: Marco Rubio and the G.O.P. Play a Dangerous Game on Immigration," *New Yorker*, Jan. 9, 2012.

209 *When Rubio's staff:* Daniel Coronell, interview by author, Oct. 31, 2011.

209 *The next day:* Alex Burgos letter to Isaac Lee, July 8, 2011.

210 *The report pointed:* Univision nightly news broadcast, July 11, 2011, http://noticias.univision.com/estados-unidos/videos/video/2011-07-11/univision-investigo-a-marco-rubio.

210 *"He was very:* Auletta, "War of Choice."

211 *Two and a half:* Marc Caputo, email to Isaac Lee, Sept. 28, 2011.

212 *The* Herald *and:* Auletta, "War of Choice."

213 *"Days before Univision:* Marc Caputo and Manny Garcia, "The Inside Story: Univision's War with Rubio over Immigration, Drug Report," *Miami Herald*, Oct. 1, 2011.

213 *Erik Fresen, a:* Erik Fresen, interview by author, Dec. 15, 2011.

214 *The letter noted:* David Rivera, Carlos Lopez-Cantera, and Erik Fresen, letter to Reince Preibus, Oct 3, 2011.

214 *"Obviously we don't:* Auletta, "War of Choice."

215 *The newsroom brought:* Richard Altabef, confidential memorandum, "Re. Evaluation of claim by Senator Rubio's office," Oct. 19, 2011.

215 *"There are some:* Erika Fry, "Univision, *The Miami Herald,* and Marco Rubio, the GOP's Rising Star," *Columbia Journalism Review*, January/February 2012.

216 *"We felt very:* Aminda Marques, interviewed by author, Apr. 10, 2012.

216 *"For us I:* Marques, interviewed by author, Apr. 10, 2012.

217 *On the night:* Gerardo Reyes, interview by author, Nov. 28, 2011.

217 *Marques said the:* Auletta, "War of Choice."

217 *Its chairman, Haim Saban:* Ibid.

217 *Saban was trashed:* Ibid.

CHAPTER TEN: THE GOLDEN DOOR

219 *"My heart goes:* Jim Ash, "Bill Targets Farm Slavery," *Palm Beach Post,* Mar. 13, 2003.

220 *"They were happy:* Tirso Moreno, interview by author, Feb. 17, 2012.

222 *"In the 15:* Jeb Bush, "Winning Hispanics Back," *Washington Post,* Jan. 26, 2012.

222 *The Obama administration:* Jordy Yaeger, "Obama's ICE Reports Record Number of Deportations of Illegal Immigrants," *The Hill,* Oct. 18, 2011.

223 *Nearly 200,000 men:* Tim Lockette, "New UF Farm Safety Program Targets 200,000 Migrant Workers," *University of Florida News,* Jun. 30, 2005, http://news.ufl.edu/2005/06/30/farmsafety/.

223 *"Upwards of three-quarters:* Greg Schell, interview by author, Feb. 17, 2012.

223 *"That's only fair:* Ibid.

223 *With Peterman, Rubio:* Todd Wright, "Legislation Would Help Farm-workers; House Version Stalls as Senate Bill Advances," *Sun-Sentinel,* Mar. 1, 2002.

224 *Rubio and Peterman:* Ash, "Bill Targets Farm Slavery."

224 *Rubio also supported:* Beth Reinhard, "Rubio Takes Tougher Stance on Illegal Immigration," *Miami Herald,* Nov. 10, 2009.

227 *"Rubio was born:* Steve Bousquet, "House Makes History with Choice of Speaker," *St. Petersburg Times,* Sept. 14, 2005.

227 *"The 34-year-old:* Associated Press, "Florida's First Cuban-American House Speaker-designate Elected," Sept. 13, 2005.

227 *The Palm Beach Post:* Alan Gomez, "Cuban-American to be Named Florida House Speaker for '06," *Palm Beach Post,* Sept. 14, 2005.

227 *And later Human:* John Gizzi, "Politics 2005: Week of October 10," *Human Events Online,* article accessed via nexis.com, Oct. 7, 2005.

227 *During the 2010 Senate race:* Beth Reinhard, "Marco Rubio Warming up Panhandle Voters," *Miami Herald,* Nov. 1, 2009.

228 *"I think that:* Transcript of *America's Nightly Scoreboard* for October 21, 2011, accessed via nexis.com.

229 *Rubio responded with:* Marco Rubio, "Marco Rubio: My Family's Flight from Castro," Politico.com, Oct. 21, 2011, available at http://www.politico.com/news/stories/1011/66567.html.

230 In the interview: NPR, "Reporter Raises Questions about Rubio's Background," *NPR*, Oct. 21, 2011, audio available at http://www.npr.org/2011/10/21/141597314/roig-franzia-discusses-questions-about-rubios-background.

230 *The Cuban passport:* Oriales Rubio passport inspected by author Oct. 20, 2011.

231 *Raul Martinez, the:* Raul Martinez, interview by author, Mar. 6, 2012.

231 *"If [Rubio] had:* Sandhya Somashekhar, "For Republicans, Spotlight Turns to Florida—and Rubio," *Washington Post*, Jan. 28, 2012.

232 *Frank Gonzalez, a:* Frank Gonzalez, interview by author, Dec. 14, 2011.

232 *Once in a February 2010:* transcript of Sean Hannity interview with Marco Rubio, Fox News, Feb. 18, 2010.

232 *once in a September 2011:* Marc Caputo, "Did the Washington Post embellish Marco Rubio's embellishments," *Miami Herald–Naked Politics blog*, http://miamiherald.typepad.com/nakedpolitics/2011/10/did-the-washington-post-embellish-marco-rubios-embellishments.html, Oct. 20, 2011.

232 *The paper reported:* Marc Caputo, "Rubio to pen autobiography," *Miami Herald*, Sept. 26, 2011.

234 *"Marco told me:* Author interview with confidential source, 2011.

234 *"A lot of us:* Reinhard, "Marco Rubio Takes Tougher Stance on Illegal Immigration."

234 *"His tone has:* Ibid.

235 *"Some have said:* Marco Rubio, "Opposing the Philosophy of Sonia Sotomayor Isn't Anti-Hispanic," Politico.com, http://www.politico.com/news/stories/0809/25788.html, Aug. 5, 2009.

236 *"His rhetoric does not:* J. C. Planas, interview by author, Oct. 11, 2011.

236 *"Nothing against immigrants:* Audio and video of Sen. Marco Rubio available at: http://www.youtube.com/watch?v=tyg1HrDJc94&feature=related.

237 *The refugee programs:* Roger Daniels, *Guarding the Golden Door: American Immigration Policy and Immigrants since 1882* (New York: Hill and Wang), 193.

237 *"I think [Rubio] unwittingly:* Somashekhar, "For Republicans, Spotlight Turns to Florida—and Rubio."

237 *Just before the:* Scott Wong, "Rubio Takes Hard Line on Immigration," Politico.com, May 23, 2011.

Notes

238 *"I gotta say:* Sandhya Somashekhar, "In Florida, GOP Candidates Praise Marco Rubio, a Favorite for Running Mate," washingtonpost .com, Jan. 26, 2012, http://www.washingtonpost.com/politics/in-florida -gop-candidates-praise-marco-rubio-a-favorite-for-running-mate/2012/ 01/26/gIQAzGicVQ_story.html.

239 *"These young people:* Author transcript of Marco Rubio remarks at Hispanic Leadership Network, Jan. 27, 2012.

239 *"I think the:* Jim Geraghty, "Rubio on the Race," *nationalreview.com,* accessed Apr. 10, 2012, http://www.nationalreview.com/articles/2948 46/rubio-race-jim-geraghty?pg=3.

239 *Ruben Navarrette, Jr.:* Ruben Navarette, Jr., "Navarette: GOP version of Dream Act holds promise," *CNN.com,* accessed Apr. 10, 2012, http://politicalticker.blogs.cnn.com/2012/04/05/navarrette-gop-version -of-dream-act-holds-promise/.

240 *Without mentioning Rubio:* Sen. Harry Reid, "Don't Keep Dreamers Waiting," *Miami Herald,* Apr. 1, 2012.

240 *"That could be:* Interview with Juan Williams, *Fox News,* Apr. 4, 2012, viewable at http://www.huffingtonpost.com/2012/04/02/marco-rubio -says-the-dream-act_n_1396824.html.

240 *His aunt and:* Luís Enrique Lastres and Irma García Lastres, Affidavit of support for Pedro Víctor García addressed to Hon. American Con-sul, Visa Division, Havana, Cuba, Nov. 10, 1956.

240 *In May 1956:* Luís Enrique Lastres and Irma García Lastres, Affidavit of support for Dominga García Rodriguez and his aunts, Adria García Rodriguez and Magdalena García Rodriguez, May 26, 1956.

240 *And that same:* Mario Rubio, Application for Immigrant Visa and Alien Registration, Foreign Service of the United States of America, May 18, 1956.

241 *"Most importantly, he:* Alfonso Aguilar, interview by author, Feb. 17, 2012.

AFTERWORD

243 *In 2012, as:* Scott Wong, "Marco Rubio Builds A-Team to Control Image, Bio," Politico, March 12, 2012.

243 *The revelation that:* Address by Marco Rubio to Hispanic Leadership Network Conference, Miami, Jan. 27, 2012, author transcript.

243 *He had to:* Ibid.

Index

Index

Index

Index

Index

Index

Index

Index

Index

Index

Index